Tournament Killer Poker
by the Numbers

BOOKS BY TONY GUERRERA

Killer Poker by the Numbers

Killer Poker Shorthanded (with John Vorhaus)

TOURNAMENT KILLER POKER BY THE NUMBERS

The Keys to No-Limit Hold'em Success

Tony Guerrera

LYLE STUART
Kensington Publishing Corp.
www.kensingtonbooks.com

LYLE STUART BOOKS are published by

Kensington Publishing Corp.
850 Third Avenue
New York, NY 10022

All Kensington titles, imprints, and distributed lines are available at special quantity discounts for bulk purchases for sales promotions, premiums, fund-raising, educational, or institutional use. Special book excerpts or customized printings can also be created to fit specific needs. For details, write or phone the office of the Kensington special sales manager: Kensington Publishing Corp., 850 Third Avenue, New York, NY 10022, attn: Special Sales Department; phone: 1-800-221-2647.

Lyle Stuart and the Lyle Stuart two spade logo are Reg. US Pat. & TM Off.

First printing: December 2008

10 9 8 7 6 5 4 3 2 1

Printed in the United States of America

ISBN-13: 978-0-8184-0723-9
ISBN-10: 0-8184-0723-9

To those who love the game, play hard,
and have neither fear nor regrets.

Contents

Foreword: Flexibility

by Annie Duke

Small multitable tournaments last several hours, but that's a sprint compared to the biggest multitable tournaments, which require that you last through several fourteen-hour—or longer!—days. Eventually, we all get tired, and once fatigue sets in, making good decisions becomes difficult. My friend John Vorhaus describes this state of mind as "oxygen-debt stupidity," and it'll definitely lead to the kind of careless mistakes that can send you to the rail. Having mental stamina, then, is a crucial part of tournament success. But how do you get it? Well, it turns out that one way to be in great mental shape is to be in great physical shape first.

The better your physical conditioning is, the longer your focus at the tables will last. Erik Seidel, Phil Ivey, and I are just a few of today's top players who subscribe to this idea. It's hard enough to beat great players when you're sharp as a tack—tackle them when you're fatigued and you're toast. Even average players can be a challenge when you're tired. You just don't have the mental juice you need when you need it. That's why I work out. Believe me, it's not because I love running up and down the same Hollywood hills every day.

If you don't have a regular exercise routine, I suggest you get one. Exercising is good for your poker, and it's good for

your health. And don't think for a minute that being physically fit is only about stamina. Being in good physical shape
means having not just stamina but also strength and flexibility. And it's to the subject of flexibility that I would now
like to turn (after all, it *is* the title of this foreword)—because
physical flexibility is one thing, but mental flexibility is
something else altogether.

Players who struggle in poker often do so because they
cling to mandates like "raise or fold" or "if you never bluff,
you're playing weak-tight." These and countless other sup-
posed tomes of poker wisdom are relics from poker's ancient
past. (And by ancient past, I mean as long ago as, hey, 1999.)
In this new age of poker, if you or I were to follow blanket
rules such as these, we'd be crushed. Today's world-class
players deviate again and again from conventional poker
wisdom. This is because conventional poker wisdom is usually directed toward players in games where straying from
ABC tight-aggressive play will lose money in the long run.
That may be the case in cash games, but it's sure not true in
tournaments!

In today's poker tournaments, you'll encounter every
conceivable type of poker player, playing every conceivable
strategy. Thus, mindlessly adhering to advice like "I shouldn't
raise with a hand worse than AQ under the gun at a fullhanded table" just won't cut it. You could refine your thinking to, "I shouldn't raise with a hand worse than AQ under
the gun at a fullhanded table because of X, Y, and Z," but
that won't cut it either. You're still playing cookie-cutter
poker, and that approach usually won't net you even a
cookie. Any poker situation you can think of will have some
recommended lines of play—but also very good reasons for
exceptions to, or even radical departures from, those lines of
play. Without flexibility, you might as well just give your
entry fee to the charity of your choice.

"It depends" seems to be the proverb of choice for any poker sage, and there's a good reason for this. You need to be flexible enough to make decisions free from the bias of pre-conceived notions. Critical, dispassionate thinking is called for as you sort through all the information at your disposal. Having a flexible, open mind, then, is the key ingredient to making decisions that yield the highest rate of long-term tournament success.

And this is where Tony Guerrera's *Tournament Killer Poker by the Numbers* comes in. Because as he did in *Killer Poker by the Numbers,* Tony has written a book that's a math wonk's dream. But he knows something about math wonks—that many of them are too closed-minded. Because they know the numbers of poker so well, they sometimes neglect on-the-spot analysis to see them through many of poker's key situations. Worse, they often rely on numbers that don't have much to do with actual playing conditions. For sure, Tony does some calculations in this book, but as in *Killer Poker by the Numbers,* they're put in the context of real play-ing situations. And they make you think, really *think,* about the relationship between poker math and poker play. Whether you come at the game from the math side or the play side, it's an eye-opener. Yes, indeed it is.

Because what Tony *really* does in this book is teach you the underlying math and the underlying thought process you need to be a shark in one of today's most popular poker forms, the no-limit hold'em tournament. That's good news, but here's even better news: even though the book talks about no-limit hold'em tournaments exclusively, many of the concepts covered will help you no matter what game you're playing.

If you're behind in the hand, should you automatically muck, or can you take advantage of a lucrative bluffing op-portunity? If you have a good hand, how can you best accu-

mulate chips with it? With what edge should you be willing
to risk your tournament life? Good players ask themselves
questions like these, and countless more, throughout every
hand they play. But when you get right down to it—and
Tony *does* get right down to it—all these questions just beg
the fundamental one: "How can I win as much as possible?"
Ultimately, going after that goal is what world-class tournament poker is all about, and lucky for you, that's what Tony
is all about in *Tournament Killer Poker by the Numbers*.

It's up to you to piece everything together to come up
with the right decisions for the unique circumstances you
find yourself in. But I do know this—by understanding the
theory that Tony puts forth in *Tournament Killer Poker by the
Numbers* and by always playing with a flexible mind, your
poker thinking will reach new levels. And those new levels
will help you reach more final tables. I look forward to seeing you at one soon!

Introduction: Soul Searching

My first time playing poker outside the realm of home games was in the summer of 2002, when I took my first trip to Commerce Casino and plunked down $40 in a $1–$2 limit hold'em (LHE) game. It was a lot of fun, and the people I observed at Commerce weren't exactly the sharpest knives in the drawer. I smelled blood and money. Unfortunately, my intelligence and the introductory online research I did before my trip weren't enough. I was just another guppy in the tank, and I lost my 20 big bets (BBs) in about 2 hours.[1]

To turn poker into a profitable endeavor, I began doing what I do best: learning. I became a very serious student of the game. I purchased *Winning Low Limit Hold'em* (Conjelco, 2000) by Lee Jones and *Hold'em Poker for Advanced Players* (Two Plus Two, 2001) by Mason Malmuth and David Sklansky. I performed tons of calculations away from the tables. And I tried to see the game as my opponents saw it, so I could do my best to exploit their mistakes.

My second and third sessions were also −20BB sessions, but I could feel myself improving. I treaded water successfully during my fourth session, and from there, I never

---

1. I use BB to signify big bets—the amount of the largest bet in a limit game. And I use bb to signify big *blinds*.

looked back. That doesn't mean I never had losing sessions.[2] But for the next year, I slowly began climbing the LHE ranks, and I also started getting my feet wet in the world of online poker. And when the *no-limit hold'em* (NLHE) explosion began in 2003, I transitioned from playing only in LHE cash games to playing primarily in NLHE cash games. My success in NLHE was pretty much immediate, and I continued to improve by devouring poker books, constantly thinking about better ways to play specific situations, performing calculations, and talking strategy nonstop with my network of talented poker-playing friends.[3]

Of course, the ineptitude of the average poker player back in those days helped. A player needed little more than the *tight-aggressive* (TAG), *hit-to-win* poker preached by the books of the time. Reflecting back on those times, I thought I knew pretty much everything I needed to know about poker. I was a whiz with probabilities and *odds,* I knew how to extract value from my made hands, and I generally knew when my good hands were beaten by even better hands.

These days, I realize that what I knew back then was, at best, a shaky foundation. Fortunately, because I was well versed in the fundamental theory of making poker decisions, I was able to evolve and compete effectively against the higher caliber of competition found in today's cash games. To this day, I continually explore new lines of play, using many of the thought processes found in *Killer Poker by the Numbers (KPBTN)* (Kensington, 2007) to evaluate their

---

2. If you're going to take advice from someone who claims never to have a losing cash game session or who claims to place in the money in something like 80% of *single-table tournaments* played, then beware, because you'll be taking advice from a liar.

3. Pretty much any successful poker player will mention the importance of discussing strategy with friends who play in the same games you do. History points us to many times where the masses have been wrong; however, the masses are correct on this one.

effectiveness.[4] This exploration is a fun and necessary part of poker. And that's why knowing "how to think" is more important than simply knowing "what to do."

When I wrote *KPBTN*, I knew that I couldn't possibly include every situation. And although I regret not emphasizing certain lines of play in *KPBTN* (bluffing and preflop 3-betting in particular), I'm confident that anyone going through the book could analyze such lines of play on their own. My job with *KPBTN* wasn't to cover every possible line of play. Instead, it was to teach readers all the tools needed to figure things out on their own. A book that tells you what to do can only get you as far as the situations it covers. A book that tells you how to think gets you far beyond.

Tournament Killer Poker by the Numbers (TKPBTN) continues in the "how to think" spirit of *KPBTN*. My experience in tournament poker emphasizes the importance of the how-to-think approach. I had been playing successfully in cash games for about a year before I started playing tournaments. When I first started playing tournaments, I played a mixture of *single-table tournaments* (STTs) and *multitable tournaments* (MTTs) online. I had some decent results, but I wanted to do better. I'm a big fan of learning from others whenever possible, so I turned to books and the Internet for whatever golden nuggets of information I could find. Everything I read pretty much reiterated the same themes:

1. Don't risk your chips in marginal confrontations because better opportunities will present themselves later on.

---

4. Don't worry if you haven't read *KPBTN*. I sincerely believe that it's a must-read for anyone who's very serious about the game (not just because I wrote it), but I've written *TKPBTN* to stand on its own.

2. Play very *tight* early in tournaments and open your
   game up as the *blinds* increase.

3. Your seat is the most valuable thing you have; all you
   need is a chip and a chair.

Items 1 and 3 compose what I refer to as the chip preservationist approach to tournaments, and item 2 is really the
result of the situations you often find yourself in when you
take the chip preservationist approach. I was something of a
preservationist when I first started playing tournaments.
After reading a bunch of seemingly sound tournament advice, I became even more of a preservationist. When it came
to my chips, I was as conservative as the sum of Pat Bu-
chanan, George W. Bush, Ann Coulter, and Alan Keyes. I was
very tight when I played in cash games and even tighter
when I played in tournaments. All the arguments support-
ing chip preservation made sense to me. Why take risks in
marginal situations when better situations will arise? Why
risk elimination when staying out of pots results in climbing
up the pay scale as opponents eliminate each other?

I was excellent at reading my opponents, and I felt like I
had an excellent grasp of tournament theory. Unfortunately, my overall results from 2003 to 2005 begged to differ.
I wasn't necessarily a beast at STTs, but I did well in them
(we'll later see that the survivalist mentality is suitable for
the early stages of STTs). Meanwhile, at best, I was mediocre
at MTTs. I don't know where I ranked exactly within my network of successful poker-playing friends, but I'm pretty sure
that I was the leader when it came to average finish and percentage of *in-the-money* (ITM) finishes. However, I'm also
pretty sure that I was dead last when it came to net profit,
and net profit is really the name of the game.

I was getting far in tournaments the most consistently,

but I wasn't getting to many final tables. For the longest time, I just thought that I was unlucky. My ability to analyze hands seemed to be dead-on, and with my relatively high ITM percentage, I thought that it was just a matter of time before I'd string together some big final tables. I sneaked my way to an occasional final table, but really, my string of big MTT paydays never came. I needed to make an adjustment, and the only place I could think of was that I was too tight when it came to risking my chips. With the same reads that I was making, my friends would be making completely different moves. Basically, they were accepting the types of marginal edges that I was forsaking. I attributed their better results to *variance* and stubbornly stuck to my chip preserving ways.

Around this time, Dan Harrington came out with his *Harrington on Hold'em* books (Two Plus Two, 2004 and 2005). Here, a well-respected tournament player was talking about tournament NLHE decisions purely in terms of *expected value* with respect to chips (*chip EV* or cEV). The "wait for better opportunities" philosophy found in the chip-preservationist literature was nowhere to be found in Harrington's books. I strongly felt that something was wrong with approaching tournaments by considering pure cEV. But Harrington's track record, combined with that of my friends, clearly indicated that I needed to do some serious soul searching when it came to NLHE tournaments. Soul searching for this atheist consisted of a bunch of calculating, debating, and experimenting. No longer satisfied with the hand-waving arguments that had seemed to make sense for so long, I set out to find out *the* truth about tournament poker. The material in *TKPBTN* is the result of this soul searching, which propelled me out of the depths of tournament mediocrity. If you're struggling with tournament poker and frustrated with your results, know that I'm writing this book with the experience of someone who's been there. If you're already crushing tournaments and you're simply looking for an additional edge, know that I'm also writing this book with the experience of coaching players just like you.

TKPBTN is being marketed as a book that's specifically about NLHE tournaments; after all, every example in this book has to do with NLHE tournaments. However, tournament theory itself is independent of NLHE. If you understand the theory I put forth and how I apply it to NLHE tournaments, you'll be able to take the theory and apply it to tournaments featuring your poker variant of choice.

Some of the math I use is stuff that you may not be comfortable with. I'm not going to advertise falsely that this book is an easy read. But I've tried to avoid what seems to be a creed of many academics and lawyers: making basic concepts sound arbitrarily difficult with a bunch of formal and obscure language so that they give the illusion of seeming much smarter than everybody else is. Try as hard as you can to follow all the math because the stronger your understanding of the theory is, the more confident you can be in your ability to deduce the best action no matter what situation you're in. And the confidence that comes with that sense of decision-making power is what separates the best from the rest.

But as much as I believe in the importance of understanding how the general theory is derived, I also believe that because of available software it's possible to apply a lot of what I cover without having to wade through all the derivations if you're not comfortable with them. If you're not entirely comfortable with things like conditional probabilities and logarithms, don't spend days being frustrated and stuck on a calculation. Instead, just skim through the derivations and skip to the results that I summarize.

Finishing *TKPBTN* has been an interesting process. When

I first submitted the book proposal, I had a road map in mind. When I got down to writing the book, something completely different—and vastly superior—resulted. Originally due in February 2007, it's now May 2008. Part of the delay was from me getting my hands in too many cookie jars for my own good (writing articles, hosting a radio show, coaching, consulting, and playing—even the Tsunami can only do so much).[5] But the delay was also due to me making sure that everything you needed to know about tournament poker was presented in a way that made sense. My understanding of tournament poker has evolved substantially during the writing process. At the risk of making your head explode, I present the full scoop without holding back any of the gory details.

Many have been eagerly waiting for the day when *TKPBTN* would be finished. The day has finally arrived, and it's time to think about poker tournaments as you've never thought of them before. I wish you much fun and success at the tables. All I ask for in return is that you give me a big shout-out[6] when you win your first WPT or WSOP event![7]

---

5. Many thanks to those who listen to *Killer Poker Analysis* on Rounder's Radio (www.roundersradio.com) for giving me this sweet nickname. I originally wanted to be Tony "Tanuki San" Guerrera, but I think that Tsunami is quite fitting—and a bit more intimidating.
6. With your permission, I'd love to post your shout-out on my website, www.killerev.com!
7. Poker is a gender-neutral game, but to avoid awkward constructions such as "he or she," I use male singular pronouns throughout. For those who object, don't blame me—blame the lack of a gender-neutral pronoun in the English language.

Acknowledgments

Thanks to Greg Dinkin and Frank Scatoni of Venture Literary for pitching my ideas, and thanks to Richard Ember and everyone else at Kensington for liking them, editing them, and publishing them. Many thanks also go to the crew at Kensington for enduring the many delays in delivering the manuscript.

Annie Duke contributed some excellent material to prior Killer Poker titles, and she returned to honor this book with an insightful foreword. Her efforts are much appreciated.

Ryan Patterson's simulations were a huge addition to *Killer Poker by the Numbers,* and his work has proven to be valuable once again. Theory is always best when complemented by solid simulation and experimentation—back dat theory up!

Many thanks go to John Vorhaus (JV) for years of great mentorship and for throwing my hat into the ring whenever the opportunity has arisen. Quite simply: "JV is *the* man!"

Thanks to my family and friends for all the support and good times. I love my life because I have all of you around to share it with me.

A very special thanks goes to my dear Evelyn for enduring countless weekends of me not being able to take her out as I finished this book:

對於妳來說，我的第一本書裡面
有太多的英文、數學和撲克牌

我的第二本書，沒有太多的數學，
可是仍有太多的英文和撲克牌

這本書仍然有太多的英文和撲克牌
可是這本書比起第一本書
有更多的數學

我要你讀我所寫的東西，
所以我想我要用中文寫一些
和數學或撲克牌無關的東西

我愛你！！

And finally—thanks to you, the reader! Poker has been a great source of fun and profit for me over the past few years; I hope my work makes poker the same for you. Visit me at killerev.com and contact me anytime. I eagerly await your stories of triumph; may your mEV always be positive! (Don't worry if you don't know what mEV is; you'll have an honorary Ph.D. in it by the time you finish this book.)

Tournament Killer Poker
by the Numbers

1

♣ ♠ ♦ ♥

CONVENTIONS

♧ ♤ ◇ ♡

Introduction

In tournament NLHE, we need to consider many variables when making our decisions:

- Payout structure
- Blind structure
- Our cards
- Our opponents' cards
- How our opponents play
- Depth of stacks

Analyses not accounting for all these variables are incomplete. This chapter describes conventions used throughout this book—conventions that make the precise description of situations concise and quick to read.

Tournament Chips vs. Money

Central to the theory of tournament poker is the idea that there's a difference between a quantity of tournament chips and the monetary value associated with a quantity of tournament chips. Suppose you're in the following tournament:

Format: Winner Take All (WTA)

Entrants: 50

Starting chips: 5,000

Buy-in: $10+$1[1]

Payout structure: 1st = $500

If you win this tournament, the (50)(5,000) = 250,000 chips you'll have will be worth $500 instead of $250,000. Now take the following example:

Format: Single-Table Tournament (STT)

Entrants: 10

Starting chips: T100

Buy-in: $100+$9

Payout Structure: 1st = $500; 2nd = $300; 3rd = $200

If you win this tournament, the T1,000 chips you have will be worth $500 instead of $1,000.

---

1. The $1 is the tournament fee, or the rake. It doesn't count toward the prize pool. An important part of intelligent tournament selection is playing in tournaments that don't carry excessive rakes. Later, we'll look at how the rake affects your bottom line.

In our coverage of tournament NLHE, we'll be flip-flopping back and forth between talking about chips and the monetary value that we can assign to those chips. To avoid confusion, a T will always precede a number of tournament chips, and an appropriate currency symbol will always precede a number referring to an amount of money.

Position

Your absolute position at the table will influence some of your decisions. Your position relative to certain players at your table will also influence your decisions. Because position is so important, we need a quick, convenient way to describe the position of players at the table. And because we can simply refer to players by their position, a quick, convenient way to describe position will also give us a quick, convenient way to refer to players.

The positions present in every hand are the *button* (B) and the *big blind* (BB). Most of the time, there will also be a *small blind* (SB). As long as at least 4 players are dealt into a hand, the player to the left of the BB (who acts first preflop) is *under-the-gun* (UTG). The player immediately to his left is called UTG+1, the player two to his left is called UTG+2, and so on, until you get to B (e.g., B at a 5-handed table, though 2 to the left of UTG, is always referred to as B instead of UTG+2).

Meanwhile, as long as 4 players are dealt into a hand, the player to the right of B is called the cutoff (CO). The person immediately to CO's right is called CO − 1, the person two to his right is called CO − 2, and so on, until you get to BB (BB is always referred to as BB). Figure 1.1 provides two examples of how this notation works.

FIGURE 1.1: Table Position Diagrams

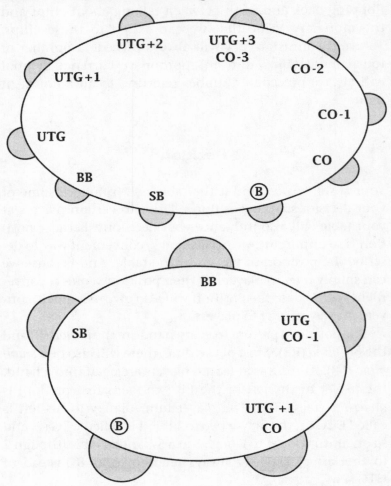

With this naming convention, it's often possible to refer to a specific player in two ways. For example, UTG at a 4-handed table where the SB and BB have been posted normally also happens to be CO. One label isn't more correct than the other is—as long as the table size is indicated, they both uniquely identify the same player. At a 10-handed table, the player 5 to the left of the BB is UTG+4 and CO -2. Since 2 is smaller than 4, this player would usually be referred to as CO -2; however, UTG+4 is still acceptable.

Hand Descriptions

Some readers didn't like the modified Mike Caro University (MCU) notation I used in *Killer Poker by the Numbers (KPBTN)* to describe the action in a hand. I'll be truthful when I say that I also thought it was too bulky—it looked better on my 20" monitors than it looked in print. But when following the action in a hand, I don't like to read through a bunch of text. I'm the "By the Numbers" guy, but I hate constantly having to update stack sizes with mental arithmetic while reading through a bunch of text. I'm very visual with my poker—I like to see the present state of affairs in front of me. Textual hand descriptions seem to dominate pretty much every poker forum on the Internet, and maybe it's because I haven't spent much time on Internet poker forums, but I'm much quicker at parsing through a well-executed graphical or tabular presentation of some sort. After some thinking, I came up with a new tabular format; see table 1.1 (p. 7) for an example hand.

This format is designed to be read from left to right in a columnar fashion:

Column #1 (Player): This column refers to players by name or position or both.

Column #2 (Stacks): This column lists each player's stack before blinds for the hand in question are posted.

Column #3 (Preflop): This column (split into subcolumns) displays preflop action. In table 1.1, sbT10 means that a small blind of 10 was posted and bbT20 means that a big blind of 20 was posted. In this column, and in general, dashes indicate folds, and numbers indicate the total number of chips a player is in for to that point in the betting round. For example, the T20s in the second subcolumn of preflop action in table 1.1 indicate that SB completed to T20 and BB checked his option. The cell in the bottom of this column displays the size of the pot at the conclusion of preflop action. In table 1.1, the pot contains T140 at the conclusion of preflop action.

Column #4 (Stacks): This column lists stacks for players still in the hand going into the flop.

Column #5 (Flop): This column shows the flop, and the subcolumns show the betting action. In table 1.1, the T0 entries indicate checks. The cell in the bottom of this column displays the size of the pot at the conclusion of flop action.

Column #6 (Stacks): This column lists stacks for players still in the hand going into the turn.

TABLE 1.1: Example Hand

	STACKS	PREFLOP	STACKS	FLOP K♣7♣3♠	STACKS	TURN 6♦	STACKS	RIVER J♣	STACKS
SB xx	T1,000	sbT10/T20	T980	T0/–					T980
BB xx	T2,000	bbT20/T20	T1,980	T0/–					T1,980
UTG xx	T1,500	T20	T1,480	T80	T1,400	T0/T300	T1,100	T0/–	T1,100
UTG+1 xx	T1,300	T20	T1,280	T80	T1,200	T150/T300	T900	T0/–	T900
UTG+2 xx	T2,500	–							T2,500
UTG+3 xx	T800	–							T800
CO-2 xx	T1,050	T20	T1,030	–					T1,030
CO-1 (8♣7♣)	T2,200	T20	T2,180	T80	T2,100	T150/T300	T1,800	T400	T3,080
CO xx	T1,750	–							T1,750
B xx	T900	T20	T880	–					T880
POT		T140		T380		T1,280		T1,680	

Column #7 (Turn): This column shows the turn, and the subcolumns show the betting action. The cell in the bottom of this column displays the size of the pot at the conclusion of flop action.

Column #8 (Stacks): This column lists stacks for players still in the hand going into the river.

Column #9 (River): This column shows the river, and the subcolumns show the betting action. The cell in the bottom of this column displays the size of the pot at the conclusion of the hand (uncalled river bets are included in this total).

Column #10 (Stacks): This column lists stacks of all players at the conclusion of the hand.

If action doesn't make it to the river, tables will exclude columns from the betting rounds not played, but the right-most stacks column will always display what the players' stacks are at the conclusion of the hand.

Hand Distributions

When our opponents act, we can *put* them on ranges of hands based on their tendencies. For opponents yet to act, we can predict things such as the hands they'll call raises with. *Hand distributions* are an essential part of the game, and we'll be talking about them a lot.

Listing out hands individually can get cumbersome quickly, so we need some notation to help us express hand distributions concisely. *Killer Poker by the Numbers* and *Killer Poker Shorthanded* used something I referred to as *interval notation* to express hand distributions. But a more common

way of referring to hand distributions is much more concise.
I'll be using the following conventions:

1. Plus signs following unpaired hole cards signify that
   you should keep the first card constant while incre-
   menting over the second card until the rank of the second card is one below the rank of the first card (e.g.,
   J7+ = {J7, J8, J9, JT}).

2. Minus signs following unpaired hole cards signify that
   you should keep the first card constant while decre-
   menting over the second card until the second card is a
   2: (e.g., 85 − = {85, 84, 83, 82}).

3. Plus signs following a pocket pair signify all pocket
   pairs equal to and higher than the indicated pocket
   pair: (e.g., JJ+ = {JJ, QQ, KK, AA}).

4. Minus signs following a pocket pair signify to include
   all pocket pairs equal to and lower than the indicated
   pocket pair: (e.g., 88 − = {88, 77, 66, 55, 44, 33, 22}).

5. A short dash between two sets of hole cards where the
   first card is the same in both signifies to include all
   hands where the first card is the same and the second
   card goes from the second card in the first set of hole
   cards to the second card in the second set of hole cards:
   (e.g., K9–K6 = {K9, K8, K7, K6}).

6. A short dash between two sets of hole cards where the
   first card is different in both signifies to include all
   hands where the first and second cards increment or
   decrement simultaneously: (e.g., JT–54 = {JT, T9, 98,
   87, 76, 65, 54}).

7. The letter *o* means that a hand is offsuit and the letter *s* means that a hand is suited. No letter designation after a hand indicates that the hole cards can be either suited or unsuited: (e.g., AKs = {A♣K♣, A♦K♦, A♥K♥, A♠K♠}; AKo = {A♣K♦, A♣K♥, A♣K♠, A♦K♣, A♦K♥, A♦K♠, A♥K♣, A♥K♦, A♥K♠, A♠K♣, A♠K♦, A♠K♥}; AK = {AKs, AKo}).

8. *{Rand}*, for random, refers to the distribution of all possible hole cards.

Chapter Summary

As we progress through our exploration of tournament NLHE, I'll be introducing additional conventions as needed. But at least we're now on the same page regarding much of what's needed to ensure that we're speaking the same language.

2

♣ ♠ ♦ ♥

PROBABILITY

Introduction

Decision making in NLHE tournaments (and pretty much all poker tournaments) is a four-step process:

1. Calculate the distribution of stacks resulting from a particular line of play.

2. Calculate the monetary value associated with this distribution of stacks.

3. Iterate steps 1 and 2 for all possible lines of play.

4. Pick the line of play resulting in the most valuable distribution of stacks.

This process relies heavily on the branch of mathematics known as *probability,* so our first step is a crash course on probability.

As you go through this primer, you'll probably be thinking something like, "How the hell does Tony expect me to use this stuff when I'm at the tables?" The answer: the really in-depth analysis we'll be doing is stuff that can only be done reasonably away from the tables. When I'm playing, the extent of what I do in my head is on the order of estimating probabilities and assessing my expected gains/losses with respect to chips.

But the purpose of this chapter isn't just academic. We want the ability to perform sophisticated analyses away from the tables so that we can come to the tables armed with a bunch of useful information that we can draw on when we need it. Therefore, when we encounter unique situations that we can't deal with on the spot, we can go home, analyze them to death, and know what to do in the future when any similar situations arise. In the end, poker isn't just about what happens at the tables. It's really an ongoing process involving learning and relearning over and over again. And by the end of this book, we'll develop a synergy between in-depth analysis away from the table and general concepts that should motivate our play when we're at the table. With that being said, it's time for Probability 101.[1]

Probability Defined

The definition of probability applicable to poker refers to relative frequencies involving sets of outcomes. The probability of a specific outcome is the number of ways that the

---

1. If you've read *KPBTN,* some of the material in this chapter will be familiar, but I suggest going through it because I cover some aspects of calculating probabilities that I didn't specifically address in *KPBTN.* I also introduce some standard notation not used in *KPBTN* to make calculations later in the book more concise. This is a new and improved version of the probability primer in *KPBTN.*

specific outcome can happen divided by the total number of ways that an event can resolve itself. This idea is expressed by equation 2.1, which will be our working definition of probability:

$$P(\text{Outcome of Interest}) = \frac{\text{Number of Ways an Outcome of Interest Can Occur}}{\text{Total Number of Ways Outcomes Can Occur}}$$

(2.1)

Example 2.1: You have a bag of 10 marbles. 3 of the marbles are red, and 7 of the marbles are blue. What's the probability of drawing a red marble from the bag?

Answer: The bag only contains 2 types of marbles, but there are really 10 total possible outcomes for drawing a marble since the bag contains 10 marbles. Of those 10 marbles, 3 are red. Therefore, the probability of drawing a red marble, written as $P(\text{Red})$ or P_{Red}, is:

$$P(\text{Red}) = P_{Red} = \frac{\text{Red Marbles}}{\text{Total Marbles}} = \frac{3}{10} = .3 \qquad (2.2)$$

Example 2.2: You have 8♥3♥, and the board is T♥5♦2♥7♣. What's the probability that you'll hit a flush on the river?

Answer: Between your hole cards and the board cards, 4 hearts are in play, meaning that 9 hearts remain in the deck. Since we know 6 cards (your 2 hole cards and the 4 board cards), $52 - 6 = 46$ cards remain in the deck. The probability of making a flush on the river is therefore $\frac{9}{46} \approx .19576$.

Example 2.3: You have two standard six-sided dice. What's the probability of rolling an 11?

Answer:

$$P(11) = \frac{\text{Number of Ways to Roll an 11}}{\text{Total Number of Possible Rolls}} \qquad (2.3)$$

What numbers should we place in the numerator (the top) and the denominator (the bottom) of equation 2.3?

One possible answer is that $P(11) = \frac{1}{11} \approx .0909$ since it appears that 11 rolls are possible: {2, 3, 4, 5, 6, 7, 8, 9, 10, 11, and 12}, and only one of them is 11.[2] However, this is wrong because each possible roll isn't equally likely. More ways exist for some numbers to be rolled compared to other numbers. To see why this is so, let's express each possible roll as (*a,b*), where *a* is the number on the first die and *b* is the number on the second die. The *outcome space* (the set of all possible outcomes) for rolling two dice is {(1,1), (1,2), (1,3), (1,4), (1,5), (1,6), (2,1), (2,2), (2,3), (2,4), (2,5), (2,6), (3,1), (3,2), (3,3), (3,4), (3,5), (3,6), (4,1), (4,2), (4,3), (4,4), (4,5), (4,6), (5,1), (5,2), (5,3), (5,4), (5,5), (5,6), (6,1), (6,2), (6,3), (6,4), (6,5), (6,6)}. 36 equally likely rolls are possible. 2 of them, (5,6) and (6,5), result in an 11. Therefore, the probability of rolling an 11 is really:

$$P(11) = \frac{\text{Number of Ways to Get 11}}{\text{Total Number of Possible Rolls}} = \frac{2}{36} = \frac{1}{18} \qquad (2.4)$$

In example 2.3, notice that we completely define the outcome space by writing every possible way to roll two dice such that each possible way is equally likely. Then, we take the number of ways to get 11 as a subset of the outcome space. If you do all your probability problems like this, you'll never go wrong. Unfortunately, individually listing every outcome in an outcome space is usually way too time-consuming in most situations. 36 outcomes are possible when rolling two six-sided dice. Imagine how many possible outcomes exist when dealing with situations arising from a deck of 52 cards!

---

2. Braces, { }, are usually used to enclose the members of a set.

Permutations

Substituting the appropriate numbers in the numerator and denominator of equation 2.1 involves knowing how to count things that are sometimes tricky to count. One concept that will help you with counting is the idea of a *permutation*. A permutation is a particular ordering of elements in a set. If a set has two objects, *a* and *b,* then the permutations of that set are {*a,b*} and {*b,a*}.

Example 2.4: List all the permutations of the flop A♣K♥Q♠.[3]

Answer: The set's permutations are A♣K♥Q♠, A♣Q♠K♥, K♥A♣Q♠, K♥Q♠A♣, Q♠A♣K♥, and Q♠K♥A♣. The first element in each permutation is the first card on the flop, the second element in each permutation is the second card on the flop, and the third element in each permutation is the third card on the flop.

One way to count permutations is to list them all individually, as we just did in example 2.4. A faster way to count permutations is to take the number of ways to choose the first element, multiply that by the number of ways to choose the second element given that you've chosen the first element, and continue until all the elements have been chosen. Following this procedure for the A♣K♥Q♠ flop, we see that there are 3 ways to choose the first element (A♣, K♥, or Q♠). Once the first element is chosen, 2 ways exist to choose the second element (if the first element is the A♣, then the second element is either the K♥ or the Q♠; if the first element is the K♥, then the second element is either the A♣ or the Q♠; and if the first element is the Q♠, the second element is

---

3. Formal set notation might express this flop as {A♣, K♥, Q♠}, but there's no need for excessive formalities. I'll drop the braces when they seem unnecessary.

either the A♣ or the K♥). And once the second element is chosen, only 1 way exists to choose the third element; the third element is completely determined because there are only three objects. Therefore, there are 3•2•1 = 6 permutations of A♣K♥Q♠.

Example 2.5: How many permutations of hole cards are there?

Answer: 52 possibilities that exist for the 1st card, and 51 remaining possibilities exist for the 2nd card given that the first card has already been chosen. The total number of permutations is 52•51 = 2,652. Again, notice that order matters when it comes to permutations. Although A♣K♣ and K♣A♣ are the same hand when it comes to the logic of playing poker, they are two distinct hands when thinking in terms of permutations.

From the definition of permutations and the definition of probability in equation 2.1, we see that one way of calculating probabilities is to take the number of permutations of an *outcome of interest* and then to divide it by the total number of permutations of all possible outcomes.

Example 2.6: Calculate the probability of seeing a flop of A♣K♥Q♠ if you're observing a table and don't know anyone's hole cards.

Answer: From example 2.4, we already know that there are 6 permutations of A♣K♥Q♠. To find the total number of permutations of flops, recognize that there are 52 possibilities for the first card, 51 possibilities for the second card given that the first card has been determined, and 50 possibilities for the third card given that the first two cards have been determined. Therefore, there are 52•51•50 = 132,600 permutations of flops, and the probability of seeing a flop of A♣K♥Q♠ is:

$$\frac{6}{132,600} = \frac{1}{22,100} \approx .00004525 \qquad (2.5)$$

Example 2.7: Calculate the probability of being dealt AKs.

Answer: First, we need to calculate the number of AKs permutations. The first card can be 1 of 4 aces or 4 kings, meaning that 8 possibilities exist for the first card. Given that the first card is an ace or king, only one possibility exists for the second card—the card of the same suit as the first card (for example, if the first card is the A♣, the second card has to be the K♣). The number of AKs permutations is $8 \cdot 1 = 8$.[5] To find $P(AKs)$, divide 8, the number of AKs permutations, by the total number of permutations for two cards, which we know from example 2.5 to be $52 \cdot 51 = 2,652$. The probability of being dealt AKs is:

$$\frac{8}{2,652} = \frac{1}{331.5} \approx .003017 \qquad (2.6)$$

Factorials

When finding how many permutations exist, we often have to multiply several numbers together where each number is one less than the preceding number. Suppose we want to find how many ways a deck can be ordered. 52 possibilities exist for the first card, 51 possibilities exist for the second card, 50 possibilities exist for the third card, and so on, all the way down to 1 possibility for the 52nd card. The number

---

4. Another way of finding the number of AKs permutations is to realize that there are four different types of AKs (clubs, diamonds, hearts, and spades) and that each type of AKs has 2 permutations (AK and KA), meaning that there are $4 \cdot 2 = 8$ permutations of AKs.

of permutations is $52 \cdot 51 \cdot 50 \ldots \cdot 3 \cdot 2 \cdot 1 \approx 8.066 \cdot 10^{67}$.[5] Writing out products of 52 numbers can be quite cumbersome, but luckily, there's a notational device to help us out: the factorial—denoted by an exclamation point. Using a factorial, $52 \cdot 51 \cdot 50 \cdot \ldots \cdot 3 \cdot 2 \cdot 1$ can be represented much more compactly as 52!. In general:

$$n! = n(n-1)(n-2) \ldots (3)(2)(1) \qquad (2.7)$$

In equation 2.7, n is a positive integer.

Example 2.8: What's 6!?

Answer: $6! = 6 \cdot 5 \cdot 4 \cdot 3 \cdot 2 \cdot 1 = 720$

Example 2.9: What's 20!?

Answer: $20! = 20 \cdot 19 \cdot 18 \cdot \ldots \cdot 3 \cdot 2 \cdot 1 = 2{,}432{,}902{,}008{,}176{,}640{,}000$

Now, imagine that you're at a 10-handed table. That means that 20 cards have been dealt, and in addition, there are 5 more cards for the flop, the turn, and the river. The number of permutations is $52 \cdot 51 \cdot 50 \ldots \cdot 30 \cdot 29 \cdot 28 \approx 7.407 \cdot 10^{39}$.[6] To express this with factorials, we can say $\frac{52!}{27!}$. The 27! in the denominator cancel out all the factors less than 28 in the numerator. To see how this works, consider equation 2.8:

---

5. $8.066 \cdot 10^{67} = 80{,}660{,}000$ That's 8,066 followed by 64 zeroes!

6. If you read *KPBTN*, you'll recognize this example. My answer here is different because the answer here is the correct answer. In *KPBTN*, the incorrect answer, 25!, snuck through the cracks. Publishing an error-free book is tough work, so I have an errata section for my books at my website, www.killerev.com. I also have a frequently asked questions (FAQ) section for my books. If you're having trouble matching a result in this book, first visit the errata and FAQ sections—chances are that your problem will be addressed in one of those sections. If that doesn't help, contact me via the form on my webpage.

$$\frac{5!}{3!} = \frac{5 \cdot 4 \cdot 3 \cdot 2 \cdot 1}{3 \cdot 2 \cdot 1} = 5 \cdot 4 = 20 \qquad (2.8)$$

Notice how the 3, the 2, and the 1 in the denominator cancel out the 3, the 2, and the 1 in the numerator.

Equation 2.9 gives the number of permutations if r objects are drawn without replacement from a pool of n objects:

$$_nP_r = \frac{n!}{(n-r)!} \qquad (2.9)$$

Notice how all the factors in the denominator will cancel with factors in the numerator—much in the same way that they do in equation 2.8.

Example 2.10: You enter a 10-player STT where the top 3 players are paid. How many permutations of *in-the-money* (ITM) finishes are there?

Answer:

$$_{10}P_3 = \frac{10!}{(10-3)!} = \frac{10!}{7!} = 10 \cdot 9 \cdot 8 = 720 \qquad (2.10)$$

Combinations

Permutations are great, but sometimes, keeping track of specific orderings isn't necessary. After all, many times when a group of cards is dealt in poker, order doesn't really matter. Permutations aren't useless for poker-related calculations; some poker calculations are easiest when thinking about permutations. However, another method of counting exists: *combinations.* When considering combinations, order doesn't matter; a combination is an unordered sampling of objects. For example, A♣K♣ and K♣A♣ are both representations of the same combination of hole cards.

One way to determine the number of AKs combinations is to list them all and count them: {A♣K♣, A♦K♦, A♥K♥,

A♠K♠}. Since order doesn't matter, we can also use a slightly different multiplication method than the one we used to find permutations by considering only one AKs ordering. Suppose the first card is an ace and the second card is a king. There are 4 aces in the deck, and for each ace, there is only 1 king of the same suit. Thus, there are 4•1 = 4 AKs combinations. Yet another way to find the number of AKs combinations is to start with the fact that there are 8 *permutations* of AKs. To find the number of AKs *combinations,* we can then divide out the permutations leading to doubly counted combinations (e.g., we don't want to double count A♣K♣ and K♣A♣ since they're the same combination). There are two cards, meaning that there are 2! = 2 permutations for each AKs combination and a total of $\frac{8}{2}$ = 4 AKs combinations.[7]

Equation 2.11 is the general formula for the number of possible combinations when *r* objects are drawn without replacement from a pool of *n* objects (referred to as "*n* choose *r*," which is denoted as $_nC_r$ or $\binom{n}{r}$):

$$_nC_r = \binom{n}{r} = \frac{n!}{r!(n-r)!} \tag{2.11}$$

Equation 2.11 comes from taking $_nP_r$ and dividing by *r*!, the number of permutations of a set containing *r* distinct objects.[8]

Example 2.11: You hold AA. How many combinations of flops are there?

---

7. A great way of checking answers is to arrive at them using multiple methods, making sure that each produces the same answer.
8. Some calculators have !, $_nP_r$, and $_nC_r$ functions built in. Check to see if yours does. If not, a web search at Google (www.google.com) should point you in the direction of an online tool that can perform these calculations. Go Internet—as long as you're skilled at separating trash from treasure, the Internet is an information gold mine!

Answer: We know two of the cards in the deck (your two aces), so we're choosing 3 cards from a deck of 50 cards. The number of combinations of flops, given that you know your two hole cards, is:

$$\binom{50}{3} = \frac{50!}{3!(50-3)!} = \frac{50!}{3!47!} = \frac{50 \cdot 49 \cdot 48}{3 \cdot 2 \cdot 1} = 19,600 \qquad (2.12)$$

In general, there are 19,600 possible flops given that you only know your hole cards.

Example 2.12: You hold AK. What's the probability that you don't hit an ace or a king?

Answer: From example 2.11, we know that there are 19,600 possible combinations of flops since you only know your 2 hole cards. Meanwhile, the flops not containing an ace or a king arise from drawing 3 cards from the pool of 44 non-aces and non-kings in the deck:

$$\binom{44}{3} = \frac{44!}{3!(44-3)!} = \frac{44!}{3!41!} = \frac{44 \cdot 43 \cdot 42}{3 \cdot 2 \cdot 1} = 13,244 \qquad (2.13)$$

The probability of not hitting an ace or a king is:

$$\frac{13,244}{19,600} \approx .6757 \qquad (2.14)$$

Example 2.13: You hold A♥K♥. What's the probability of flopping exactly two hearts?

Answer: Again, from example 2.11, we know that there are 19,600 possible combinations of flops since you only know your 2 hole cards. Regarding the flops containing exactly two hearts, you're choosing 2 cards from the pool of 11 hearts and then choosing 1 of the remaining 39 non-hearts in the deck:

$$P(2 \text{ Hearts}) = \frac{\binom{11}{2}\binom{39}{1}}{19,600} = \frac{2,145}{19,600} \approx .1094 \qquad (2.15)$$

Example 2.14: You have QQ, and you put your opponent on AA, KK, QQ, JJ, TT, 99, 88, AK, AQ, AJ, AT, A9s, or A8s. What's the probability that your opponent has AA or KK?

Answer: To answer this question, we need to break your opponent's distribution down in terms of the number of combinations available for each possible holding.

- AA, KK, JJ, TT, 99, and 88 have 6 combinations each. Take AA for example. There are 4•3 = 12 permutations of AA, meaning that there are $\frac{4\cdot3}{2!} = \frac{12}{2} = 6$ combinations of AA (we divide by 2! to get rid of the double counts because there are 2! permutations of 2 objects).

- QQ has only 1 combination since there are only 2 queens left in the deck.

- AK, AJ, and AT have 16 combinations each. Take AK, for example. There are 4 aces and 4 kings in the deck, and 4•4 = 16.

- AQ has 8 combinations. There are 4 aces in the deck and 2 queens (since you already hold 2 queens), and 4•2 = 8.

- A9s and A8s have 4 combinations each. Take A9s for example. The only ways to have A9s are to have A♣9♣, A♦9♦, A♥9♥, or A♠9♠.

In total, your opponent's hand distribution comprises 6(6) + 1(1) + 16(3) + 8(1) + 4(2) = 101 combinations. AA and KK represent 12 of those combinations. Therefore, the probability that your opponent has AA or KK is $\frac{12}{101} \approx$ .1188.

Whether you use permutations or combinations to find probabilities will be a question of convenience. Sometimes, it's more natural to use permutations to describe a situation. Other times, it's more natural to use combinations to describe a situation. Just make sure that you stay consistent. If you begin doing a problem using permutations, make sure that *all* the work in that problem is in terms of permutations. If you begin doing a problem using combinations, make sure that *all* the work in that problem is done in terms of combinations.

Mutual Exclusivity and Complements

Instead of considering the probability of not flopping an ace or a king when holding AK, let's instead consider the probability of flopping at least one ace or king. Let's call an ace or a king a matching card (MC, for short). Equation 2.16 gives the probability of flopping at least one MC:

$$P(\text{At Least One MC}) = P(1MC) + P(2MCs) + P(3MCs) \quad (2.16)$$

We can add P(1MC), P(2MCs), and P(3MCs) because 1MC, 2MCs, and 3MCs are outcomes that have no overlap; it's impossible for a flop to meet more than one of these conditions. In math speak, outcomes with no overlap are said to be mutually exclusive.[9]

If you were to follow equation 2.16, you would find P(1MC), P(2MCs), and P(3MCs), and then you would add them together. You would get the correct answer, but mutual exclusivity provides a shortcut. The entire outcome space of flops is {0MCs, 1MC, 2MCs, 3MCs}. Since the sum of the probabilities of all the outcomes in a properly defined outcome space have to add up to 1:

$$P(0MCs) + P(1MC) + P(2MCs) + P(3MCs) = 1 \quad (2.17)$$

$$(P(1MC) + P(2MCs) + P(3MCs)) = 1 - P(0MCs) \quad (2.18)$$

9. We didn't say this before when talking about outcome spaces, but all the outcomes in a properly defined outcome space are mutually exclusive.

Flopping 0 MCs is said to be the complement of flopping at least 1 MC. In general, a set of outcomes, plus its complement, comprises the entire outcome space of an event. The idea of complements can be used to find the probability of flopping at least 1 MC:

Step 1: Find the probability of the complement (flopping 0 MCs).

Step 2: Subtract the probability of the complement from 1 to get the probability of flopping at least 1 MC.

In example 2.12, we found that $P(0MCs) = \frac{13,244}{19,600} \approx .6757$. Therefore, the probability of flopping at least 1 GC is:

$$1 - \frac{13,244}{19,600} = \frac{6,356}{19,600} \approx .3243 \tag{2.19}$$

If you're calculating a probability that requires you to add the probabilities of a bunch of mutually exclusive events, determine whether it's possible to use complements to make things easier.

Example 2.15: You're playing in an STT where first pays $100, second pays $60, and third pays $40. You're one of four remaining players. Prior to posting the blinds, the stacks are:

SB: T2,000

BB: T3,000

UTG: T5,000

B: T5,000

Blinds are T150–T300, and action folds to SB—who shoves all-in. SB is somewhat short-stacked, with just over 6bb after posting. Normally, players in SB's position are somewhat liberal with the hands they'll shove all-in with, but this particular player has been very *tight,* and he's folded in similar situations before—indicating that he's not shoving with any two. You put him on {AK–A9, AA–55}. You have AJ; what's the probability that you're not dominated by a higher ace or facing a pocket pair higher than TT?

Answer: First, calculate the total number of hand combinations in SB's range. 12 combinations each are possible for AK, AQ, AT, and A9 (3 aces times 4 possibilities for the kicker); 9 combinations are possible for AJ (3 aces times 3 jacks), 3 combinations each are possible for AA and JJ ($_3C_2 =$ 3); and 6 combinations each are possible for KK, QQ, TT, 99, 88, 77, 66, and 55 ($_4C_2 = 6$). In total, SB's shoving range comprises $12(4) + 9(1) + 3(2) + 6(8) = 111$ combinations. Of those, 24 combinations are a higher ace (AK or AQ) and 18 combinations are a pocket pair higher than TT (AA, KK, QQ, or JJ). The probability of being against one of these hands is $\frac{42}{111}$, so the probability of not being against one of these hands is $\frac{69}{111}$.

Example 2.16: You have A♣K♦, and the flop is 9♦8♣2♠. You're heads-up on the flop, and your opponent *pushes* all-in. If you call, what's the probability that you'll catch at least one ace or king?

Answer: This problem doesn't give us any information about the opponent who pushed all-in. Therefore, you're drawing from a deck of 47 cards containing 3 aces and 3 kings.

The best way to find the probability of hitting at least one ace or king is to use complements. We'll find the probability of hitting no aces or kings and then subtract that probability from 1 to get the probability of hitting at least one ace or king.

Not hitting an ace or a king on the turn and the river is a joint event, meaning that the probability of it happening is the probability of it not happening on the turn multiplied by the probability of it not happening on the river (given that it didn't happen on the turn). The probability of not hitting an ace or a king on the turn is $\frac{41}{47}$ since there are 41 cards that are neither aces nor kings in the deck of 47 cards. Given that the turn is neither an ace nor a king, the probability that the river is neither an ace nor a king is $\frac{40}{46}$. Therefore, the probability of missing the turn and the river is $\left(\frac{41}{47}\right)\left(\frac{40}{46}\right) \approx .7586$. The probability of hitting at least one ace or king is the complement of this probability: $1 - .7586 = .2414$.

Example 2.17: You're SB with JTs. The blinds are T200–T400, and you have T2,000. If you push all-in, your opponent, who has T3,000, will call with AA, KK, QQ, JJ, TT, 99, 88, AK, or AQ. What's the probability that you steal the blinds after pushing all-in?

Answer: To figure out the probability that your opponent folds to your all-in bet, we first need to express his calling distribution in terms of combinations for each possible holding:

- AA, KK, QQ, 99, and 88 have 6 combinations each. Take AA, for example. There are $4 \cdot 3 = 12$ permutations of AA, meaning that there are $\frac{4 \cdot 3}{2!} = \frac{12}{2} = 6$ combinations of AA (we divide by 2! to get rid of the double counts because there are 2! permutations of 2 objects).

- JJ and TT have 3 combinations each. Take JJ, for example. Because you have a jack in your hand, there are only 3 jacks left in the deck, meaning that there are $\frac{3 \cdot 2}{2!} = 3$ combinations of JJ. Since you have a T in your hand, the same is true for TT.

- AK and AQ have 16 combinations each. Take AK, for example. There are 4 aces and 4 kings in the deck, and $4 \cdot 4 = 16$.

In total, your opponent will call your all-in with 6(5) + 3(2) + 16(2) = 68 combinations. Since you know your hole cards, there are 50 cards left in the deck, meaning that there are $\frac{50 \cdot 49}{2!}$ = 1,225 possible combinations of hole cards that your opponent might hold. Your opponent will fold 1,225 − 68 = 1,157 combinations, meaning that the probability that you steal the blinds is $\frac{1,157}{1,225} \approx .9445$.

Joint Probabilities, Conditional Probabilities, and Independent Events

A joint probability is the probability of an event that actually comprises many individual outcomes. For example, being dealt AK is a joint event because being dealt an ace and being dealt a king are considered individual events that both must happen for one to hold AK. We've just tossed this term "joint probability" into the mix, but we've already been finding joint probabilities using permutations and combinations. Another useful way of finding a joint probability is to take the probability of the first outcome and to multiply it by the probability of the second outcome given that the first outcome happened. If there's a third outcome, then multiply by the probability of the third outcome given that the first and second outcomes happened. Continue this process until you cover all the individual outcomes comprising the joint outcome of interest.

Consider the probability of rolling two dice and getting a 12. To roll a 12, you need to roll a 6 on the first die and a 6 on the second die. If we call rolling a 6 on the first die A and rolling a 6 on the second die B, then we can write the probability of rolling a six on both dice symbolically as $P(A \cap B)$; the "$\cap$" symbol means "and." $P(A \cap B)$ is equal to the probability of A happening times the probability of B happening given that A happens. The probability of B happening given that A happens can be written as $P(B|A)$; the symbol "|" means "given." $P(B|A)$ is referred to as a *conditional probability*. Equation 2.20 gives the expression for $P(A \cap B)$:

$$P(A \cap B) = P(A)P(B|A) \qquad (2.20)$$

Equation 2.20 not only applies to the dice example, but it also applies any time you have two outcomes, A and B, that compose a joint event.

Going back to our dice, the outcome of the first roll doesn't influence the outcome of the second roll. This means that $P(B|A) = P(B)$. Whenever $P(B|A) = P(B)$, events A and B are said to be independent. Meanwhile, whenever $P(B|A) \neq P(B)$, events A and B are said to be dependent (what a shocker). The probability of getting a 12 is therefore $P(12) = P(A \cap B) = P(A)P(B) = \left(\frac{1}{6}\right)\left(\frac{1}{6}\right) = \frac{1}{36}$.

The rolls of the first die and the second die are said to be independent of each other because the outcome of the first roll doesn't affect the outcome of the second roll; the probability of rolling a 6 on the second die is $\frac{1}{6}$, regardless of what number is rolled on the first die. Equation 2.21 is the joint probability of an event comprising two independent events:

$$P(A \cap B) = P(A)P(B) \qquad (2.21)$$

Probability textbooks tend to make a big deal out of the difference between equations 2.20 and 2.21. After all, the concept of independent events is pretty important. But really, equation 2.21 is nothing more than a special case of equation 2.20, where $P(B|A) = P(B)$.

When calculating the probabilities for joint events, you're always multiplying probabilities. Make sure that you're multiplying the correct probabilities, and you're good to go.

Example 2.18: What's the probability of being dealt pocket aces?

Answer: The probability that the first card is an ace is $\frac{4}{52}$. Given that the first card drawn is an ace, the probability that the second card in an ace is $\frac{3}{51}$.

$$P(\text{AA}) = \left(\tfrac{4}{52}\right)\left(\tfrac{3}{51}\right) = \tfrac{12}{2,652} = \tfrac{1}{221} \approx .004525 \qquad (2.22)$$

Probabilities Depend on Knowledge

The outcome of any probability calculation depends on what we know about a situation. Examples 2.19 and 2.20 illustrate this point.

Example 2.19: What's the probability of seeing a flop containing 3 aces?

Answer: The way this situation is worded, we must assume that the flop is being drawn from a deck of 52 cards. A flop of 3 aces results from drawing 3 aces from the pool of 4 aces in the deck. The total number of possible flops is given by the number of combinations that exist for drawing 3 cards from a pool of 52 cards.

$$P(\text{AAA}) = \frac{\binom{4}{3}}{\binom{52}{3}} = \tfrac{4}{22,100} = \tfrac{1}{5,525} \approx .0001810 \qquad (2.23)$$

Example 2.20: What's the probability of seeing a flop containing 3 aces given that you hold AK?

Answer: A flop of 3 aces results from drawing 3 aces from the pool of 3 aces in the deck. The total number of possible flops is given by the number of combinations that exist for drawing 3 cards from a pool of 50 cards.

$$P(\text{AAA}) = \frac{\binom{3}{3}}{\binom{50}{3}} = \frac{1}{19,600} \approx .00005102 \qquad (2.24)$$

When calculating probabilities, it's very important to keep track of whether events are independent of each other. You also need to be aware of your state of knowledge concerning the situation you're calculating probabilities for. Whenever you write down a probability, check to see if it makes sense according to what's physically happening. For example, if you draw an ace from a deck of cards, there's no possible way that the probability of the second card being an ace can also be $\frac{4}{52}$ because after drawing the first ace, there are only 3 aces remaining in a 51-card deck. By constantly checking yourself along the way, you should minimize the likelihood of making a mistake when calculating probabilities.

Example 2.21: Take the situation from example 2.2 (you have 8♥3♥, and the board is T♥5♦2♥7♣). Except now, you put your opponent on JTs or T9s. What's the probability that you'll hit a flush on the river?

Answer: You know your 2 hole cards and the 4 board cards. You also know what your opponent has. Since the T♥ is on the board, there's no way that your opponent can hold the J♥ or 9♥. With respect to hearts versus non-hearts, you effectively know 8 cards in the deck, 4 of which are hearts. This means that there are 9 hearts remaining in a deck of 44 cards. The probability that you make a flush on the river is $\frac{9}{44} \approx .205$. Notice how knowledge of your opponent's hole cards resulted in an answer different from the one we got for example 2.2. However, also notice how this knowledge didn't dramatically increase your probability of winning.

The Binomial Distribution

When playing poker, we often have information pertaining to the frequency with which actions happen. For example, a particular opponent has raised 2 out of 15 hands when UTG, or a particular opponent has attempted to steal blinds 4 out of 11 times action has folded to him and he's been in late position. Whenever a player raises or doesn't raise or whenever a player steals or doesn't steal are two types of situations in which an opponent's action can be thought of as binary—that is, where an opponent either executes a particular action or doesn't execute a particular action. Suppose the probability that an opponent will execute a specific action is p. This means that the probability that an opponent won't execute that action is $1 - p$. If the choice to execute the particular action in question is made n times and we let r represent the number of times the action is executed, then equation 2.25 is the probability of seeing the event executed r times out of n:

$$\binom{n}{r}p^r(1 - p)^{n-r} \qquad (2.25)$$

$\binom{n}{r}$ is in this expression because there are $\binom{n}{r}$ combinations for which the event with a probability of p can take place r out of n times.

Example 2.22: If you're dealt 50 hands, what's the probability that you'll be dealt AA at least 2 times?

Answer: This question is best answered using equation 2.25 along with the idea of complements. From example 2.18, we know that $P(AA) = \frac{6}{1,326} = \frac{1}{221}$. The probability of being dealt AA at least 2 times in the span of 50 hands is equal to:

$$1 - \binom{50}{0}\left(\frac{1}{221}\right)^0\left(\frac{220}{221}\right)^{50} - \binom{50}{1}\left(\frac{1}{221}\right)^1\left(\frac{220}{221}\right)^{49} \approx .02172 \qquad (2.26)$$

(In equation 2.26, $\binom{50}{0}\left(\frac{1}{221}\right)^0\left(\frac{220}{221}\right)^{50}$ is the probability of getting dealt AA exactly 0 times, and $\binom{50}{1}\left(\frac{1}{221}\right)^1\left(\frac{220}{221}\right)^{49}$ is the probability of getting dealt AA exactly 1 time.)

Sigma Notation

Sometimes, something called sigma notation is useful when expressing calculations to be done with the binomial distribution. Sigma notation is a shorthand way of expressing sums. For example, the sum of integers from 1 to 10 looks like equation 2.27 in regular notation and equation 2.28 in sigma notation.

$$1 + 2 + 3 + 4 + 5 + 6 + 7 + 8 + 9 + 10 = 55 \qquad (2.27)$$

$$\sum_{n=1}^{10} n = 55 \qquad (2.28)$$

This notation tells us to start with $n = 1$, and to continue summing until $n = 10$.

Example 2.23: $\displaystyle\sum_{n=2}^{7} n = ?$

Answer: $2 + 3 + 4 + 5 + 6 + 7 = 27$

Example 2.24: $\displaystyle\sum_{r=3}^{5}\binom{5}{r}p^r(1 - p)^{5-r} = ?$

Answer: $\binom{5}{3}p^3(1 - p)^2 + \binom{5}{4}p^4(1 - p)^1 + \binom{5}{5}p^5(1 - p)^0$

Approximations: Independence

Doing precise analysis of tournament situations can be challenging and extremely time-consuming at times. And often, getting answers correct to several decimal places isn't necessary. All we need are easy-to-use approximations that yield results good enough to work with.

Your opponents' hands aren't independent of each other. But dealing with all the conditional probabilities involved can quickly become a nightmare—especially when doing analysis of preflop all-in scenarios. Since treating the hands of multiple opponents as independent of each other makes analysis much easier, let's see how much error this introduces.

My good friend, Ryan Patterson, ran computer simulations consisting of 1 billion hands each. In each simulation, we were UTG, and we assigned a particular calling distribution to all our opponents. Each simulation found out the probability of not being called as a function of the number of players remaining to act. This probability was then compared to the probability of not being called when opponents' hands are treated as being independent of each other. For example, if you hold 22 and you have one opponent who'll call with AA–JJ, the probability that he'll fold is .980. If you have two opponents who'll call with AA–JJ, simulation 1 shows that the probability that they both fold is .961. Take .980 and square it (the *independence* approximation), and you get .960. The difference between the simulation result and the independence approximation is .001 (i.e., treating the hands as independent introduces an error of .001). The distributions used for each of the simulations are in table 2.1:

TABLE 2.1: Opponent's Calling Distributions for Each Independence Simulation

Simulation 1	{AA-JJ}
Simulation 2	{AA-22}
Simulation 3	{AK, QJ, T9, 87, 65, 43, 22}
Simulation 4	{AA–88, AK–AT}
Simulation 5	{AA-22, AK–A2, KQ–KT, QJ–QT, JT, 98s–65s}

Some of these distributions—especially the one used in simulation 3—aren't realistic calling distributions. But the goal of these simulations is to see if the error introduced by assuming independence is small for a wide range of calling distributions.

The difference between the simulation results and the independence approximation increases as the number of opponents increases. The largest difference for each simulation was:

- Simulation 1: .005

- Simulation 2: .005

- Simulation 3: .005

- Simulation 4: .022

- Simulation 5: .021

In simulations 4 and 5, errors on the order of .01 were encountered beginning with about 4 opponents.

This study is by no means exhaustive, but it at least suggests that treating opponents' hands as independent won't introduce significant errors in our analyses. Therefore, I'll reserve the right to treat opponents' hands as independent from time to time to make this no more of a math textbook than it already is. And I'll encourage you to assume that your opponents' hands are independent of each other to make the analyses you engage in much more manageable.[10]

---

10. Please don't misunderstand this section and assume that it's *always* okay to treat dependent events as independent. This section is very specific in that it's about opponents' hand distributions.

Approximations: Clumping

Having solely considered the hand distributions of players remaining to act behind you, let's now consider the impact that your opponents' actions have on the probabilities associated with players remaining to act. Specifically, let's address the notion of clumping: when players in *early position* (EP) fold, it's more likely that players in later position will have good hands since the players in EP threw away bad hands.

Performing analyses that ignore clumping is much easier than performing analyses accounting for clumping, so just like what we did in the last section, we want to investigate the error introduced by ignoring clumping. Once again, my friend, Ryan, ran simulations consisting of 1 billion hands each. We assigned folding distributions to the players in front of us and calling distributions to the players behind us. As a function of the number of players who folded in front of us, we found the probability that all the opponents behind us would fold as a function of the number of opponents behind us. Simulations were performed for all numbers of players in front and behind (for all table sizes). As expected, the case for which clumping has the largest effect is when you're SB at a 10-handed table where 8 players have folded to you. Table 2.2 (p. 36, top) lists the playing distributions for players acting before us (meaning that players who fold in front of us are on the complements of these distributions).

Distribution 4, {None}, represents the situation in which the players in front of us fold no matter what. Information-wise, this is equivalent to being first to act. The calling distributions for players behind us, given that you push all-in, are given in table 2.3 (p. 36, middle).

We looked for differences between Distributions 1–3 and Distribution 4. If clumping isn't a significant effect, we shouldn't see much difference.

TABLE 2.2: Playing Distributions for Players in Front of Us (Clumping Simulations)

Distribution 1	{AA–77, AK–A9, KQ}
Distribution 2	{AA–22, AK–A2, KQ–KT, QJ–QT}
Distribution 3	{AA–22, AK–A2, KQ–KT, QJ–65, QT}
Distribution 4	{None}

TABLE 2.3: Calling Distributions of Players Behind You (Clumping Simulations)

First Caller	[AA,22] || [AK,A2] || [KQ]
Second Caller	[AA,QQ]
Third Caller	[AA]
Fourth Caller	[AA]

TABLE 2.4: Clumping Errors as a Function of the Number of Folders in Front of You

FOLDERS	DIST. #1 MIN.	DIST. #1 MAX.	DIST. #2 MIN.
1	0	0	0
2	0	.01	.01
3	0	.01	.01
4	.01	.01	.01
5	.01	.01	.02
6	.01	.02	.02
7	.01	.02	.03
8	.01	.02	.04

Table 2.4 suggests that we can't completely ignore clumping when in late position at *fullhanded* tables since distributions #2 and #3 are representative of the types of distributions that players in front of you will be playing. The effect isn't huge, but it does come into play. Fortunately, an easy solution exists. Just take the numbers from the approximate error column and apply an on-the-fly adjustment to the numbers you get when not accounting for clumping. Use corrections on the lower end when EP players are on tight distributions, and apply corrections on the upper end when EP players are on *loose* distributions.

Example 2.25: You're SB at a 10-handed table. All 8 players before you fold. You have 52o, and if you go all-in, you think BB will call with {AA–22, AK–A2}. About what percentage of the time will BB fold?

Answer: First assume that clumping isn't a factor. {AA–22, AK–A2} is $11(6) + 2(3) + 10(16) + 2(12) = 256$ combinations. Your opponent holds 1 of $_{50}C_2 = 1,225$ combinations. Therefore, without accounting for clumping, the probability that BB will fold is $\frac{969}{1,225} \approx .79$. Since 8 players folded in front of you, clumping will come into play, so apply a clumping cor-

DIST. #2 MAX.	DIST. #3 MIN.	DIST. #3 MAX.	APPROX. ADJUSTMENT
.01	0	.01	≈ .00–.01
.01	.01	.01	≈ .01
.02	.01	.02	≈ .01–.02
.03	.01	.03	≈ .01–.03
.04	.02	.04	≈ .01–.03
.05	.02	.05	≈ .02–.04
.06	.03	.06	≈ .02–.05
.07	.04	.07	≈ .02–.06

rection based on the numbers in table 2.4. Based on table 2.4, we should apply a correction in the range of .02 to .06. The middle of this range is .04. The probability that BB folds is more accurately approximated to be somewhere around .75.

Chapter Summary

Probability calculations are a large component of most poker analyses. Although you won't be using everything covered in this chapter at the table, understanding this material is important if you want to do your own analyses of unique situations away from the table. And quality away-from-the-table analyses are a big component of winning play.

3

DISTRIBUTIONS

Introduction

Chapter 2 began by outlining the decision-making process you should use when playing NLHE tournaments:

1. Calculate the distribution of stacks resulting from a particular line of play.

2. Calculate the monetary value associated with this distribution of stacks.

3. Iterate steps 1 and 2 for all possible lines of play.

4. Pick the line of play resulting in the most valuable distribution of stacks.

In this and the next few chapters, we'll focus on step 1 of this process.

At times, it's possible to deduce the exact cards that an opponent is holding and the precise lines of play an opponent will take with those cards. But in general, the best you can do is to come up with ranges of hands and actions based on the information you've gained by being actively engaged in the process of observing how your opponents play. This whole notion of ranges may seem at first to reduce poker into a guessing game. But your success in tournaments will largely depend on how good you are at putting your opponents on ranges. Putting opponents on ranges is less of a guessing game and more of a practice in the arts of observation and deduction.

The ranges you deduce are the information that you must process to arrive at your decisions. Poker is a game involving many things, but at its heart, poker is a game of distributions.

Putting Opponents on Hand Distributions

The range of hands that an opponent may have is his hand distribution. Put your opponents on hand distributions that are too narrow and you're making a mistake. Put your opponents on hand distributions that are too wide and you're also making a mistake. You need to put your opponents on the most accurate distributions possible. If an opponent is pushing all-in with any two cards, then his pushing distribution is {Rand}, and assigning any other distribution would lead to you to fold more hands than you should. If an opponent is only reraising with AA-QQ, then putting him on {AA–JJ, AK} when he reraises would lead you to play too many hands.

Putting opponents on hand distributions is an exercise in processing two types of data: betting patterns and physical tells. When I play poker, I largely rely on betting-pattern information. If I happen to observe any physical tells, I use them to make appropriate adjustments to my betting-pattern dependent reads. Suppose I know that an opponent typically raises from EP with {TT+, AQ+}. One time he raises from EP, I notice that his hands tremble and that he announces his raise at a barely audible level. These physical cues would prompt me to shift his hand distribution from {TT+, AQ+} to KK+. The topic of physical tells can take up an entire book, and, in fact, some great books exist on the topic.[1] For starters, here are some common tells to look for:

- Players who don't pay attention to other players and who muck their hands quickly preflop are sitting around waiting for good cards.

- Players who don't pay attention to other players and have a bit of a clueless, blank stare tend to be somewhat loose-passive. Players like this do a lot of calling with questionable hands—bluffing them is tough. But the word *"passive"* in the loose-passive label is very important. When players like this start playing *aggressively,* they typically have very good hands.

- Players who pay close attention to the action when they're not in hands are usually dangerous opponents in the sense that they're usually playing both their cards *and* their opponents.

- Unsophisticated players who tend to act weak when strong and act strong when weak.

---

1. I highly recommend *Caro's Book of Tells* (Cardoza, 2003) and *Phil Hellmuth Presents Read 'em and Reap: A Career FBI Agent's Guide to Decoding Poker Tells* (Collins, 2006). For additional recommendations pertaining to tells or any other poker topic, check out my extensive book reviews at www.killerev.com.

- Sophisticated players who try to exploit inexperienced players and tend to act weak when strong and act strong when weak.

- Players who exhibit reverse tells; they act strong when strong and act weak when weak.

- A player whose neck vein pulsates typically has a very good hand.

- A player whose hand trembles typically has a very good hand.

- A player who makes a fast bet is more likely to be bluffing (this is a timing tell that can also be applied online).

- A player who makes a slow bet is more likely to have a very good hand (this is also a timing tell that can be applied online—my experience seems to dictate that online, the slow bet tell is a bit more reliable than the fast bet tell).

- A player who asks for a chip count is figuring out *implied odds* for a draw, feigning weakness, or trying to extract a tell from you.

- Players who seem to think of decisions purely in terms of who has whom covered place a high emphasis on survival and typically believe that their opponents do as well. These types of players have the potential to become reckless bullies when they become chip leaders.

- Players who put chips in their hands before it's their turn to act. This practice, known as bet loading, can mean a few different things: 1. the person intends on putting all the chips in his hand(s) in the pot, 2. the person intends to put at least some of the chips in his hand(s) in the pot, 3. the person doesn't want you to bet and has the chips in his hands simply to dissuade you from betting, or 4. nothing because the player habitually keeps the same number of chips in his hands at all times.

- A player with sunglasses who has them up but puts them down after looking at his hole cards is intending on playing the hand (obviously, this tell is only effective if that player looks at his hole cards immediately after receiving them).

This laundry list should be helpful, but realize that none of these tells are 100 percent reliable. In addition, what about tells not on this list? Perhaps the most important lesson I can impart regarding tells is the following: observing physical tells is really about establishing baseline behaviors for each of your opponents and figuring out what deviations from those baselines mean. With that being said, I do rely heavily on the first three tells on my laundry list when I'm at a brick-and-mortar table with unknown players.

Let's proceed to the other important piece of information you'll be logging: betting patterns. The number of betting patterns that you can observe is practically endless. The following are just some of the questions I try to answer when I'm probing for betting patterns:

- What are my opponents' preflop raising distributions as a function of position?

- What are my opponents' preflop reraising distributions as a function of relative position (i.e., if I have experience playing with a group of players, do they play differently as a function of who are specifically to their right and left)?

- Does a *limp-reraise* automatically mean QQ+?

- Does a player call instead of reraising with QQ+; in other words, is this opponent apt to slow play?

- Who at my table looks to steal blinds?

- Are there any bullies who play very loosely and aggressively when they have position?

- Do different bet sizes mean different things?

- What bet sizes allow me to extract value?

- What bet sizes allow me to steal pots?

- How do my opponents play postflop?

- Who calls down with middle or bottom pair?

- Who *check-raises* bluffs?

- Who employs *stop-and-goes*?

- Who folds unless he has top pair or better?

- Who *continuation bets* (CB)?

- Who doesn't continuation bet?

- Do players who check on the flop often fold on the turn?

- Who fires two bullets?

- Who fires three bullets?

- Who floats (i.e., calls bets or raises with the intention of bluffing later on in the hand)?

- Who plays draws passively?

- Who habitually semibluffs draws?

- Who's willing to bluff a missed draw?

- Who plays phantom *outs* (i.e., bluff when cards that appear to help draws hit even when not drawing)?

- etc., etc., etc.

The number of such questions I ask about my opponents is practically endless. The number of such questions *you* ask about *your* opponents should be just as long. I can't put every possible betting pattern in this book along with what each betting pattern means for every type of opponent you'll face. The main idea is that betting patterns are there if you look for them; if you aren't looking for them, you're doing your expected profits a big disservice.

By not knowing your opponents' betting patterns, you won't know whom to resteal against preflop; you won't know whom to check-raise bluff on the flop; you won't know how to extract as many chips as possible when you hit a monster; and in short, you'll be walking through a maze with a blindfold. Knowing your opponents' betting patterns as well as possible will allow you to exploit the holes in your opponents' games as profitably as possible.

Default Profiles of Unknown Opponents

Reading betting patterns is great, but what do you do when a tournament just starts, when new players are moved to your table, or when you're moved to another table? You can't afford to sit back idly while you learn *everything* about your opponents. Certain blind structures simply don't give you the time. Gun slinging is quite tough unless you have some idea as to how your opponents play. Fortunately, if you have a bit of playing experience under your belt, you actually have information about your opponents before you even sit at the table. That's right—you have information about players you've never seen in your life!

Before you even play a single hand, you have all your past poker-playing experience to draw on, meaning that you can assign a default player profile to any opponents you've never faced. This default profile will be the average of all the players you've ever played against. It takes both betting patterns and tells into account, and an accurate default player profile is essential to your success in tournament poker. Since poker evolves, the default profile I assign to my opponents now isn't the same as the default profile I assigned to my opponents two years ago, and most likely, it won't be the same as the default profile I assign to my opponents two years from now.

The more accurate this default profile is, the less trouble you'll get yourself into during the first orbit or two against fresh faces. However, this default profile is *not* enough to get you through an entire tournament. No matter how good a default profile is, you must identify as quickly as possible how each of your opponents deviates. As soon as your opponents show their true colors, you can then assign them to more specific player profiles—let's call these more specific player profiles archetypes.[2]

However, assigning archetypes still isn't enough. After all, archetypes are nothing more than slightly more specific versions of default player profiles. In reality, your job is never really done; your goal is to acquire as much nuanced information as possible about each of your opponents. And remember that it's possible to learn new things about players you've played thousands of hands against (you also need to

2. In *Killer Poker Shorthanded* (Lyle Stuart, 2007), JV and I put forth several player archetypes that we commonly encounter in shorthanded NLHE cash games. Check them out if you're looking for some inspiration.

monitor such frequently encountered foes for adjustments).
In the end, your primary goal is learning as much as possible
about your opponents, so you can work with the most accurate hand and action distributions possible.[3]

Example 3.1: Early in an MTT, action folds to you, and you
raise to 3bb with A♥J♠. CO and the blinds call your raise. You
and your opponents are all about 100bb deep. The flop is
A♠T♦2♣. You bet 5bb; CO folds; SB calls; BB folds. The turn is
5♣. SB checks; you bet 8bb; SB calls. The river is 7♦. SB checks;
you bet 10bb; SB calls. SB shows A♣3♠, and you take down
the pot. What conclusions do you make about this player?

Answer: The player's preflop call with A3o indicates that
he'll play any ace—even for a raise when he's *out of position*
(OOP). Some players who overvalue AX don't necessarily
overvalue other hands, but some do. I wouldn't immediately put hands like K7 and Q9 into the distribution of
hands he calls raises with, but I'd keep them in mind as postflop play evolves. And speaking of postflop play, note that
this player was content to call down with his hand. This is
the type of controllable player you'd love to engage in future
hands. If he has something really good, he'll probably be aggressive and let you know. If he happens to slow play big
hands, you'll find out when he calls down with a monster.
But regardless of how he plays his big hands, if you have
something marginal, like top pair with a medium kicker,
this player won't put you to any tough decisions—you can
value bet the flop, turn, and river—confident that this guy
won't try to pull a move like a check-raise bluff that can
move you off your hand.

3. And again, remember that accurate isn't the same thing as narrow. If an
    opponent is shoving all-in with any two cards, then the most accurate
    distribution assignable is "any two cards." The distributions you assign
    can't be too big, and they can't be too small. They need to be just right.

An important note about example 3.1 is that if you have any doubts about your opponent's playing style and the pot is really large with respect to your stack on the river, taking a free showdown with a hand that figures to be marginally ahead of your opponent's calling distribution isn't the worst thing you can do if you still have a decent number of big blinds in your stack. Suppose the pot is 60bb on the river, and your stack is 60bb. If your opponent checks to you, trying to eke out a 15bb–20bb value bet on the river might not be worth it if it's possible that you'll make a mistake where you either fold the winning hand to a check-raise bluff or call a check-raise with a losing hand.

Too Tight Is Better Than Too Loose

When coming up with the default player profile you assign to your opponents, there's an interesting phenomenon that you should be familiar with. Suppose that the default distribution you assign to EP raisers is {AT+, 77+}. If you see Skillz2PayDaBillz raise from EP with 33, you know that you should adjust his EP raising distribution to {AT+, 33+}. And you probably wouldn't be incorrect to argue that 22 and some other hands should also be included. Certainly, if you also observe that he raises from EP with KQ, then you should add KQ to his EP raising distribution and be on the lookout for raises with hands such as KJ, QJ, and JTs.[4]

---

4. Don't necessarily add hands like KJ, QJ, and JTs to his EP raising distribution, but definitely be on the lookout for them—especially if post-flop action indicates he might have one of these hands. Remember that hands of NLHE take place across four betting rounds (stacks permitting), and sometimes what happens during a later round of betting may indicate that you need to adjust a conclusion made during an early round of betting.

Still supposing that the default distribution you assign to EP raisers is {AT+, 77+}; let's now consider DragonSlayer. He's raised preflop twice from EP. Both of those hands went to showdown, and you got to see that he raised from EP with AK and JJ. This information isn't even close to being adequate for trimming DragonSlayer's EP raising distribution down to {AK, JJ+}. Tightening up hand distribution reads requires much more data than loosening up hand distribution reads.

Example 3.2: The default preflop 3-betting distribution you assign to players in the early rounds of MTTs is {AA–88, AK–AQ}. One player 3-bets 10 times within the first 50 hands. Miraculously, all hands go to showdown, and he has AA 2 times, KK 2 times, AK 3 times, QQ 2 times, and JJ 1 time. Assuming that this player's true 3-betting range is {AA–88, AK–AQ}, what's the probability that over the span of ten 3-bets, this player won't be seen raising with {TT–88, AQ}?

Answer: AA–88 is 7 hands with 6 combinations each, making 42 total combinations. AK–AQ is 2 hands with 16 combinations each, making 32 total combinations. In total, the {AA–88, AK–AQ} distribution comprises 74 combinations. Of those, {TT–88, AQ} comprise 6(3) + 16(1) = 34 combinations. The probability that this player doesn't show {TT–88, AQ} in 10 hands—given that he's on {AA–88, AK–AQ}—is $\left(\frac{40}{74}\right)^{10} \approx .002130$. This very low percentage indicates that {AA–88, AK–AQ} is probably wider than this player's actual preflop 3-betting distribution.

Example 3.3: Take the situation from example 3.2, except now, find the 3-betting distribution for which there's a 10 percent chance of seeing 3-bets from {AA–JJ, AK}.

Answer: First, solve equation 3.1 for x, the number of combinations in the distribution:

$$\left(\tfrac{40}{x}\right)^{10} = .10 \tag{3.1}$$

$$\left(\tfrac{40}{x}\right) = \sqrt[10]{.10} \tag{3.2}$$

$$\frac{40}{\sqrt[10]{.10}} = x \tag{3.3}$$

$$50.3570 \approx x \tag{3.4}$$

Since {AA–JJ, AK} make up 40 combinations, we're looking for about 10 more combinations. TT is 6 more combinations; meanwhile AQ is 16 more combinations. After seeing someone 3-bet 10 consecutive times with {AA–JJ, AK}, the widest possible distribution you can reasonably assign is along the lines of {AA–TT, AK} or {AA–JJ, AK–AQ}.

Another important consideration when it comes to default distributions is the amount of chips you'll lose, on average, as a function of whether the default distributions you assign are too loose or too tight:

1. Reads that are too loose tend to result in losing chips that shouldn't be lost.

2. Reads that are too tight tend to result in not winning chips that should be won.

Of these mistakes, #1 generally costs more chips than #2. However, don't take this to mean that mistake #2 is acceptable. Excessive preflop folding quickly adds up to many lost opportunities to win chips. And folding too many winning hands on the turn and the river is catastrophic.[5]

---

5. This doesn't mean that you should call with every hand that has just a slim shot at winning. Again, it's about how the hand you hold stacks up with respect to your opponents' distributions. But if the distributions

However, tight reads are easier to adjust, and they don't lead you to making big mistakes early—giving you the opportunity to figure your opponents out. Therefore, if your reads aren't going to be perfect to begin with, err a tad toward being too tight. But you should quickly look for evidence to loosen your reads where appropriate. And if after a few tournaments, you're finding that your default reads are systematically too tight, go ahead and loosen them up a bit. Refining default distributions and player archetypes is a process that never stops.

Finding the Narrowest and Widest Hand Distributions

Example 3.3 is a specific instance of a more general problem. When playing, you get to observe the frequency with which opponents make certain actions. Sometimes, you're fortunate enough to see a showdown. But when you're not fortunate enough to see a showdown, you can still get lots of information.

First, imagine that you've seen the same situation a practically infinite number of times against a particular opponent. For example, of the 100,000,000 hands you've played against him when he's been UTG at a 9-handed table, he's raised 5,000,000 times. $\frac{5,000,000}{100,000,000} = .05$ is a great estimate of the proportion of hands this player raises with. Since there are 1,326 combinations of hole cards, you can assume that

---

you assign to your opponents are off in a way that leads you to fold a very large percentage of winning hands on the turn and the river, then you're essentially leaking the chips that you put in during earlier betting rounds *and* not winning the chips that your opponents put in during earlier betting rounds.

this player is raising with .05(1,326) = 66.3 hole card combinations. AA–TT represents 30 combinations, and AK–AQ represents 32 combinations—making 62 total combinations. The additional 4.3 combinations could come from the fact that this player might be a tad bit looser or tighter with his raising requirements as a function of the table. And an important point about this type of analysis is that it's probably tough to pin down an opponent's distribution precisely because of such considerations. But that doesn't mean that this analysis is useless. Consistently pinning opponents to hand distributions that are accurate to within just one or two sets of hole cards will help you tremendously.

Very rarely, if ever, will you have played 100,000,00 hands against a particular opponent, so let's imagine a more typical situation:

Example 3.4: You're playing in an online STT that started with 10 players. Action is down to 4 players. As is typical for this type of tournament, no one has above 10bb. Since action has been down to five players, Stackalacker has *open* shoved all-in 4 of the 9 times he's had the chance to open. What's the narrowest hand distribution he could be on such that the probability that he's on the distribution is .1?

Answer: We need to employ a process similar to that used in example 2.22. Since we're considering the narrowest distribution possible, we're looking for the distribution such that the probability that he'd raise at least 4 times out of 9 is .1. We need to solve equation 3.5:

$$\sum_{r=4}^{9} \binom{9}{r} p^r (1 - p)^{9-r} = .1 \qquad (3.5)$$

This is doable by hand, but I don't want to turn this into any more of a math textbook than some of you might already think it is. I used a TI-83 graphing calculator to solve this equation, and got $p \approx .2104$, which corresponds to $.2104(1,326) = 278.9904$ combinations.[6] AA–22 is $6(13) = 78$ combinations. AK–A2 is $12(16) = 192$ combinations. In total {AA–22, AK–A2} comprises 270 combinations, which is very close to 279. Adding KQ to the mix bumps the narrowest possible distribution up to {AA–22, AK–A2, KQ}. Earlier in a tournament, when stacks are deep and postflop playability factors into many players' decisions, it's possible that hands like KJ, KT, and QJ would be in the distribution instead of the low aces or the low pocket pairs or both. But in the endgame, when postflop playability is no longer a concern, it usually makes the most sense to fill distributions with pocket pairs and unpaired aces first.

Example 3.5: Same situation as described in example 3.4, but now what's the widest distribution such that the probability that he's on the distribution is .1?

Answer: Since we're considering the widest distribution possible, we're looking for the distribution such that .1 is the probability that he'd raise 4 times out of 9. We need to solve equation 3.6:

$$\sum_{r=1}^{4}\binom{9}{r}p^r(1 - p)^{9-r} = .1 \qquad (3.6)$$

Like equation 3.5, this is doable by hand, but I used a TI-83 graphing calculator to solve this equation. The result: $p \approx$

---

6. If you have a graphing calculator and you love getting down to details like this, then great. If this is a bit too "By the Numbers" for you, don't worry. This topic is important for presenting a comprehensive treatment of tournament poker theory, but skimming over it won't detract you from understanding the overall idea, which is that there can be quite a range of distributions possible given that you have limited data on an opponent—the more data you get, the tighter your reads can become.

.6990, which corresponds to .6990(1,326) = 926.874 combinations. At this point, it's easier to enumerate the combinations that aren't in the distribution: 1,326 − 926.874 = 399.126. It's probably safe to assume that this player is shoving with any pocket pair, so this means we need to come up with about 399 combinations of unpaired hole cards. Thus, 16 combinations are possible for a specific set of unpaired hole cards, so we're looking for $\frac{399}{16}$ = 24.9375 starting hands. The worst 22 starting hands are something like {T2–32, T3–63, T4–74, T5–85, T6–96}. Who knows whether a player shoving this wide values a hand like T6 more than a hand like 53? And perhaps this player shoves with some hands only when they're suited.[7] The bottom line is that the widest possible distribution is very wide—much wider than the best 50 percent of hole cards.

The results from examples 3.4 and 3.5 show just how important just one showdown can be. When playing in a tournament, it's difficult to see situations repeated a large number of times. This doesn't mean that inferences can't be made, but it does mean that you need to be aware that playing poker is all about making informed inferences.

Example 3.6: You're in an online $20+$2 MTT. FacesOfDeath has entered the pot 0 out of 5 times when UTG. What's the widest possible distribution that you could reasonably assign to him playing UTG (again, use 10 percent as your cutoff).

Answer: Let p denote the probability that FacesOfDeath won't play a hand UTG. The probability that he won't play 5 consecutive hands is p^5, meaning that we want to solve p^5 =

---

7. Which isn't necessarily a bad idea. Although the edge to be derived from being suited is small, it's not at all negligible when considering the typical edges one has in preflop all-in scenarios.

.1. Taking the fifth root of both sides, we get that $p \approx .6310$. This means that the widest possible distribution that this person could reasonably be playing UTG consists of $(1 - .6310)(1,326) = 489.294$ combinations. {AA–22, AK–A2, KQ–K7, QJ–Q8, JT, T9s–54s, T8s–53s}, consists of 494 combinations. It's hard to know whether the widest possible distribution may favor hands like unsuited *connectors* as opposed to K7 or Q8, but at least this is somewhat of an approximation of what this player's widest range may be. Of course, it's most likely that this player is on a much narrower distribution, but identifying the widest possible distribution is important with respect to keeping your mind open postflop when unsuspected things happen.

Tournament-Specific Conditions Affecting Hand Distribution Reads

When profiling your foes in tournaments, keep in mind that tournament-specific dynamics can change how a player has been typically playing or how a previously faced opponent may be playing in the particular tournament you are in. Some variables to look for are the following:

Stacks Relative to the Blinds: Players who are typically tight may become *loose-aggressive* (LAG) when their stacks become short. Typically loose players may become tight as their stacks become short. Players who end up with gigantic stacks might play much more loosely than they'd been playing or might end up sitting on their stacks—content with waiting out into the money as far as possible. Some players go into shove/fold mode preflop with stacks shorter than 8bb. Meanwhile, others are content to limp weak hands regardless of how short-stacked they are. Some short-stacked pushbots will min raise or limp AA or KK with really short stacks, but others will shove all-in with them—just like the other hands they shove all-in with. I can't cover the full spectrum; just know that your opponents will change how they play based on how their stacks measure up with respect to the blinds. Furthermore, your better opponents will realize that players will be making adjustments based on how deep their stacks are with respect to the blinds, and they'll make adjustments in response to these adjustments. For example, if TightRock senses that MadPusher is shoving all-in to 5bb often, then TightRock may widen the range of hands he enters when MadPusher has shoved all-in as a short stack.

Stacks Relative to Other Stacks: Big stacks typically don't like to tangle with other big stacks in large pots. This means that if you're a big stack and a similarly stacked opponent makes a large bet against you, you can be fairly confident that he has the goods. This concept also manifests itself in a slightly different way. Some players keep track of their stacks, not in terms of big blinds, but instead in terms of their opponents' stacks. Players like these will sometimes take reckless gambles when their stacks are below average—even if they still have lots of big blinds.

Rebuy/Add-On Period: In tournaments featuring rebuys and/or add-ons, many players play much differently while rebuys and add-ons are still available. You need to deduce how your opponents are playing during the first part of the tournament as quickly as possible so that you can accumulate chips in the way that maximizes long-term profits. But then you usually need to throw most of that data out of the window once the second part of the tournament begins. Think of tournaments with re-buys and add-ons as two subtournaments.

Blind Structure: Players who you've played in other tournaments may adjust their play depending on how fast the blinds go up. Tight rocks in tournaments with slow blind structures can become loose cannons in tournaments with fast blind structures. And when it comes to default player profiles, it's safe to assume that players in tournaments with fast blind structures will be play-ing looser and more aggressively than players in tournaments with slow blind structures are. Just be on the lookout for players who enter tournaments with fast blind structures, intending simply to fold into the money. On the extreme, players of this mold might go so far as to stall whenever it's their decision to act.

Payout Structure: Players who you've played in other tournaments may adjust their play depending on how top-heavy the payout structure is. In many tournaments, you'll identify players who play sub-optimally with respect to the payout structure. Make sure you keep tabs on the general principle driving your opponents' play. For example, suppose action is down to 11 players in a *satellite* that gives seats to the top 10 players. You're tied for last with 5bb. Action folds to you, and you're SB with a ragged hand. BB is in 7th place with 8bb. If BB is aware of the flat payout dynamic, he'll fold everything here—including AA. If he's the last float in the clueless parade, he'll call with a wide range of hands simply because you're most likely stealing.[8] The biggest mistake you can make in this spot is to shove all-in with 32o against an opponent who'll call with {Rand}.

Bubble Play: Many otherwise aggressive opponents may tighten up right before the money. Players who've been relatively tight may open their games right before the money—taking advantage of those just trying to eek out a payday. Once the money *bubble* bursts and players have just gotten into the money, many small and medium stacks may play recklessly, hoping to acquire a huge stack by winning a lucky gamble or two. The money bubble isn't the only bubble; some players value making final tables, meaning that they might tighten up a lot right before the final table. Always be aware of the money bubble and the final table bubble—and look very carefully for opponents who seem to change up their play during these two periods.

Example 3.7: You're in a $100+$9 STT. First pays $500, second pays $300, and third pays $200, and action is down to five players. You're BB with KTo. Prior to posting blinds, the stacks are as follows:

SB: T2,000

BB (You): T2,000

UTG: T3,000

8. I should acknowledge Mr. Killer Poker, John Vorhaus, here since I often hear him use the phrase, "the last float in the clueless parade."

CO: T1,500

B: T6,500

Blinds are T150–T300. UTG limps, and everyone else folds. UTG has been observed to be trapping, but he's been limping with a wide range of hands—stuff along the lines of A3, K5, Q7, and 54. What do you do?

Answer: We haven't talked about the monetary equity associated with moves yet, but it's quite clear here that this is a great time to pick up a bunch of chips because your KT is way ahead of the limper's range. If he's trapping, so be it. Push all-in.

Example 3.8: You're in an MTT with a top-heavy payout structure. The top 30 spots pay, and 35 players remain. Blinds are 200–400, and you have 3,000 chips—which puts you in about thirtieth place in the chip standings. You're in the SB with A5o. Action folds to CO, a 10,000 stack who raises to 1,000. Then B folds. Recently, this player has been 2/2 when it comes to raising in situations in which he has the option to open from late position (LP). Should you shove with your A5o?

Answer: In a few chapters, we'll see how simply surviving into the bubble is severely overrated in MTTs with top-heavy payout structures. If CO is abusing the bubble, you should shove since your A5o is way ahead of his hand distribution; this is a great opportunity to accumulate chips. If CO isn't abusing the bubble, then folding your A5o is probably best. If you're new to the table, then wait one more time before assuming that he's abusing the bubble.[9] If you've been playing with CO

9. "Third time's the adjustment" is something that JV and I have both talked about in prior Killer Poker titles.

for a while, just ask yourself how aggressive he's been in general in blind stealing scenarios. If he's been even slightly more proactive than a typical player has been when it comes to stealing blinds, then you don't need to wait for the third time to make the adjustment. Otherwise, you should wait for the third time before shoving with a hand like A5o.

Action Distributions

Putting opponents on hand distributions is taxing, but it's only half the battle. We also need to predict how our opponents will respond to our actions:

1. If your hand compares unfavorably to your opponents' hand distributions, lines of play may exist that will force your opponents to fold often enough for you to show a long-term profit. For example, a middle-position (MP) player raises and an LP player calls. You're BB with 22, and you call, looking to spike a set. The flop is A96. You check, and your opponents check. The turn is another 6. Even though there's a good chance that one of your opponents has a pocket pair higher than your 22, there's also a very good chance that none of your opponents have an ace. Occasionally, some opponents will check a pair of aces on the flop either to be tricky or to control the size of the pot. But since you could have checked to the preflop raiser with a pair of aces, this is a great time to represent the ace. Try to take the pot down with a bet even though you probably don't have the best hand.

2. Suppose you put an opponent on a weak hand that's better than your hand—something like ace high, for

example. As much as you want to believe that an opponent with such a hand should fold to a bluff, bluffing is only a good play if your opponent will actually fold. A great example of this is a situation in which you have something like 87 on a paired flop of 556. You semi-bluff the flop, and your opponent calls. A 2 falls on the turn. You fire a second bullet, and your opponent calls. The river is another 2. You highly suspect that your opponent has an ace to go along with the two pair on the board. Although you showed strength by firing two bullets, you think it's highly likely that your opponent will call a third bullet despite the vulnerability of his hand. Therefore, save your chips and check.

3. If your hand compares favorably to your opponents' hand distributions, you need to figure out the lines of play that will extract the most value. In particular, size your bets so that you extract value or take pots down immediately depending on the size of the pot and the probability of whether your opponents will catch up later in the hand.

4. Figure out which opponents will put you on to tricky decisions when you have good, but not great, hands, and then employ lines of play against them that allow you to see showdowns relatively easily. Typically, this means controlling the size of the pot so that you're not stuck having to make tough decisions for large chunks of your stack.

Once you're able to put your opponents on accurate hand and action distributions, you can have complete control over your table. You'll know how to make as many chips as possible with your very good hands, you'll know how to maximize value while minimizing losses with your decent—but not great—hands, and you'll find ways to accumulate chips even when you're not getting good hole cards or hitting flops.

Example 3.9: You're in a $50+$5 STT. First pays $250, second pays $150, and third pays $100. Action goes down as described in table 3.1:

TABLE 3.1: Betting Action for Example 3.9

	STACKS	PREFLOP
YOU (98s)	T2,000	sbT200 / ?
BB	T3,000	bbT400
UTG	T5,000	-
B	T5,000	-

Blinds are T200–T400, and action folds to you. You have 98s. If you shove all-in, you're confident that BB's calling distribution is something on the order of {AA–55, AK–A7}. If you push all-in, what's the probability that BB will call?

Answer: Your opponent holds 2 cards from a pool of 50 remaining cards in the deck, meaning that the hand he holds is one of $_{50}C_2 = 1,225$ combinations. {AA–TT, 77–55} is 8 hands, each with 6 possible combinations. 99–88 is 2 hands, each with 3 possible combinations. {AK–AT, A7} is 5 hands, each with 16 possible combinations. A9–A8 is two hands, each with 12 possible combinations. In total, BB's calling distribution consists of 8(6) + 2(3) + 5(16) + 2(12) =

158 combinations. The probability that BB will call an all-in is $\frac{158}{1,225} \approx .1290$.

Example 3.10: You're in a $200+$30 MTT taking place in an LA card room. Action goes down as described in table 3.2 (p. 64).

What's your action after your opponent checks to you on the river?

Answer: This board isn't the most benign board for your AJ. Players like to call raises with connected cards, *1-gaps,* and medium pocket pairs, and this board hits a wide range of those hands hard enough to beat your one pair. However, opponents who'll call raises with connected cards, 1-gaps, and medium pocket pairs tend also to call raises with {KJ, QJ, JT, J9}. If your AJ were crushed, your opponent most likely would have check-raised at some point or led the river, fearing that you wouldn't bet the river with a pair of jacks. Although you have 16.6667bb in your stack, the pot is much bigger than your stack—the size of your stack is the size of a natural value bet that's a little bit over one third of the pot. The board is scary, but there doesn't seem to be huge evidence that you're beaten. Go all-in here to accumulate extra chips. If you had more chips in your stack, checking behind would become preferable to betting the river because taking the free showdown would prevent your opponent from check-raise bluffing you off a big pot.

TABLE 3.2: Betting Action for Example 3.10

	STACKS	PREFLOP	STACKS	FLOP J♥8♣7♠	STACKS	TURN 6♦	STACKS	RIVER 2♠
SB xx	T2,000	sbT15 / –						
BB xx	T2,500	bbT30 / –						
UTG xx	T1,000	–						
UTG+1 xx	T1,500	T30 / T100	T1,400	T0 / T200	T1,200	T0 / T300	T900	0
UTG+2 xx	T2,000	–						
YOU (A♣J♦) xx	T1,100	T100	T1,000	T200	T800	T300	T500	?
CO−1 xx	T750	–						
CO xx	T2,500	T100	T2,400	–				
B xx	T500	–						
POT		T345		T745		T1,345		

Chapter Summary

In this chapter, we covered the process of thinking in terms of hand and action distributions. When putting your opponents on distributions, you *will* be wrong sometimes. Like with anything, the more you engage yourself in the process, the better you'll become at it. But no matter how good you become at assigning distributions to your opponents, being comfortable in the realm of uncertainty is an important part of the process.

As humans, we have an urge to want to know everything. Sometimes, to satisfy ourselves psychologically, we convince ourselves that we know the answers to questions that we actually don't know the answers to. Ironically, saying "I don't know" or "I'm not sure" can reflect more wisdom and understanding than saying something like "the answer to A is B." Keep this in mind the next time you want to put your opponent on a specific set of hands. In the end, you need to throw all hope and other biases away, and you simply need to keep your reads honest with respect to your state of knowledge. Honestly assess all scenarios, and you'll be doing a great service to your poker game.

4

PLAYER TRACKING
SOFTWARE

Introduction

If you only play brick-and-mortar tournaments, you have
only your memory to help you. If you play tournaments online, then software exists that can help you incredibly. Part
of the reason I've gotten intense with the math in some sections leading up to this point is that I want to teach you how
to do the most thoughtful analyses possible away from the
table. I want your skills to be so great that you can ask any
question—and come up with the answer instead of
hopelessly trying to plod through poker forums in the hopes
that someone has written something that addresses your
question. But the other reason I got intense with the math is
for those of you who play online.

Player tracking software has existed for years. But to this
date, online players exist who know nothing about it. And
those who may have been using the software for the past few
years still don't necessarily know how to interpret the numbers properly. Once you're done with this chapter, you'll no
longer be in either camp. You'll know about the various types

of player tracking software, the meaning of commonly used statistics, and the way to analyze any player tracking software statistics not covered in this chapter on your own. If you don't play online, this chapter might be optional, but you might still want to read it because you might pick up some things that you can take with you to the brick-and-mortar setting.

Player Tracking Software Overview

In *Killer Poker Online/2* (Lyle Stuart, 2006), JV referred to player tracking software *sniffers*. As the name implies, sniffers track players and give you information that can give you a huge edge. I originally wrote an appendix about sniffers for JV in *Killer Poker Online/2* (see "Appendix B: Information Overlord"). The appendix in *Killer Poker Online/2,* my initiation into the world of poker writing, serves as a good introduction to interpreting the numbers, but a lot has changed since 2006. And even though the analysis I do there is a good start, it doesn't get into some of the subtler sides of interpreting statistics from sniffers.

With all the progress that's been made, there doesn't seem to be a ton of room left for sniffers to evolve—at least with respect to the type of information they collect. These days, the best sniffers output extremely nuanced information that can be easily parsed. If you know what to look for— and by the end of this book you'll know what to look for—today's sniffers put a wealth of extremely powerful information at your fingertips. If you play tournaments online at sites that allow sniffers and are supported by sniffers, you simply can't do without them—especially if you multitable.[1]

1. And if you want to make serious money playing tournaments online, you'll need to multitable. More about this in the section in the final chapter entitled "Hourly Win Rate."

Two different classes of sniffers exist: The first class of sniffers consists of software packages that record data only from tables you play at. Worthwhile software packages from this class of sniffers give you access to the following five functions:

1. Detailed statistics regarding preflop play as well as play on the flop, the turn, and the river (broken down with respect to position when appropriate).

2. A customizable *heads-up display* (HUD) that allows you to overlay your opponents' stats on your online tables in real time.

3. A customizable pop-up display that contains detailed stats.

4. Graphical replays of tournaments (and cash game sessions).

5. Advanced filters that allow you to target specific situations so that you can find leaks in your game, find leaks in frequently encountered opponents' games, or attempt to come up with reasonable default player profiles and player archetypes.

As of June 2008, the only two sniffers from this class worth your time are Hold'em Manager (www.holdem manager.net) and Poker Tracker (www.pokertracker.com).[2]

---

2. My apologies to the makers of other sniffers, but unless you give the same detailed statistics that Hold'em Manager and Poker Tracker provide, your software isn't good enough. If you've developed a piece of software that you deem to be a worthy rival, don't hesitate to contact

Don't waste your money on anything else. Poker Tracker version 2, used with the helper application Poker Ace HUD, has been the standard for years. The only improvement really needed was to report some of the more nuanced statistics in a way that could be immediately interpreted. And just recently, Hold'em Manager crashed onto the scene and addressed the issue of making nuanced statistics accessible by including things in its HUD including preflop stats broken down with respect to position, 3-betting frequency, stop-and-go frequency, and much more.

Poker Tracker responded by releasing version 3, and now, the decision between Hold'em Manager and Poker Tracker V3 will purely be a function of individual preference with respect to the interface (if I'm wrong, it wouldn't be the first time in my life I've made a bad read—but I'm confident on this one so let's see how it holds up). You should try them both (hooray for free trials), and then purchase the one you're more comfortable using.[3]

The second class of sniffers is software and websites that data mine poker sites. Think about having a version of Hold'em Manager or Poker Tracker that gives you information for players you've never played against! None of the data mining sniffers give you extremely nuanced information to work with; however, since poker is a battle of information, being able to jump immediately from default player

---

me through my website (www.killerev.com). I'll be more than happy to do a review of your software to put up at my site.

3. Yes, I said the word "purchase." Not everything on the Internet is free—especially pieces of quality software like Hold'em Manager and Poker Tracker. The money you'll spend on one (or both) of these software packages is equal to a few tournament buy-ins at most and is well worth the minor expense. You'll get a great return on your investment in no time.

profile to player archetype is a huge advantage. For tournaments, two of the major data mining tools are Shark Scope (sharkscope.com) and Official Poker Rankings (officialpoker rankings.com). They allow you to see the complete results history of the players at your tables. And while just knowing whether someone is a long-term winner or loser won't tell you exactly how to play, you can usually make some inferences. Combine Hold'em Manager or Poker Tracker with the results from a data mining sniffer, and you'll be properly equipped to battle in the modern age of online poker tournaments.[4]

Different poker sites have different policies regarding the software they permit. Before using a sniffer of any type, make sure that these two requirements are met:

1. The sniffer you're interested in operates on the site(s) you play.

2. The terms of service for the site(s) you play permit the use of the sniffer you want to use.

After all, you don't want to spend money on a piece of software and then end up not being able to use it at your site of choice. And you especially don't want the double whammy of having wasted money and being banned from your favorite site. Just like with everything else, be smart and do your research when it comes to sniffers.

---

4. By "modern age," I mean something on the order of post-2006, when even the average player has a decent degree of skill and knowledge.

VPIP

Interpreting the statistics from sniffers is a two-part battle:

1. Understanding how they are calculated.

2. Not extrapolating and interpreting meaning beyond what a particular statistic means.

Perhaps the most commonly cited statistic is VPIP, which is the percentage of times a player Voluntarily Puts chips In the Pot. It's calculated as follows:

$$VPIP = \left(\frac{\text{\# of Hands a Player Voluntarily Puts Chips in Preflop}}{\text{Total \# of Hands Played}} \right)(100\%) \quad (4.1)$$

The term voluntarily is important here. VPIP isn't the same as percentage of flops seen. If I post the big blind and see the flop in a pot that was unraised preflop, this hand wouldn't count in the numerator of equation 4.1—the big blind is a forced bet.

VPIP can help determine your opponents' preflop hand distributions. At the most basic level, a player with a VPIP of x is probably playing the top x% of hands. Since 1,326 combinations of hole cards exist (if you haven't committed this number to memory yet, this is your chance—it's a very important number), a player with a VPIP of x is playing a number of combinations equal to x% of 1,326. And from this number of combinations, we can come up with hand distributions much in the way that we were doing in chapter 3.

Moving a step beyond this basic level, realize that your opponents will have VPIPs that are functions of position at the table. Intuitively, players tend to play fewer hands from out of position and more hands when in position. So, one way to use VPIP is to take x% of 1,326 and to assume that the EP distribution is smaller and that the LP distribution is wider. But not all opponents account for position. Fortunately, today's player tracking software let's you know who's who—there's no need for guesswork. The HUDs include drop-down menus, so in a click, you can see a player's VPIP as an explicit function of position.

Taking yet another step beyond the basics, keep in mind that quite a few scenarios arise even when just considering preflop play and that many players will play varying distributions of hands depending on the scenario. Players will enter raised pots with a hand distribution different from the one they enter unraised pots with. Players may have different hand distributions they play as a function of the number of players in the pot. To get the full story regarding an opponent's preflop play, you can't just consider VPIP alone. VPIP really needs to be considered in the context of the other statistics.

Fortunately, today's best sniffers give you these statistics. Use them, and you won't have to extrapolate the hand distribution with which an opponent will call a raise; they flat-out tell you things like what percentage of times a player has called a preflop raise and what percentage of times a player has 3-bet when confronted with the option (you should customize your HUD to make these statistics easily accessible while you're playing).

The one thing that's really tough for sniffers is a tournament-specific nuance. Players change how they play as stack depths and table sizes change. The statistics you have on a player for the first few levels of play might not apply once blinds increase or the bubble approaches. And unfortunately, it's tough to get enough numbers on a player who you don't have any prior history on. Getting enough hands per blind level is something you can only do when you've played multiple tournaments against the same player. The best you can do is to take your HUD data and use it as a reference point. If a player makes a play that seems contrary to the stats, make an immediate note of it.

We're starting to get into the realm of differentiating between passive preflop play and aggressive preflop play. And for that, we'll need to talk about another statistic. But first, it's important to address what's perhaps the most common mistake made when interpreting VPIP. The higher a player's VPIP is, the more hands that player is entering pots with. And although players who are loose preflop are sometimes loose postflop, players who are loose preflop aren't always loose postflop. Sometimes, players float around looking to hit flops and promptly exit when given a chance once they've missed. Putting chips in with suspect holdings against such players is a great way to reduce the size of your stack. Using VPIP to infer postflop play is one of the biggest mistakes made by sniffer users. Avoid it!

PFR

PFR is a player's *preflop raising percentage.* It's calculated using equation 4.2:

$$PFR = \left(\frac{\text{\# of Hands a Player Raises Preflop}}{\text{Total \# of Hands Played}} \right)(100\%) \qquad (4.2)$$

Many of the issues pertaining to PFR are similar to those pertaining to VPIP. First, players typically have different raising distributions depending on their position and the action that's happened before them. Second, players who are very aggressive preflop aren't necessarily hyperaggressive postflop.

Since PFR doesn't differentiate between different types of preflop raising (raises, 3-bets, 4-bets, and so on, are all lumped together), another big mistake that players make is assuming that someone with a high PFR has a loose 3-betting distribution. Sure, some players with high PFRs will have them as a result of 3-betting more often than other players do. But many ways exist to build up a high PFR, including raising a large percentage of pots from MP and LP when no one else has entered the pot. To get a handle on an opponent's 3-betting behavior, you should really look at the actual percentage of times an opponent 3-bets when given the opportunity.[5]

Example 4.1: 40 hands into an online MTT, $hipItFool has a VPIP of 50% and a PFR of 30%—numbers signifying that this player is very loose-aggressive preflop. Table 4.1, opposite, describes the betting action.

Should you call the 450-chip bet on the river?

Answer: This type of question is very typical of web forums. Posters will describe a hand all the way to the river, give their opponents' VPIP and PFR, and ask for advice. But really, there isn't enough information to answer this question. Your ATo is way ahead of $hipItFool's distribution preflop, but that's about as far as this information allows us to go. If we assume that $hipItFool is like most players in that he typically continuation bets on the flop, ATo is way ahead of his distribution on the flop. But that's about as far as you should be comfortable extrapolating. It's pretty much impossible to tell where you are on the turn and the river. With no other information to go on, and about one third of your stack on the line in a situation in which the board is highly connected, folding is probably the best move.

---

5. Hold'em Manager and Poker Tracker allow you to customize the heads-up display and the pop-up display. You should customize your heads-up display to include the preflop 3-betting percentage.

TABLE 4.1: Betting Action for Example 4.1

	STACKS	PREFLOP	STACKS	FLOP T♠8♣5♠	STACKS	TURN 6♦	STACKS	RIVER J♣
SB xx	T2,200	sbT15 / –						
BB xx	T3,000	bbT30 / –						
UTG xx	T2,000	–						
UTG+1 xx	T1,220	–						
UTG+2 xx	T4,000	–						
CO – 2 xx	T2,500	T90	T2,410	T100	T2,310	T150	T2,160	T450
SHIPITFOOL xx	T3,000	–						
CO xx	T750	–						
YOU **(A♥7♠)**	T1,750	T90	T1,660	T100	T1,560	T150	T1,410	?
POT		T225		T425		T725		

Because this player has already been in so many hands, you should have more nuanced data. In particular, since this player has raised preflop 30% of the time in the span of 40 hands, this player has raised preflop 12 times. If this player has fired three bullets four or fewer times, assume that $hipItFool has a hand that beats your ATo. Meanwhile, consider calling if $hipItFool has fired three bullets at least 8 times. It's hard to know where you are in the gray area between 4 and 8, but unless you've seen a three-barrel bluff shown down, you should assume that this player has a good hand.

Just like with VPIP, the key to using PFR effectively is to look at it in the context of other variables:

Example 4.2: You're in a satellite that pays the top 10 places. 15 players remain (including you). You're in 11th place with 12,000 chips, and blinds are 300–600. Action folds to $CO-2$ (13th place with 9,000 chips) who limps. B and SB fold, and you're BB with AT. $CO-2$ has a VPIP of 18% and a PFR of 13% over the span of 100 hands. What's your action?

Answer: This player is either trapping or limping with hands that are at the bottom of his range. 18% of 1,326 is 238.68 and 5% of 1,326 is 66.3, meaning that we first need to come up with a distribution of about 239 combinations and then take the bottom 66 combinations to figure out his limping distribution (assuming for a moment that he's not trapping with a monster).

AA–22 is 78 combinations and AK–A2 is 192 combinations. $192 + 78 = 270$; taking away 30 combinations from this distribution amounts to eliminating something like {44–22, A2}, leaving {AA–55, AK–A3}. The bottom 66 combinations from this distribution are something like A6–A3. Another possibility is that $CO-2$'s entire playing distribution is something like {AA–55, AK–A9, KQ–KT, QJ–QT, JT}. The bottom 66 combinations from this distribution looks something like {KT, QJ–QT, JT}.

In either situation, your AT is a big favorite against the bottom 5% of this player's range. The only thing you should be worried about is the possibility of a trap. With the stacks and the blinds where they are, this is the time in a tournament where a crafty player might limp with a huge hand preflop. But raising to about T2,000 should be big enough to get your opponent to fold his typical limping hands and small enough to give you the opportunity to fold should he go over the top.

Alternatively, there's no harm in checking and then leading about T600–T900 chips on the flop pretty much regardless of the flop, unless it's something like KQX, KJX, or QJX (where X isn't an ace). This line of play controls the size of the pot—which can be a good thing to do given the circumstances. Remember that playing postflop isn't a bad thing!

If a player's VPIP is equal to his PFR, then he's raising *every* time he enters the pot. Meanwhile, no matter how high a player's VPIP is, he's raising with a very small range if his PFR is something like 2%. Investing any chips against a raiser with something like a 50% VPIP and a 2% PFR is a horrible idea unless you have AA or KK or stacks are deep and you believe you'll get him to go for stacks when you flop a set with a smaller pocket pair.

When it comes to preflop aggression, one additional statistic you should take particular note of is the percentage of times an opponent attempts to steal blinds (ASB) when the opportunity arises. At tables where EP and MP players enter pots a lot, it's possible that a player with a very low PFR could be a somewhat aggressive blind stealer. And if you go by PFR

alone, you might miss important restealing opportunities—
which become very important in mid- and late-tournament
play as stacks shrink with respect to the blinds.

Example 4.3: You're one of four players remaining in a
$100+$9 STT with a 50/30/20 payout structure. Table 4.2,
below, describes the action. Through 60 hands, B has a VPIP
of 18.3% (11/60), a PFR of 6.7% (4/60), and an ASB of 100%
(4/4). What's your action?

TABLE 4.2: Action for Example 4.3

	STACKS	PREFLOP
YOU (7♥7♣)	T4,000	sbT150 / ?
BB	T3,000	sbT300
UTG	T4,500	-
B	T3,500	T800

Answer: This is far from being an easy situation—especially
without *independent chip modeling* (ICM) (which we'll get
to in chapter 6). This player's PFR of 6.7% suggests that,
to within a first-order approximation, he's raising with
.067(1,326) = 88.842 combinations. {AA–88, AK–AJ} represents 7(6) + 3(16) = 90 combinations. If this is B's actual
hand distribution, it should be pretty clear that 77 doesn't
fare well here at all—B needs to fold a huge percentage of
times to a 3-bet to justify going over the top against his hand
distribution.

However, the ASB stat seems to tell a different story. The fact that this player has raised all four times he's had the chance to steal indicates that this player may highly covet the right to open from late position. And the reason why this player hasn't raised in other situations may simply be that the opposition has repeatedly preempted him.

Nonetheless, getting involved in this pot is a big gamble. Given the relative stacks and the fact that you have over 10BB, folding is probably your best move. If you had something like 2,500 chips, then shoving all-in would probably become the move of choice.

Example 4.4: You're in the third round of an online MTT. Table 4.3 (p. 80, left) describes the action.

After 40 hands, UTG has a VPIP of 7.5% (3/40) and a PFR of 2.5% (1/40). UTG+1 has a VPIP of 25% (10/40) and a PFR of 15% (6/40). CO − 2 has a VPIP of 20% (8/40) and a PFR of 7.5% (3/40). What's your line of play?

Answer: Without any stats, this situation would normally dictate a preflop raise to about T150–T200. However, UTG's stats change everything. There's a good chance that a player like this is trapping with AA or KK. Since two other players have already limped, you might as well limp and hope that you spike a set. If you end up flopping an overpair, look to keep the pot small by playing passively postflop—and if UTG ends up making pot-sized bets on the flop *and* the turn, seriously consider mucking on the turn.

Example 4.5: You're in the middle of a 50/30/20 STT. Table 4.4 (p. 80, right) describes the action.

After 50 hands, CO has a VPIP of 16% (8/50) and a PFR of 10% (5/50). He hasn't called a preflop raise, and postflop, he's folded to 4/5 bets on the flop. What's your line of play?

TABLE 4.3: Betting Action for Example 4.4

	STACKS	PREFLOP
SB xx	T3,200	sbT20
BB xx	T5,200	bbT40
UTG xx	T2,500	T40
UTG+1 xx	T3,400	T40
UTG+2 xx	T4,600	–
UTG+3 xx	T750	–
CO−2 xx	T1,600	T40
CO−1 xx	T2,000	–
YOU (Q♦Q♠)	T3,250	?
B	T1,900	

TABLE 4.4: Action for Example 4.5

	STACKS	PREFLOP	STACKS	FLOP K♣T♥9♥	STACKS	TURN 6♦
SB xx	T2,600	sbT50 / –				
BB xx	T3,100	bbT100 / –				
UTG xx	T1,300	–				
UTG+1 xx	T4,350	–				
CO xx	T1,300	T100 / T350	T950	T0 / T300	T650	–
B (K♥J♦)	T2,350	T350	T2,000	T300	T1,700	?
POT		T850		T1,450		?

Answer: At times like this, it helps to think about the hands that you can possibly have beaten. Honestly, I can't think of a single hand that you can beat here. KQ would probably be this player's most likely holding, but I wouldn't be surprised to see this player trap with two pair, a set, or a straight. If you're lucky, your opponent has KJ and you chop. Just check and hope for a free showdown. If your opponent bets on the river, you should fold.

AF

The aggression factor (AF) is the last variable that players typically refer to when talking about their opponents. As the name implies, AF is an attempted measure of how aggressively someone plays. It's calculated using equation 4.3:

$$AF = \frac{Bets + Raises}{Calls} \qquad (4.3)$$

Note that checks and folds don't count toward AF. If I bet 2 times, raise 3 times, call 5 times, check 3 times, and fold 7 times, my AF would be $\frac{2+3}{5} = 1$.

Really, a bunch of different AFs exist. You can consider AF as including all 4 betting rounds, preflop action only, flop action only, turn action only, river action only, or flop + turn + river action. Since VPIP and PFR effectively give the same information as the preflop AF, you won't see the preflop AF referred to much, and it's something you won't be using. You only need to be concerned with the postflop AF—in either its lumped form or its broken-down forms.

If you go to web forums, you'll often see people describe their opponents as VPIP/PFR/AF. For example, if RazorEdge is 25/12/3, his VPIP is 25, his PFR is 12, and his AF is 3. The AF here is always a player's lumped postflop AF.

At first glance, AF may seem like a great way to determine how to play against an opponent who shows aggression. Unfortunately, it falls short:

Example 4.6: Imagine an opponent who folds everything but the *nuts* when bet into—and who only raises with the nuts. What will this player's AF be?

Answer: This player never calls, so the denominator of equation 4.3 will be zero; this player's AF will be infinite. To compound problems, we don't have any real information regarding how this player acts in pots in which no one has bet. Maybe he bets all the time on the flop when no one else has bet, or maybe he never bets the flop when no one else has bet.

By itself, AF doesn't come close to telling the entire story. To be useful, you really need to combine AF with stats like the percentage of times an opponent folds to a bet, the percentage of times a player continuation bets, and the percentage of times a player employs stop-and-goes (sometimes pejoratively referred to as *donk* bets).

Past Tournament Performances

If you're using some type of data mining software to supplement Hold'em Manager or Poker Tracker, then you're really looking to get a jump right in the beginning of a tournament, when you've only played a small sample of hands. The two big statistics you'll be looking at are ITM percentage and return on investment (ROI).

A player's ITM percentage measures what percentage of tournaments a player places in the money. The baseline against which you should measure the ITM percentage is the percentage of players who normally get paid. In many on-line MTTs, somewhere around 10%–15% of the field gets paid. Meanwhile, in 10-handed STTs with 50%/30%/20% payout structures, 30% of the field places ITM. Interestingly, the ITM percentage isn't necessarily the greatest metric by which to measure tournament performances—especially in MTTs. Recall in my introduction that I had a very high ITM percentage for MTTs, but I had an ROI that wasn't much better than 0. The two things to look out for with ITM percentages are players with very high ITM percentages and very low ITM percentages.

Players with very high ITM percentages tend to be survivalists; they won't go broke early in a tournament with hands like top-pair-top-kicker (TPTK) postflop or AK preflop. In other words, unless you have close to the nuts, you shouldn't even think of engaging a high ITM player in a big pot early on. As blinds increase, players with high ITM percentages tend to take on different faces—particularly in STTs. In STTs, players with ITM percentages greater than 40% tend to play very tight early, but even on the bubble, when facing elimination, they can become extremely aggressive with preflop all-ins.

Players with very low ITM percentages are the players

you're looking to value bet and stack early on in tournaments. You should typically have no qualms about going to war for stacks against these players with hands like TPTK. One of the most useful aspects of data mining software is that without having played any hands, you have at least a general idea of whom you should engage in big pots early on.

For STTs, players with very high ITM percentages tend to be the elite players. In MTTs, players with high ITM percentages are those who you don't want to tangle with early, but they aren't necessarily the best players. To separate the survivors from those who thrive, we need to consider ROI: the percentage of tournament buy-ins a player wins or loses. Equation 4.4 is the formula for ROI (the buy-in includes the *rake*):

$$\text{ROI} = \left(\tfrac{\text{Prize Money} - \text{Buy-Ins}}{\text{Buy-Ins}}\right)(100\%) \tag{4.4}$$

The numerator of equation 4.4 is your net profit or loss, and by dividing it by the total amount you've spent on buy-ins, you get a metric that's normalized with respect to the stakes being played. A player with a positive ROI is a winning player; a player with a negative ROI is a losing player.

Example 4.7: You play 5 $20+$2 STTs where first pays $100, second pays $60, and third pays $40. You get one first place finish and one third place finish. What's your ROI and, on average, your net profit/loss per tournament?

Answer: You got $100 + $40 = $140 in prize money, and you spent 5($22) = $110 in buy-ins. Plugging these numbers into equation 4.4, we get:

$$\left(\tfrac{\$140 - \$110}{\$110}\right)(100\%) = \left(\tfrac{\$30}{\$110}\right)(100\%) \approx +27.2727\% \tag{4.5}$$

To figure out your net profit/loss per tournament, just take your ROI, convert from a percentage to a decimal, and multiply by the tournament buy-in:

$$\text{Net per Tournament} \approx (.272727)(\$22) \approx \$6 \quad (4.6)$$

Example 4.8: You play 5 \$20+\$2 STTs, where first pays \$100, second pays \$60, and third pays \$40. You get one second-place finish and one third-place finish. What's your ROI, and on average, how much did you make per tournament?

Answer: You got \$60 + \$40 = \$100 in prize money, and you spent 5(\$22) = \$110 in buy-ins. Plugging these number into equation 4.4, we get:

$$\left(\tfrac{\$100 - \$110}{\$110}\right)(100\%) = \left(\tfrac{-\$10}{\$110}\right)(100\%) \approx -9.0909\% \quad (4.7)$$

To figure out your net profit/loss per tournament, just take your ROI, convert from a percentage to a decimal, and multiply by the tournament buy-in:

$$\text{Net per Tournament} \approx (-.090909)(\$22) \approx -\$2 \ (4.8)$$

The more positive a player's ROI is, the better that player is. In MTTs, players with the highest ROIs don't necessarily have the largest ITM percentages—they're usually willing to take calculated risks no matter what point a tournament is in (and those calculated risks typically entail aggression). As a result, you can sometimes trap the highest ROI players in tournaments for chunks of chips. But you shouldn't make it a habit to entangle yourself with lots of marginal confrontations against them—especially when they have position.

For STTs and MTTs, about two thirds of the poker-playing population have negative ROIs. One hundred percent is the benchmark for elite MTTers, and 20% is the benchmark for top STTers. But really, opponents with even marginally positive ROIs should be players that you look out for, and you shouldn't necessarily underestimate players with slightly negative ROIs—especially if they haven't logged at least a few hundred tournaments because it takes many tournaments for the ROI statistic to converge to a reliable figure.

Example 4.9: You're midway through level 1 of an MTT with a top-heavy payout structure and a slow blind structure. Table 4.5, below, describes the action.

Through 5 hands, CO −1 has a VPIP of 100% (5/5), a PFR of 0% (0/5), and he's called 100% of preflop raises (3/3). You've already seen two showdowns. One involved a three-barrel bluff, and another involved him calling down with bottom board pair. Official Poker Rankings indicates that his ROI is −50% over the past 100 tournaments he's played. What's your line of play?

Answer: CO −1 has shown aggression already in this tournament, and his losing history suggests that he's good at getting chips in when he's behind in situations like this. The

TABLE 4.5: Action for Example 4.9

	STACKS	PREFLOP	STACKS	FLOP K♣T♦9♥
SB xx	T2,000	sbT5 / −		
BB xx	T2,100	bbT10 / −		
UTG xx	T1,800	T10 / T45	T1,755	T0 / −
UTG+1 xx	T1,500	T10 / T45	T1,455	T0 / −
UTG+2 xx	T2,500	−		
YOU (A♣J♣)	T1,970	T45	T1,925	T80 / ?
CO −1	T1,050	T45	T1,005	T300
CO	T2,620	−		
B	T2,460	−		
POT		T195		

pot contains T575, and CO −1 only has T705 left; go all-in when you know you're ahead—and there's a good chance of being called. Don't even allow for the possibility of a scare card that will kill your action.

Chapter Summary

Poker is a battle of information. The difference between success and failure in tournaments is often a matter of just a handful of key decisions. If you play online, player tracking software is necessary if you want as much information as possible about your opponents.

The material in this chapter surveyed some important statistics offered by player tracking software. But sniffers provide many more statistics than the ones we just covered. Furthermore, similar sounding statistics offered in multiple sniffers may be completely different because they use slightly different formulas. To use sniffers effectively, it's your responsibility to research the formulas sniffers use when calculating statistics to ensure that the statistics you're using mean what you think they do. And when using statistics, only use them for the information they give: don't extrapolate. With the wealth of statistics at your fingertips, there's no need even to attempt extrapolating in the first place!

Even though sniffers are powerful, don't forget to observe the action at your table(s). Statistics are very useful, but sometimes the information you get from just one showdown can be worth as much as 100 hands' worth of sniffer data (and remember that for sniffer data to be useful, you need a decent sample size—even the tightest player can easily have a VPIP of 100% after 1 hand). The best online tournament players observe their opponents, take notes, and use sniffers—you should do the same.

5

♣ ♠ ♦ ♥

EXPECTED VALUE

♧ ♤ ◇ ♡

Introduction

Having covered probability and the art of putting opponents on hand and action distributions, we're now in a great
position to assemble the remaining pieces of the tournament puzzle. This chapter will cover the mathematical concept of *expected value*. Expected value, also known as
expectation value or EV, is at the heart of the poker decision-
making process.[1]

EV Defined

EV is the average payout of a random event. Given a *random
event* with N possible outcomes, where k represents a partic-

---

1. If you don't know the probabilities associated with preflop all-in
   matchups or those associated with postflop play (things such as drawing, the probability of flopping a pair, etc.), now is a good time to check
   out appendices A and B. I put this material in the appendices because
   there didn't seem to be a good place to put them in the main text that
   didn't disrupt the development of the tournament theory itself.

ular outcome, equation 5.1 gives us our operating definition:

$$EV = \sum_{k=1}^{N} [P(k)][\text{Payout of } k] \qquad (5.1)$$

Equation 5.1 tells us that EV is nothing more than a weighted average.

Example 5.1: You're at your favorite Las Vegas casino. You stroll by the roulette tables, and you see Gamblin' Gary put $5,000 on red. What's his EV?

Answer: In Las Vegas, the roulette wheels have 38 numbers: 18 are red, 18 are black, and 2 are green. The probability that the wheel will come up red is $\frac{18}{38}$, and the probability that it won't come up red is $\frac{20}{38}$. If the wheel comes up red, Gary will be +$5,000. If the wheel doesn't come up red, then Gary will be −$5,000. Gary's EV is:

$$\left(\tfrac{18}{38}\right)(\$5,000) - \left(\tfrac{20}{38}\right)(\$5,000) \approx -\$263.16 \qquad (5.2)$$

On average, Gary will lose $263.16 per every $5,000 bet he places on red.

When performing EV calculations like the one in example 5.1, we often have a choice regarding how to express payouts: we can express payouts relatively or absolutely. Relative payouts are termed as changes—in other words, relative payouts are net results. We used relative payouts in example 5.1 when we said that Gary would be +$5,000 or −$5,000. Another way to do EV calculations is to think of absolute payouts (i.e., how much you expect to have in total after the random event is resolved). Suppose that Gary has $100,000 total in front of him before placing his $5,000 bet. If Gary wins, he'll have $105,000; if he loses, he'll have $95,000. The EV of Gary's stack is:

$$(\$105,000)\left(\tfrac{18}{38}\right) + (\$95,000)\left(\tfrac{20}{38}\right) = \$99,736.84 \qquad (5.3)$$

Since $99,736.84 is less than the $100,000 Gary started with, this would lead again to the same conclusion that this bet loses money in the long run:

$$\$99,736.84 - \$100,000 = -\$263.16 \qquad (5.4)$$

This is the same expected loss per spin found using equation 5.2.

In a way, EV is a quantity that only makes sense when thinking of the long term. In example 5.1, it's impossible for Gary to be down $263.16 after a single spin—the only two possibilities after a single spin are:

1. He's up $5,000.

2. He's down $5,000.

Neither of these possibilities is − $263.16. But after many spins, Gary's average loss per spin will approach $263.16. After 100 spins, we expect his total losses will be somewhere in the neighborhood of $26,316. After 1,000 spins, we expect Gary to lose a total of somewhere around $263,160. In the short term, Gary may actually log enough wins to believe that his bets are profitable. Only in the long term will Gary find out that he's really just lighting money on fire.

Unlike Gary, suppose you're making +EV bets.[2] Anything can—and will—happen in the short term. Being +EV and winning every bet you make are two separate things. The nature of random processes is that you can never guarantee anything. But if you repeatedly make +EV bets, you're doing all that you can to position yourself to end up profitable in the long run.

---

2. A +EV wager is one that is profitable in the long run, and a − EV wager is one that isn't profitable in the long run.

Advertisers have brainwashed us into thinking about instant gratification.[3] It's tough to dissociate from a mentality that's constantly pushed on us; however, to make good poker decisions, we can't use the type of thinking that tells us to get payday loans in order to purchase gas-guzzling GMC Yukons with blingy 24″ spinners. From the outside, tournament poker appears to be entirely a battle of short-term outcomes. Beneath the dramatized TV coverage of huge all-in confrontations, making good tournament poker decisions is all about long-term thinking. Sure, you may be knocked out of any individual tournament, but over the span of many tournaments, the players who make the best decisions are the ones who stand to make the highest total amounts of money across all tournaments. As long as you're making the most profitable decisions possible, you shouldn't care about your results in any particular tournament. And if you have some psychological hang-up that makes you terrified about the prospect of being eliminated from a tournament, just remember that there's always another tournament around the corner these days. Hell, you may be playing seven or more other tournaments at the same time if you're playing online!

Chip EV

Throughout a tournament, we battle for chips. Every possible move in a tournament has an EV with respect to chips. This type of EV is known as *chip EV* (cEV). Theoretically, cEV is relatively straightforward to calculate given that you have the proper information; the better you are at reading your

---

3. The "us" here refers to my readers residing in the United States. But unfortunately, I suspect that my readers outside the United States may also identify with me on this one.

opponents' hand distributions and predicting their actions, the more accurate your cEV calculations will be. Practically, the uncertainty in your information makes precise cEV calculations pretty much impossible in many circumstances. But as long as you're good at making educated guesses, the results of your cEV calculations will be informative.

Example 5.2: Action is down to five players in an online $100+$9 STT:

TABLE 5.1: Hand for Example 5.2

	STACKS	PREFLOP
SB xx	T2,000	sbT100
BB xx	T3,000	sbT200
UTG xx	T2,500	-
UTG+1 xx	T6,000	-
YOU (A♣2♥)	T1,500	?-

If you push all-in, you think the blinds will call with something like {AA–22, AK–A8}. Furthermore, if SB calls/ shoves, you think that BB will only enter the pot with {JJ+, AK}. What's the cEV of shoving?

Answer: In total, 12 possibilities exist if you shove:

SB and BB fold: SB's calling distribution comprises $1(3) + 11(6) + 1(3) + 6(12) = 144$ combinations. The probability that SB calls is $\frac{144}{1,225}$. Therefore, the probability that SB folds is $\frac{1,081}{1,225}$. Since SB and BB are on the same calling distribution and we're employing an independence approximation, the probability that BB folds is also $\left(\frac{1,081}{1,225}\right)$. If both the SB and BB fold, you're +T300:

$$\left(\tfrac{1,081}{1,225}\right)\left(\tfrac{1,081}{1,225}\right)(+T300) = +T233.61 \qquad (5.5)$$

SB calls, BB folds, and you win: The probability that SB calls is $\frac{144}{1,225}$. If SB calls, BB is only calling with $1(3) + 3(6) + 1(12) = 33$ combinations. The probability that SB calls and BB folds is $\left(\frac{144}{1,225}\right)\left(\frac{1,192}{1,225}\right)$. According to Poker Stove (www.pokerstove.com), you'll win about 25.83% against SB's calling distribution. When SB calls, BB folds, and you win, you're +T1,700:

$$\left(\tfrac{144}{1,225}\right)\left(\tfrac{1,192}{1,225}\right)(.2583)(+T1,700) = +T50.23 \qquad (5.6)$$

SB calls, BB folds, and you tie: The probability that SB calls and BB folds is $\left(\frac{144}{1,225}\right)\left(\frac{1,192}{1,225}\right)$. According to Poker Stove, you'll tie about 5.86% against SB's calling distribution. When SB calls, BB folds, and you tie, you're +T100:

$$\left(\tfrac{144}{1,225}\right)\left(\tfrac{1,192}{1,225}\right)(.0586)(+T100) = +T.67 \qquad (5.7)$$

SB calls, BB folds, and you lose: The probability that SB calls and BB folds is $\left(\frac{144}{1,225}\right)\left(\frac{1,192}{1,225}\right)$. According to Poker Stove, you'll lose about 68.30% against SB's calling distribution. When SB calls, BB folds, and you lose, you're −T1,500:

$$\left(\tfrac{144}{1,225}\right)\left(\tfrac{1,192}{1,225}\right)(.6830)(-T1,500) = -T117.19 \qquad (5.8)$$

SB folds, BB calls, and you win: The probability that SB folds is $\left(\frac{1,081}{1,225}\right)$. The probability that BB calls when SB folds is $\frac{144}{1,225}$. According to Poker Stove, you'll win about 25.83% against BB's calling distribution. When SB folds, BB calls, and you win, you're +T1,600:

$$\left(\tfrac{1,081}{1,225}\right)\left(\tfrac{144}{1,225}\right)(.2583)(+T1,600) = +T42.87 \qquad (5.9)$$

SB folds, BB calls, and you tie: The probability that SB folds is $\frac{1,081}{1,225}$. The probability that BB calls when SB folds is $\frac{144}{1,225}$. According to Poker Stove, you'll tie about 5.86% against BB's calling distribution. When SB folds, BB calls, and you tie, you're +T50:

$$\left(\tfrac{1,081}{1,225}\right)\left(\tfrac{144}{1,225}\right)(.0586)(+T50) = +T.30 \qquad (5.10)$$

SB folds, BB calls, and you lose: The probability that SB folds is $\frac{1,081}{1,225}$. The probability that BB calls when SB folds is $\frac{144}{1,225}$. According to Poker Stove, you'll lose about 68.30% against BB's calling distribution. When SB folds, BB calls, and you lose, you're −T1,500:

$$\left(\tfrac{1,081}{1,225}\right)\left(\tfrac{144}{1,225}\right)(.6830)(-T1,500) = -T106.27 \qquad (5.11)$$

SB and BB call, and you win: The probability that SB calls is $\frac{144}{1,225}$. When SB calls, the probability that BB calls is $\frac{33}{1,225}$. According to Poker Stove, you win about 14.00% when SB and BB call. When SB and BB call, and you win, you're +T3,000:

$$\left(\tfrac{144}{1,225}\right)\left(\tfrac{33}{1,225}\right)(.1400)(+T3,000) = +T1.33 \qquad (5.12)$$

SB and BB call, and you tie with the SB: The probability that SB calls is $\frac{144}{1,225}$. When SB calls, the probability that BB calls is $\frac{33}{1,225}$. Figuring out the probability of tying with the SB is a little bit tricky from Poker

Stove's output, but it's doable. Poker Stove claims that your pot equity from tying is about .98%, SB's equity from tying is about 1.47%, and BB's equity from tying is about 1.27%. If we let A denote the probability that you'll tie with SB, B denote the probability that you'll tie with BB, C denote the probability that you'll tie with both SB and BB, and D denote the probability that SB ties with BB, we can write the following system of equations:

$$\frac{A}{2} + \frac{B}{2} + \frac{C}{3} = .98 \tag{5.13}$$

$$\frac{A}{2} + \frac{C}{3} + \frac{D}{2} = 1.47 \tag{5.14}$$

$$\frac{B}{2} + \frac{C}{3} + \frac{D}{2} = 1.27 \tag{5.15}$$

$$A + B + C + D = 3.72 \tag{5.16}$$

Solving this system of equations (either by hand or by using a free solver found online), yields that A = 1.18%, B = .78%, C = 0.00%, and D = 1.76%. Therefore, you'll tie about 1.18% with SB. When SB and BB call and you tie with SB, you're +T750:

$$\left(\tfrac{144}{1,225}\right)\left(\tfrac{33}{1,225}\right)(.0118)(+T750) = +T.03 \tag{5.17}$$

SB and BB call, and you tie with the BB: The probability that SB calls is $\frac{144}{1,225}$. When SB calls, the probability that BB calls is $\frac{33}{1,225}$. From the preceding, you'll tie about .78% against BB. When SB and BB call and you tie with BB, you're +T750:

$$\left(\tfrac{144}{1,225}\right)\left(\tfrac{33}{1,225}\right)(.0078)(+T750) = +T.02 \tag{5.18}$$

SB and BB call, and you tie with both: The probability that SB calls is $\frac{144}{1,225}$. When SB calls, the probability that BB calls is $\frac{33}{1,225}$. From the preceding, you'll tie about 0.00% against SB and BB. When SB and BB call and you tie against SB and BB, you're +T0:

$$\left(\tfrac{144}{1,225}\right)\left(\tfrac{33}{1,225}\right)(.0000)(+\text{T}0) = +\text{T}0 \qquad (5.19)$$

SB and BB call, and you lose: The probability that SB calls is $\tfrac{144}{1,225}$. When SB calls, the probability that BB calls is $\tfrac{33}{1,225}$. According to Poker Stove, you lose about 82.28% when SB and BB call. When SB and BB call and you lose, you're $-\text{T}1,500$:

$$\left(\tfrac{144}{1,225}\right)\left(\tfrac{33}{1,225}\right)(.8228)(-\text{T}1,500) = -\text{T}3.91 \qquad (5.20)$$

Summing the results of all 12 outcomes, the cEV of shoving is +T101.69.

In the foregoing example, example 5.2, note that since BB was on a tight overcalling distribution, the situations in which both SB and BB call contribute very little to the overall cEV of shoving. Also note that ties were negligible since the probability of tying was low and the change in chips associated with tying was also low.

Example 5.3: You're in level 2 of a large MTT. Blinds are T10–T20, and players began the tournament with T5,000 (see table 5.2, p. 98).

If you call, you think that there's a very good chance that SB and BB will fold. Suppose UTG won't put any more chips in the pot if a spade hits on the turn or the river. If you call the T80 bet on the flop, how big does UTG's bet on the turn have to be to make drawing $-\text{cEV}$?

Answer: If you hit on the turn, you're +T180; if you hit on the river, you're $+\text{T}(180 + X)$, where X is the size of UTG's bet on the turn. If you miss on the turn and the river, you're $-\text{T}(80 + X)$. The probability that you hit your flush on the turn is $\tfrac{9}{47}$, the probability that you miss your flush on the

TABLE 5.2: Hand for Example 5.3

	STACKS	PREFLOP	STACKS	FLOP K♦7♠3♠
SB xx	T4,000	sbT10 / T20	T3,980	T0 / −
BB xx	T5,500	bbT20 / T20	T5,480	T0 / −
UTG xx	T5,000	T20	T4,980	T80
UTG+1 xx	T7,000	−		−
UTG+2 xx	T3,200	T20	T3,180	
CO−2 xx	T2,000	−		
CO−1 xx	T9,000			
CO (T♠8♠)	T6,500	T20	T6,480	?
B (A♣J♦)	T12,000	−		
POT		T100		

turn and hit your flush on the river is $\left(\frac{38}{47}\right)\left(\frac{9}{46}\right)$, and the proba-bility that you miss your flush on the turn and the river is $\left(\frac{38}{47}\right)\left(\frac{37}{46}\right)$. To figure out the value of X that makes this line of play $-$cEV for you, solve inequality 5.21 for X:

$$\left(\tfrac{9}{47}\right)(+180) + \left(\tfrac{38}{47}\right)\left(\tfrac{9}{46}\right)(+180 + X) + \left(\tfrac{38}{47}\right)\left(\tfrac{37}{46}\right)(-180 - X) < 0 \quad (5.21)$$

$$\left(\tfrac{9}{47}\right)(180) + \left(\tfrac{38}{47}\right)\left(\tfrac{9}{46}\right)(180) + \left(\tfrac{38}{47}\right)\left(\tfrac{9}{46}\right)X$$
$$- \left(\tfrac{38}{47}\right)\left(\tfrac{37}{46}\right)(80) - \left(\tfrac{38}{47}\right)\left(\tfrac{37}{46}\right)X < 0 \quad (5.22)$$

$$\left(\tfrac{9}{47}\right)(180) + \left(\tfrac{38}{47}\right)\left(\tfrac{9}{46}\right)(180) - \left(\tfrac{38}{47}\right)\left(\tfrac{37}{46}\right)(80)$$
$$< \left(\tfrac{38}{47}\right)\left(\tfrac{37}{46}\right)X - \left(\tfrac{38}{47}\right)\left(\tfrac{9}{46}\right)X \quad (5.23)$$

$$10.9158 < .4921x \qquad (5.24)$$

$$22.1804 < X \qquad (5.25)$$

Your opponent, if both you and he play as described, only needs to bet T23 or more to make this line of play −cEV for you.

The answer to example 5.3 brings up an important point about drawing. Suppose you knew that your opponent in example 5.3 would bet exactly T30 on the turn. The size of this bet would make calling on the turn −cEV. Therefore, when calling on the flop, you're calling with two cards to come, and since you're at 35% to hit your flush with two cards to come, you're apparently getting the proper price to call on the flop. The problem is that the bet on the turn means that you're actually getting worse than T180:T80 with two cards to come. If you understand this dynamic of drawing across multiple rounds of betting, you can:

- Avoid calling in seemingly +cEV situations that are actually −cEV.

- Bet smaller and still successfully defend against draws (assuming you don't cough up huge implied *odds*), giving you the additional opportunity to extract value from the nondrawing hands in your opponents' distributions (such as second or third pair).

Example 5.4: You're at the point in a tournament where a few players have less than 10bb. Action folds to a player who pushes all-in to 8bb. Then action folds to you, and you're BB with 22. What's the cEV of calling if you put the all-in player on {AA–22, AK–A2, KQ–KT} and you have him covered?

Answer: According to Poker Stove, your equity in the pot against {AA–22, AK–A2, KQ–KT} is 44.046%. If you call, the pot will be $(8)(2) + .5 = 16.5$bb, and 44.046% of 16.5bb is about 7.27bb. Since it's 7bb to call, the cEV of calling is $+.27$bb. The cEV of this play is extremely marginal—this is the type of call you should only be making in tournaments with extremely top-heavy payout structures.

Example 5.5: Suppose action folds to you, and you're on the button. If you open to 2.5bb, what percentage of the time do your opponents have to fold to show an immediate profit with respect to chips (ignore postflop play—assume that no matter what you have on the flop, your opponent bets into you, and you fold)?

Answer: When the blinds fold immediately, you're +1.5bb. Using the assumption put forth regarding postflop play, you're -2.5bb whenever you're called. Letting x denote the probability that both blinds fold:

$$1.5x - 2.5(1 - x) > 0 \qquad (5.26)$$

$$1.5x - 2.5 + 2.5x > 0 \qquad (5.27)$$

$$4x > 2.5 \qquad (5.28)$$

$$x > \tfrac{2.5}{4} \qquad (5.29)$$

The blinds need to fold at least 62.5% of the time.

Taking things a step further, let's see what type of hand distribution the blinds need to play. The probability that both blinds fold needs to be at least .625. Letting y denote the probability that a particular blind will fold:

$$y^2 = .625 \qquad (5.30)$$

$$y = .791 \qquad (5.31)$$

If neither of the blinds will defend more than about 21% of the time, this raise will show a profit even if you were simply to open muck your hand 100% of the time postflop. 21% of hands corresponds to about 278 combinations. {AA–55, AK–A8, KQ–K9, QJ–QT, JT} comprises 284 combinations. It's perfectly reasonable to assume that opponents will defend the blinds with a distribution something along these lines. Once postflop lines of play are accounted for, it's clear that opening to 2.5bb with a wide range of hands here will enable you to accumulate a lot of chips while, simultaneously, not risking a huge chunk of your stack to do so. The great thing about this 2.5bb opening raise is that it'll also enable you to extract a good amount of value with your very good hands, and by playing your stealing hands and premium hands identically, you set your opponents up to make big mistakes.

Example 5.6: Same situation as in example 5.5, but now consider when you open to 4bb instead of 2.5bb.

Answer: When the blinds fold immediately, you're +1.5bb. Using the assumption put forth regarding postflop play, you're −4bb whenever you're called. Letting x denote the probability that both blinds fold:

$$1.5x - 4(1 - x) > 0 \qquad (5.32)$$

$$1.5x - 4 + 4x > 0 \qquad (5.33)$$

$$5.5x > 4 \qquad (5.34)$$

$$x > \tfrac{4}{5.5} \qquad (5.35)$$

The blinds need to fold at least 72.73% of the time.

Taking things a step further, let's see what type of hand distribution the blinds need to play. The probability that both blinds fold needs to be at least .7273. Letting y denote the probability that a particular blind will fold:

$$y^2 = .7273 \tag{5.36}$$

$$y = .8528 \tag{5.37}$$

If neither of the blinds will defend more than about 15% of the time, this raise will show a profit even if you were simply to open muck your hand 100% of the time postflop. 15% of hands corresponds to about 199 combinations. {AA–77, AK–AT, KQ–KT, QJ–QT} comprises 192 combinations. Aggressive opponents will defend the blinds with something along these lines, but more timid foes will probably defend against 4bb with an even tighter range than this. But of course timid foes will defend against a 2.5bb raise with a range tighter than {AA–55, AK–A8, KQ–K9, QJ–QT, JT} because they typically don't want to risk being dominated. And since you shouldn't really be in the business of stealing naked against aggressive foes, the smaller 2.5bb opening raise from LP will generally serve you better.

Understanding cEV is important because −cEV propositions will cost you money in the long run.[4] But ultimately, cEV isn't really the quantity we're concerned with when playing tournaments.

---

4. That's assuming you're playing in a tournament where better prizes go to higher places. Sometimes, web forums host online tournaments with wacky payout structures (e.g., something along the lines of 1st = $5, 2nd = $3, 3rd = $2, 4th = $1, 5th = $10). In addition, if you play charity tournaments that give out prizes instead of cash, you may be in a situation where only certain prizes are desirable (maybe you're okay with the 1st-, 3rd-, and 5th-place prizes, but you want neither the 2nd- nor 4th-place prizes).

Monetary EV

You can't simply cash out of a tournament at any time. A tournament can only be resolved for you in one of three ways:

1. You win outright and take 1st place.

2. Someone eliminates you, and you take the payout corresponding to whatever place you finish in.

3. You make a deal with the remaining players in which everyone agrees on a way to split up the remaining prize pool.

Without considering dealmaking opportunities, your *monetary EV* (mEV) is given by equation 5.38.[5]

$$mEV = \sum_{k=1}^{N}[P(k\text{th Place})][\text{Payout of } k\text{th place}] \quad (5.38)$$

Unless you're trying to project the prize pool in the early stages of a tournament with rebuys and add-ons, you know the payouts corresponding to every place, so determining your mEV in a tournament reduces to figuring out your probability of finishing in each place (i.e., your finishing distribution). We'll address this problem specifically in chapter 6.

---

5. Dealmaking won't be covered until chapter 9. Killer tournament dealmaking involves much more than being satisfied with getting your equitable share of the prize pool. If you can anticipate the mistakes your opponents will make in the dealmaking process, you can actually incorporate the projected results from tournament deals into your monetary EV calculations!

Payout Structure

Determining the finishing distribution associated with a decision is a large part of the decision-making process in tournament NLHE. But sometimes, it's enough just to think about a tournament's payout structure.

Example 5.7: You're in a $100+$0 winner-take-all (WTA) STT with 6 entrants.[6] Action is down to 3 players. Before blinds are posted, you and your opponents have 3,000 chips each, and the blinds are at 200–400. You're in the big blind with AA, and both the button and the small blind are all-in. What should you do with your AA?

Answer: Given that everybody in a tournament plays identically, your probability of winning a tournament is equal to the fraction of total chips in your stack.[7] If you fold, you'll have 2,600 chips left, and your probability of winning the tournament will be $\frac{2,600}{9,000} \approx .2889$. We don't necessarily know the precise hand distributions your opponents are on, but given the distributions that players are typically on in this type of scenario (pocket pairs, any ace, and maybe hands like KQ and KJ), you're probably around 70% to win this hand—and therefore the tournament—if you call. Calling here boosts your probability of winning by about .4.

This result assumes that you and your opponents play identically. But even if you're the world's best heads-up player when stacks are short, you should still call for these two reasons:

6. Tournaments with no fees are awesome, and they aren't just figments of my imagination: go home games and special promotions! Tournaments with excessively high fees can be the downfall of even the most skilled tournament players. This will be another issue addressed in the final chapter.
7. This assumption will be the cornerstone of much of our analysis. It'll be proven in the next chapter.

1. Situations where you're at least 70% able to win a hand that goes to showdown aren't very common in Texas Hold'em. And while it's nice to think that it's possible to win pretty much every hand you play without going to showdown, that's simply not the reality of the game—no matter how good you are at reading your opponents and bluffing.[8]

2. Players who excel at heads-up STTs, where players start with the same amount of chips, win just a little more than 60% of their matches. Are you good enough to win over 60% of the time when you start at a 6,400 to 2,600 deficit? I know I'm not. If you are, let me know— I'd love to get some coaching from you!

Example 5.8: You're in the same situation described in example 5.7, except that first and second place each pay $300. Now what should you do with your AA?

Answer: From example 5.7, we know that if you call, you'll probably win about 70% of the time. This means that you'll lose and place out of the top two spots about 30% of the time. If you fold, there's a very small chance that your opponents will tie. This means that if you fold, one of your opponents will be eliminated almost 100% of the time, netting you $300 almost 100% of the time. Since first and second have identical payouts, folding is the correct play.

Examples 5.7 and 5.8 show that situations identical in every aspect except for payout structure might require completely different lines of play to maximize profits.

---

8. Fine. Annette_15 supposedly won a 180-player tournament that she played completely blind. I've never seen the video, but I would be shocked if she made it through the tournament without a showdown besides the last hand of the tournament.

Chapter Summary

In this chapter, we laid the foundation that will enable us to develop a comprehensive approach to tournament analysis. We defined EV to be the long-term expected payout associated with a random event. From there, we discussed cEV and mEV. Although cEV can be useful in eliminating lines of play since −cEV lines of play are also −mEV, we ultimately need to be concerned with mEV. After all, playing tournament NLHE is about making as much money as possible.

mEV is a function of two things: your finishing distribution and the payout structure. Although we haven't covered how to calculate your finishing distribution, we were still able to do some work having to do with accounting for the payout structure of a tournament. Before you jump headfirst into chapter 6, just keep the following in mind:

1. The more top-heavy the payout structure is, the less you should prize survival—especially early on.[9] In other words, don't be quick to pass up marginal edges—even if you think that there will be bigger edges to exploit later on.

2. Proper strategy in some situations with flat payout structures will be to fold *all* of your hands.

---

9. Roughly, a top-heavy payout structure is one where a hefty percentage of the prize pool is awarded to the top few places; a flat payout structure is one where the prize pool is evenly distributed among a decent percentage (something like 15%–30%) of the entrants; and a linear payout structure is one where the payout difference between places is relatively constant throughout the pay scale and a decent percentage (something like 15%–30%) of the entrants get paid.

6

INDEPENDENT CHIP MODELING

Introduction

Your mEV is a function of your finishing distribution. Figuring out your finishing distribution is one of the trickiest parts of tournament NLHE analysis. In this chapter, we'll demystify the process and study ICM, a mathematical model that deduces finishing distributions as a pure function of stack distributions (i.e., the number of chips that everybody has).

Derivation

Let's assume that all players in a tournament are implementing the same strategy. We now have a pure math problem—deducing finishing distributions as a pure function of the relative stacks in a tournament.

To begin, let's figure out your probability of finishing in 1st. Let T represent the total number of chips in a tournament, let S represent the total number of chips in your stack, and let E represent your long-term cEV. We're assuming everyone is playing identically, so you expect to neither gain nor lose chips in the long run. Therefore, $E = S$. If you finish in 1st, you'll have T chips. If you finish in any other place, you'll have 0 chips. Therefore, it's also true that $E = P(1st)T$. Since S and $P(1st)T$ both equal E:

$$S = P(1st)T \tag{6.1}$$

$$\tfrac{S}{T} = P(1st) \tag{6.2}$$

Equation 6.2 represents the commonly held assumption that your probability of finishing in first place equals the percentage of total tournament chips in your stack.[1]

With $P(1st)$ established, we can proceed to solve for $P(n$th$)$. To get an idea of what's going on, let's start by considering $P(2nd)$. Suppose you're in a tournament consisting of k players (including yourself). If you finish in 2nd, you effectively win a subtournament consisting of $k - 1$ players before losing the heads-up match. The probability of winning a subtournament is $\frac{S}{T-S_i}$, where S_i is the current stack size of the player who is presumed to finish in first. Letting $P(x,y)$ represent the probability that player x finishes in yth place, your probability of finishing in 2nd is (you're player k):

$$P(2nd) = P(1,1)\tfrac{S}{T-S_1} + P(2,1)\tfrac{S}{T-S_2} + P(3,1)\tfrac{S}{T-S_3} + \dots$$

$$+ P(k-1,1)\tfrac{S}{T-S_{k-1}} = \sum_{i=1}^{k-1}\left[P(i,1)\tfrac{S}{T-S_i}\right] \tag{6.3}$$

With all its symbols, equation 6.3 looks really intimidating, but the process of calculating $P(1st)$ and $P(2nd)$ isn't so bad:

1. If you're an empiricist, check out appendix C, which has the results from simulations that a friend of mine performed. The results of the simulations coincide with equation 6.2.

Example 6.1: You're in a satellite that pays the top two. Stacks are as follows:

You: T4,000

P1: T6,000

P2: T2,500

P3: T2,500

Assuming that you and your opponents play identically, what's the probability that you'll finish in first or second?

Answer: In total, T15,000 is in play. Since you have T4,000, $P(1st) = \frac{4,000}{15,000} = \frac{4}{15}$. Three ways exist in which you can get second place:

1. P1 finishes in first (after you effectively win a T9,000 subtournament consisting of you, P2, and P3).

2. P2 finishes in first (after you effectively win a T12,500 subtournament consisting of you, P1, and P3).

3. P3 finishes in first (after you effectively win a T12,500 subtournament consisting of you, P1, and P2).

The probability that you finish in second place is therefore:

$$\left(\tfrac{6,000}{15,000}\right)\left(\tfrac{4,000}{9,000}\right) + \left(\tfrac{2,500}{15,000}\right)\left(\tfrac{4,000}{12,500}\right) + \left(\tfrac{2,500}{15,000}\right)\left(\tfrac{4,000}{12,500}\right) = \tfrac{64}{225} \qquad (6.4)$$

Given that you and your opponents play identically, the probability that you finish in first or second is:

$$\tfrac{4}{15} + \tfrac{64}{225} \approx .5511 \qquad (6.5)$$

Now, let's consider the formula for P(3rd) if you have three opponents. With three opponents, you can finish in 3rd in 6 ways:

1. P1 takes 1st, and P2 takes 2nd.

2. P1 takes 1st, and P3 takes 2nd.

3. P2 takes 1st, and P1 takes 2nd.

4. P2 takes 1st, and P3 takes 2nd.

5. P3 takes 1st, and P1 takes 2nd.

6. P3 takes 1st, and P2 takes 2nd.

Analogous to what we said when considering $P(2nd)$, finishing in 3rd is equivalent to winning a subtournament consisting of the players not finishing in the top 2 before being eliminated. When finishing 3rd in a 4-player tournament, you're effectively eliminated after winning a heads-up match against the player who finishes in 4th place. P(3rd) in a four-player tournament is:

$$P(3rd) = P(1,1)P(2,2)\frac{S}{T-(S_1+S_2)} + P(1,1)P(3,2)\frac{S}{T-(S_1+S_3)} +$$

$$P(2,1)P(1,2)\frac{S}{T-(S_2+S_1)} + P(2,1)P(3,2)\frac{S}{T-(S_2+S_3)} +$$

$$P(3,1)P(1,2)\frac{S}{T-(S_3+S_1)} + P(3,1)P(2,2)\frac{S}{T-(S_3+S_2)} \qquad (6.6)$$

To generalize this process, account for all the ways that players can finish ahead of you and find the probability of winning the subtournament consisting of the players not finishing ahead of you for each particular combination.

Let $F_i(k,n)$ represent the probability associated with the ith particular finishing distribution of players ahead of you in a k player tournament where you finish in nth place. To illustrate what this notation means, here's $F_i(k,n)$ for a 4-player tournament where you finish in 3rd:

$$F_1(4,3) = P(1,1)P(2,2)$$

$$F_2(4,3) = P(1,1)P(3,2)$$

$$F_3(4,3) = P(2,1)P(1,2)$$

$$F_4(4,3) = P(2,1)P(3,2)$$

$$F_5(4,3) = P(3,1)P(1,2)$$

$$F_6(4,3) = P(3,1)P(2,2)$$

The particular assignments of the F_i subscripts don't matter—you're good as long as each finishing distribution is unique and all finishing distributions are accounted for.

If we generalize S_i and let it denote the sum of the stacks of the players who finish ahead of you, equation 6.7 is the expression for $P(n$th$)$ where n is greater than or equal to 2:

$$P(n\text{th}) = \sum_{\substack{i=1 \\ n \geq 2}}^{\frac{(k-1)!}{(k-n)!}} \left[F_i(k,n) \frac{S}{T - S_i} \right] \tag{6.7}$$

ICM and mEV

Equations 6.2 and 6.7 constitute the mathematical model known as ICM. With the theory behind ICM in place, we're now in a position to find the mEV associated with a stack distribution and a payout structure since:

$$\text{mEV} = \sum_{k=1}^{N} [P(k\text{th Place})][\text{Payout of } k\text{th place}] \tag{6.8}$$

Don't worry if your head is spinning from all the fancy-looking notations and equations used so far in this chapter.

At this point, the main idea is the following: assuming that you and your opponents play identically, ICM finds the probability of finishing in each place as a pure function of your and your opponents' stacks, and from there, you can use your finishing distribution and the payout structure of the tournament to find your mEV.

In practice, doing ICM calculations by hand can be quite time-consuming. Fortunately, software exists that finds the mEV associated with a stack distribution. For example, check out the free ICM calculator I have at killerev.com. With an ICM calculator in hand, finding the mEV of a line of play involves the following steps:

1. Figure out the stack distributions resulting from the line of play.

2. Use an ICM calculator to compute the mEV of each stack distribution.

3. Take a weighted average of the mEVs using the probability of each stack distribution.

In some cases, like all-in scenarios with no further action, determining the stack distributions is relatively straightforward (the trickiest part is ensuring that your reads are correct). In other cases, such as those in which play across multiple betting rounds needs to be considered, deducing the stack distributions becomes a daunting task.

Example 6.2: You're 1 of 12 players remaining in a $24+$2 MTT on Full Tilt (fulltiltpoker.com). The tournament started with 1,068 players, and the payout structure is:

1st Place: $5,767.20

2nd Place: $3,652.56

3rd Place: $2,704.18

4th Place: $2,114.64

5th Place: $1,602

6th Place: $1,153.44

7th Place: $768.96

8th Place: $576.72

9th Place: $410.11

10th Place: $230.69

11th Place: $230.69

12th Place: $230.69

The stack distribution is as follows:

P1: T550,500

P2: T450,000

P3: T375,775

P4: T346,600

P5: T300,000

P6: T225,500

P7 (You): T222,365

P8: T205,555

P9: T183,300

P10: T176,000

P11: T115,835

P12: T52,570

You're in the hand shown in table 6.1 (p. 114).

TABLE 6.1: Hand for Example 6.2

	STACKS	ANTE	STACKS	PREFLOP
SB xx	T550,500	T1,000	T549,500	sbT5,000 / –
YOU (K♦Q♦)	T222,365	T1,000	T221,365	bbT10,000 / ?
UTG xx	T183,300	T1,000	T182,300	–
UTG+1 xx	T346,600	T1,000	T345,600	–
CO xx	T450,000	T1,000	T449,000	–
B xx	T52,570	T1,000	T51,570	T51,570
POT		T6,000		

B is short stacked, so you put in on a liberal pushing distribution: {AA–22, AK–A2, KQ–K2, QJ–Q6, JT, T9s–54s, J9s–53s}. Use ICM to figure out the mEV of calling versus the mEV of folding.

Answer: Table 6.2 (opposite) gives the stack distributions if you fold, call and win, call and tie, and call and lose (along with the mEV of each stack distribution as found with the ICM calculator at killerev.com).

According to Poker Stove, when you call, P(Win) = .5547, P(Tie) = .0350, and P(Lose) = .4102. The mEV of calling is therefore as follows:

$$(.5547)(\$1,772.97) + (.0350)(\$1,520.19) +$$
$$(.4102)(\$1,245.31) = \$1,547.50 \qquad (6.9)$$

According to ICM, the mEV of calling is higher than the mEV of folding. ICM suggests calling here.

Example 6.3: Same situation as in example 6.2. But instead of putting B on a range, simply calculate the minimum P(win) required to make calling better than folding according to ICM [make an approximation and ignore ties—assume that P(Tie) = 0].

TABLE 6.2: mEV of Stack Distributions Arising from All Possible Lines of Play

	YOU FOLD	YOU CALL AND WIN	YOU CALL AND TIE	YOU CALL AND LOSE
P1	T544,500	T544,500	T544,500	T544,500
P2	T449,000	T449,000	T449,000	T449,000
P3	T375,775	T375,775	T375,775	T375,775
P4	T345,600	T345,600	T345,600	T345,600
P5	T300,000	T300,000	T300,000	T300,000
P6	T225,500	T225,500	T225,500	T225,500
P7 (YOU)	T211,365	T283,935	T226,865	T169,795
P8	T205,555	T205,555	T205,555	T205,555
P9	T182,300	T182,300	T182,300	T182,300
P10	T176,000	T176,000	T176,000	T176,000
P11	T115,835	T115,835	T115,835	T115,835
P12	T72,570	T0	T57,070	T114,140
YOUR mEV	**$1,447.92**	**$1,772.97**	**$1,520.19**	**$1,245.31**

Answer: Using the numbers in table 6.2 and letting X denote the probability of winning, we can set up equation 6.10:

$$(\$1,772.97)X + (\$1,245.31)(1 - X) > \$1,447.92 \quad (6.10)$$

$$\$1,772.97X + \$1,245.31 - \$1,245.31X > \$1,447.92 \quad (6.11)$$

$$\$527.66X > \$1,447.92 - \$1,245.31 \quad (6.12)$$

$$\$527.66X > \$202.61 \quad (6.13)$$

$$X > \tfrac{\$202.61}{\$527.66} \quad (6.14)$$

$$X > .3840 \quad (6.15)$$

ICM suggests that calling is better than folding as long as you'll win more than 38.40% of the time.

The result of example 6.3 is interesting. Calling in example 6.3 is +cEV as long as X is greater than $\frac{41,570}{114,140} \approx .3642$. When it comes to calling, ICM will sometimes give results such that +cEV propositions are −mEV. And in some cases, like bubble play in STTs, ICM suggests folding even in huge +cEV situations. To get comfortable with ICM's suggestions, it is best to spend some time every day away from the table running calculations on a wide range of situations.

The work in example 6.2 shows that working with ICM can be tedious—even with an ICM calculator. Fortunately, when it comes to analyzing preflop all-in situations involving open shoves and calling open shoves, software exists that does *all* the work for you. Input the stacks, the payout structure, and the players' pushing and calling ranges, and the software will figure out all possible stack distributions, figure out the probability of each stack distribution, find the mEV of each stack distribution using ICM, and take the weighted average of all mEVs. Three popular mEV calculators that I recommend are:

1. ICM Applicator (icmpoker.com)

2. Sit-n-Go Power Tools (sitngo-analyzer.com)

3. SitNGo Wizard (sngwiz.com/index.php)

Experiment and use the one you like best. (Note that these pieces of software sometimes make some approximations to simplify what can be very complicated calculations. For example, they often deal with ties by not accounting for the stack distribution resulting from a tie and, instead, distribute P(Tie) evenly between P(Win) and P(Lose). For most situations, this approximation won't matter too much; but it is something you should be aware of.)

Preflop All-Ins

Traditionally, ICM has been used extensively to analyze the preflop jam/fold endgame of STTs. Examples 6.2 and 6.3 use ICM to analyze a situation outside of STTs. And though they address a preflop all-in scenario, mastering preflop jam/fold analysis is an important part of becoming an elite tournament player. Some more examples follow.

Example 6.4: You enter a $30+$3 STT that seats 10 players. It's a standard 50/30/20 payout tournament, so first pays $150, second pays $90, and third pays $60. About forty-five minutes into things, you're 1 of 4 remaining players. Blinds are T250–T500, and prior to the blinds being posted, the stacks are as follows:

P1 (UTG): T3,000

P2 (Button): T3,500

P3 (Small Blind): T2,500

P4 (You) (Big Blind): T6,000

Action folds to P3, who pushes all-in from the small blind. You put him on {AA–22, AK–A2, KQ–KT, K9s–K2s, QJ–QT, JTs–54s, J9s–53s}. You have 22 in the BB. According to ICM, should you call, or should you fold?

Answer: The decision to call or fold is based purely on which is larger: the mEV of calling or the mEV of folding. To find the mEV of calling, we need to take the weighted average of the mEVs resulting from all the possible stack distributions that arise from calling. Three outcomes are possible if you call: you can win, you can tie, or you can lose. According to Poker Stove (pokerstove.com), P(win) = .4470, P(tie) = .0137, and P(lose) = .5393 given your opponent's hand distribution. Table 6.3, opposite, shows the stack distributions arising from all possibilities—along with their mEVs.

The overall mEV of calling is therefore (.4470)($120.42) + (.0137)($99.20) + (.5393)($72.63) = $94.36. The mEV of folding is $0.11 higher than the mEV of calling. According to this calculation, you should fold your 22.

Thinking in terms of chips, your equity is $P(win) + \frac{P(tie)}{2} = .4538$. Your cEV is positive as long as your *pot odds* are better than .5462:.4538 ≈ 1.204:1. In this situation, you're getting T3,000:T2,000 = T1.5:T1, which is better than 1.204:1. Your cEV is positive, but again, your mEV is negative.

TABLE 6.3: mEV of Stack Distributions Arising from All Possible Lines of Play

	YOU FOLD	YOU CALL AND WIN	YOU CALL AND TIE	YOU CALL AND LOSE
P1	T3,000	T3,000	T3,000	T3,000
P2	T3,500	T3,500	T3,500	T3,500
P3	T3,000	T0	T2,500	T5,000
P4 (YOU)	T5,500	T8,500	T6,000	T3,500
YOUR mEV	$94.47	$120.42	$99.20	$72.63

Example 6.5: You're in the same tournament from example 6.4. After folding your 22, about three orbits pass, and the stacks are as follows prior to the blinds being posted:

P2 (UTG): T3,500

P3 (Button): T3,500

P4 (You) (Small Blind): T4,000

P1 (Big Blind): T4,000

The blinds are T300–T600, and action folds to you. You're in the small blind with 32o. If you push all-in, you think your opponent will call with {AA–22, AK–A2}. Is a blind steal profitable here?

Answer: To answer this question, we need to compare the mEV of pushing to the mEV of folding. To find the mEV of pushing, we need to take the weighted average of the mEVs resulting from all the possible stack distributions that arise from pushing. Four outcomes are possible if you push: your opponent folds, your opponent calls and you win, your opponent calls and you tie, or your opponent calls and you lose. The following are the stack distributions arising from pushing:

TABLE 6.4: mEV of Stack Distributions Arising from Pushing

	P1 FOLDS	P1 CALLS; YOU WIN	P1 CALLS; YOU TIE	P1 CALLS; YOU LOSE
P2	T3,500	T3,500	T3,500	T3,500
P3	T3,500	T3,500	T3,500	T3,500
P4 (YOU)	T4,600	T8,000	T4,000	T0
P1	T3,400	T0	T4,000	T8,000
YOUR mEV	$85.15	$117.74	$78.22	$0

Since you know 2 cards, there are $\frac{50 \cdot 49}{2} = 1{,}225$ combinations of possible hole cards that your opponent can hold. Of those, AA–44 represent 6 combinations each, 33–22 represent 3 combinations each, AK–A4 represent 16 combinations each, and A3–A2 represent 12 combinations each. In total, the {AA–22, AK–A2} distribution represents 256 combinations. The probability that your opponent will call is $\frac{256}{1{,}225}$. The probability that your opponent will fold is $\frac{969}{1{,}225}$. Poker Stove tells us that P(win) = .2660, P(tie) = .0102, and P(lose) = .7238 if your opponent calls. The overall mEV of pushing is:

$$\left(\tfrac{969}{1{,}225}\right)(\$85.15) + \left(\tfrac{256}{1{,}225}\right)(.2660)(\$117.74) + \left(\tfrac{256}{1{,}225}\right)(.0102)(\$78.22)$$
$$+ \left(\tfrac{256}{1{,}225}\right)(.7238)(\$0) = \$74.07 \qquad (6.16)$$

Meanwhile, if you fold, the corresponding stacks and your mEV are shown in table 6.5.

The mEV of folding is $0.47 higher than the mEV of calling according to an ICM-based mEV calculation. This calcu-

TABLE 6.5: mEV of Stack Distributions Arising from Folding

P2	T3,500
P3	T3,500
P4 (YOU)	T3,700
P1	T4,300
YOUR mEV	**$74.54**

lation indicates that you shouldn't necessarily be shoving all-in with *any* two cards as you become short stacked with respect to the blinds. But the small mEV differential indicates that with sufficient *fold equity,* you should be shoving all-in with very wide ranges when short-stacked with respect to the blinds.

Postflop Play and Play Across Multiple Rounds of Betting

ICM has long been reserved for analysis of the STT endgame, where action is pretty much all-in or fold preflop. However, ICM can be applied to situations extending well beyond—including situations in which play across multiple betting rounds is considered. In extending ICM beyond preflop all-in scenarios, you need to project all the possible lines of play that can evolve from where you are in the hand, find the stack distribution arising from each line of play, and evaluate the mEV of each line of play.

Really, the same process is used in evaluating the preflop all-in scenarios we just considered. But practically, it can be more involved because of the sheer number of possibilities involved—the different lines of play available in any situation can quickly branch out to a large number.

But this doesn't mean that ICM is irrelevant for such cases. It's just that the analysis can become very involved very quickly. And unfortunately, software doesn't exist that accounts for playing across multiple betting rounds.[2] You'll need to go in with a plain ICM calculator for each possible stack distribution. It's far from undoable, and exploring various lines of play—especially those not involving large percentages of your stack—will be very important in forming your low blind play strategy.

Example 6.6: You're in a $100+$9 online STT where 1st pays $500, 2nd pays $300, and 3rd pays $200. Blind levels are 10 minutes each, and blinds are currently T200–T400. Table 6.6 describes the action:

TABLE 6.6: Betting Action for Example 6.6

	STACKS	PREFLOP	STACKS	FLOP J♥8♣7♠
SB (Q♥T♥)	T4,000	sbT200 / T400	T3,600	T0 / ?
BB xx	T3,500	bbT400 / T400	T3,100	T1,000
UTG xx	T3,000	–		
BB xx	T4,500	T400	T4,100	T1,000
POT		T1,200		T3,200

You checked the flop because BB and B have been playing straightforwardly at this stage. They'll bet if they have a king, and they'll check if they don't. Given the bet and the

2. Though I see such software being available in the near future . . . maybe at killerev.com.

call, you know that either BB or B has a king (possibly both). What's your action?

Answer: You're on the bubble, so you probably have some fold equity against a king—but not much. With only 9 outs and minimal fold equity, a check-raise semibluff is a poor choice. Your choices on the flop are calling or folding. If you fold, the following represent the most likely outcomes of the hand (the stack distributions are listed as (SB (You), BB, UTG, B)):

1. BB and B check down to the river; BB wins: (T3,600, T5,300, T3,000, T3,100): mEV = $248.087

2. BB and B check down to the river; B wins (T3,600, T2,100, T3,000, T6,300): mEV = $256.848

3. BB and B check the turn; BB shoves on the river; B folds (T3,600, T5,300, T3,000, T3,100): mEV = $248.087

4. BB and B check the turn; BB shoves on the river; B calls; BB wins (T3,600, T7,400, T3,000, T1,000): mEV = $275.984

5. BB and B check the turn; BB shoves on the river; B calls; B wins (T3,600, T0, T3,000, T8,400): mEV = $308.545

6. BB and B check the turn; BB checks the river; B shoves the river; BB folds (T3,600, T2,100, T3,000, T6,300): mEV = $256.848

7. BB and B check the turn; BB checks the river; B shoves the river; BB calls; BB wins (T3,600, T7,400, T3,000, T1,000): mEV = $275.984

8. BB and B check the turn; BB checks the river; B shoves the river; BB calls; B wins (T3,600, T0, T3,000, T8,400): mEV = $308.545

9. BB shoves the turn; B folds (T3,600, T5,300, T3,000, T3,100): mEV = $248.087

10. BB shoves the turn; B calls; BB wins (T3,600, T7,400, T3,000, T1,000): mEV = $275.984

11. BB shoves the turn; B calls; B wins (T3,600, T0, T3,000, T8,400): mEV = $308.545

12. BB checks the turn; B shoves; BB folds (T3,600, T2,100, T3,000, T6,300): mEV = $256.848

13. BB checks the turn; B shoves; BB calls; BB wins (T3,600, T7,400, T3,000, T1,000): mEV = $275.984

14. BB checks the turn; B shoves; BB calls; B wins (T3,600, T0, T3,000, T8,400): mEV = $308.545

Of course, the possibility exists that neither BB nor B will shove; perhaps BB will make something like a T750 blocking bet on the turn or the river. But typical STTers tend to shove in situations like these, preferring not to put themselves in positions where they might have to make tough decisions in later betting rounds.[3]

Assuming that each of these outcomes is equally likely when you fold, the mEV of folding is as follows:

3. This isn't to imply that shoving is bad for either player here. But the main motivation for an action should never be fear of having to play

$$\$248.087\left(\tfrac{1}{14}\right) + \$256.848\left(\tfrac{1}{14}\right) + \$248.087\left(\tfrac{1}{14}\right) + \$275.984\left(\tfrac{1}{14}\right) +$$

$$\$308.545\left(\tfrac{1}{14}\right) + \$256.848\left(\tfrac{1}{14}\right) + \$275.984\left(\tfrac{1}{14}\right) + \$308.545\left(\tfrac{1}{14}\right) +$$

$$\$248.087\left(\tfrac{1}{14}\right) + \$275.984\left(\tfrac{1}{14}\right) + \$308.545\left(\tfrac{1}{14}\right) + \$256.848\left(\tfrac{1}{14}\right) +$$

$$\$275.984\left(\tfrac{1}{14}\right) + \$308.545\left(\tfrac{1}{14}\right) \approx \$275.209 \qquad (6.17)$$

(Go ahead and assign different probabilistic weights or additional outcomes if you choose. The important thing is that you understand the thought process going into this calculation, so you can perform similar analysis on whatever situations you wish.)

Having deduced the mEV of folding, it's now time to consider the lines of play resulting from calling on the flop. First, let's figure out if you should call a bet on the turn when you miss. To do this, consider the best case scenario when you miss: you hit a Q or a T on the turn (potentially giving you 5 additional outs), BB shoves, and B calls (meaning you're getting the best possible pot odds)—see table 6.7, page 126.

When you call, the following outcomes are possible:

1. You win: (T11,500, T0, T3,000, T500): mEV = $451.810

2. You lose: (T0, T?, T3,000, T?): mEV = $0

To win, you need to river a heart, a Q, or a T. Any other time, you lose, because we're assuming that both of your opponents have you beaten. Since you have 14 outs, and

TABLE 6.7: Possible Line of Play for Example 6.6

	STACKS	PREFLOP	STACKS	FLOP K♥7♥5♦	STACKS	TURN Q♦
SB (Q♥T♥)	T4,000	sbT200 / T400	T3,600	T0 / T1,000	T2,600	T0 / ?
BB xx	T3,500	sbT400 / T400	T3,100	T1,000	T2,100	T2,100
UTG xx	T3,000	–				
B xx	T4,500	T400	T4,100	T1,000	T3,100	T3,100
POT xx		T1,200		T4,200		

the deck contains 46 cards, the mEV of calling on the turn is:

$$\$451.810\left(\tfrac{14}{46}\right) \approx \$137.507 \qquad (6.18)$$

Meanwhile, if you fold on the turn, the following outcomes are possible:

1. BB wins: (T2,600, T8,400, T3,000, T1,000): mEV = $239.609

2. B wins: (T2,600, T0, T3,000, T9,400): mEV = $285.429

Assuming each of these outcomes is equally likely, the mEV of folding is:

$$\$239.609\left(\tfrac{1}{2}\right) + \$285.429\left(\tfrac{1}{2}\right) \approx \$262.519 \qquad (6.19)$$

(If you work out the cEV of the call on the turn, you'll find that the call is highly favorable. When on the bubble in STTs, the buffer between neutral cEV and neutral mEV can be huge—the necessary probability of winning can differ by more than 20% in some cases!)

Because you're forced to fold to a bet on the turn, the

most likely case is that you're drawing on the flop with just one card to come. But let's be optimistic and assume you'll get to see the river for free if you miss the turn. Furthermore, let's assume that you'll always double-up against B when you hit your flush. If that's the case, then the following scenarios are possible:

1. You hit your flush, trips, or two-pair, and double up: (T9,400, T2,100, T3,000, T500): mEV = $414.294

2. You miss and BB wins with no further bets that are called: (T2,600, T6,300, T3,000, T3,100): mEV = $203.778

3. You miss and B wins with no further bets that are called: (T2,600, T2,100, T3,000, T7,300): mEV = $215.099

4. You miss and BB wins after BB and B go all-in: (T2,600, T8,400, T3,000, T1,000): mEV = $239.609

5. You miss and B wins after BB and B go all-in: (T2,600, T0, T3,000, T9,400): mEV = $285.429

The probability that you improve to two-pair or better with two cards to come is:

$$1 - \left(\tfrac{38}{47}\right)\left(\tfrac{37}{46}\right) + \left(\tfrac{6}{47}\right)\left(\tfrac{5}{46}\right) = \tfrac{393}{1,081} \qquad (6.20)$$

Assuming that outcomes 2–5 are equally likely when you don't win, the mEV of calling on the flop given the most optimistic case (besides when both players call when you improve to two-pair or better) is:

$$\$414.294\left(\tfrac{393}{1,081}\right) + \$203.778\left(\tfrac{688}{1,081}\right)\left(\tfrac{1}{4}\right) + \$215.099\left(\tfrac{688}{1,081}\right)\left(\tfrac{1}{4}\right) +$$

$$\$239.609\left(\tfrac{688}{1,081}\right)\left(\tfrac{1}{4}\right) + \$285.429\left(\tfrac{688}{1,081}\right)\left(\tfrac{1}{4}\right) = \$300.806 \ (6.21)$$

Now, let's assume the exact opposite—the worst-case scenario where you don't get a free card if you miss on the turn and have absolutely no implied odds if you hit. In that case, the following stack distributions are possible:

1. You hit your flash on the turn: (T6,800, T2,100, T3,000, T3,100): mEV = $353.102

2. You miss and BB wins after betting and winning uncontested: (T2,600, T6,300, T3,000, T3,100): mEV = $203.778

3. You miss and B wins after betting and winning uncontested: (T2,600, T2,100, T3,000, T7,300): mEV = $215.099

4. You miss and BB wins after BB and B go all-in: (T2,600, T8,400, T3,000, T1,000): mEV = $239.609

5. You miss and B wins after BB and B go all-in: $285.429

Assuming that outcomes 2–5 are equally likely, the mEV of calling on the flop is:

$$\$353.102\left(\tfrac{9}{46}\right) + \$203.778\left(\tfrac{37}{46}\right)\left(\tfrac{1}{4}\right) + \$215.099\left(\tfrac{37}{46}\right)\left(\tfrac{1}{4}\right) +$$

$$\$239.609\left(\tfrac{37}{46}\right)\left(\tfrac{1}{4}\right) + \$285.429\left(\tfrac{37}{46}\right)\left(\tfrac{1}{4}\right) = \$258.700 \quad (6.22)$$

The results of equations 6.21 and 6.22 show that the best-case scenario results in an mEV that's $25.597 higher than folding on the flop and that the worst-case scenario results in an mEV that's $16.509 lower than folding on the flop. The difference between calling and folding will be determined by how often the probable best-case scenario happens with respect to the probable worst-case scenario—in addition to the spectrum of all other possibilities. Because it will be relatively easy for your opponents to put you on a flush draw if you just call on the flop, it's probably safe to assume that you don't have great implied odds. Therefore, folding immediately on the flop is probably the best move.

Chapter Summary

The fundamental assumption of ICM is that all players are implementing the same strategy. Obviously, real playing conditions dictate that this isn't the case at all. Even though high-blind play in tournaments often reduces to a preflop jam/fold game, the jamming and calling distributions will most likely vary from player to player. Some players might call all-ins to five big blinds with {AA–22, AK–A2, KQ–K8, QJ–QT, JT} while others might fold everything except {AA–99, AK–AJ}. ICM really gives a window into optimal, nonexploitable play as opposed to exploitative play. In other words, ICM allows one to calculate how everybody should play. Playing optimally won't make you the most money against all your opponents' strategies, but it'll ensure that your opponents can't profit from your decisions.

If you're trying to play exploitatively and make the most money from your opponents' mistakes (which most of your opponents will make), then the step beyond ICM is to model each player's jamming and folding distribution as a function of stack distribution and position and to derive your optimal decisions by simulating tournaments all the way. Theoretically, this sounds much nicer than implementing it. As a result, a practical route toward exploitative play is to use ICM calculations and to make qualitative adjustments based on actual playing conditions. Combine the model with your first-hand experience, and you'll put yourself in a position to make quality tournament decisions.

And even though ICM is usually just applied to tournament endgame scenarios—particularly those arising in STTs—it can really be applied to a much wider range. This includes situations in MTTs and play across multiple rounds of betting.

7

N-UP MODELING

Introduction

When it comes to tournament poker, the traditional advice given by most authors is to play very conservatively in the early stages, avoiding any confrontations that might put your entire stack at risk. The rationale behind this advice is that if you're highly skilled, you can pass off marginal edges in the present because of bigger edges that you'll have in the future. Understanding this concept is extremely important if you're to be a successful tournament player. However, some players take this concept to extremes that are ultimately detrimental to their results.

Tournament poker is about balancing the ideas of chip preservation and chip accumulation. On one hand, as you survive longer in a tournament, your payout goes up. There's an intrinsic value simply to having a seat. On the other hand, you can't simply sit and avoid playing hands. You need to get chips to keep up with the increasing blinds. Players who *constantly* pass off opportunities to accumulate chips in anticipation of better future opportunities cost themselves prize-pool equity in the long run.

The question we really need to answer is this: what's the minimum edge that you should accept when risking all your chips in the early stages of a tournament? For example, if you're something like a 57/43 favorite, should you risk all your chips or fold in anticipation of a better opportunity? ICM is a pure theoretical look at this question. In this chapter, we're going to switch to applying some mathematical analysis to the results of top tournament players. If you're traditionally a big chip preservationist in MTTs with top-heavy payout structures, your views of how to play such tournaments will change considerably after reading this chapter.

Derivation

Consider your path through a tournament to be a series of double ups. The probability that you'll win a tournament like this is given by D^n. In this expression, D is the probability that you'll win an all-in confrontation and double up, and n is the number of double ups you need to win. Assuming that you and everyone else in the tournament is equally skilled, the probability of you doubling up when you're all-in is .5. For a 16-player tournament, $P(win) = (.5)^4 = \frac{1}{16}$. This is what we'd expect—if you and your 15 competitors are equally skilled, then you all should have a $\frac{1}{16}$ probability of winning.

If you play better than your opponents do, then your probability of winning each double up will be greater than .5. The big question is how much bigger than .5? Suppose you've played one hundred 16-player WTA tournaments and you've found that your EV is 2 buy-ins (in other words, your average profit per tournament is 1 buy-in). In a 16-player tournament, an EV of 2 buy-ins translates into a P(Win) of $\frac{2}{16}$ instead of $\frac{1}{16}$. Let D denote the probability of winning a double-up. Since you need 4 double ups to win the tournament:

$$P(\text{Win}) = D^n \qquad (7.1)$$

$$\tfrac{2}{16} = D^4 \qquad (7.2)$$

$$\tfrac{1}{8} = D^4 \qquad (7.3)$$

$$\sqrt[4]{\tfrac{1}{8}} = D \qquad (7.4)$$

$$.5946 \approx D \qquad (7.5)$$

If your edge in this tournament is 1 buy-in, then the probability of your winning each all-in is about .5946.

Modeling a tournament as a series of double ups may seem silly since it's not how the actual dynamics of tournament poker play out. Although many players play NLHE as if it were "double up or fold" poker, the reality is that well-played NLHE is about much more than doubling up or folding. Early tournament play, when blinds are low, is largely about playing effective small ball: extracting maximal value with made hands and taking lucrative stabs at pots with bets representing only a small fraction of your stack. As we continue through this chapter, just keep in mind that we're simply developing a model that will give us some important insight.

Example 7.1: You're in a WTA tournament consisting of 128 players, and your EV is still 2 buy-ins. Modeling this tournament as a series of double ups, what's your probability of winning each double up?

Answer: The following math gives us your value of D for this tournament:

$$P(\text{Win}) = D^n \tag{7.6}$$

$$\frac{2}{128} = D^7 \tag{7.7}$$

$$\frac{1}{64} = D^7 \tag{7.8}$$

$$\sqrt[7]{\frac{1}{64}} = D \tag{7.9}$$

$$.552 \approx D \tag{7.10}$$

D for a 128-player tournament with an mEV of 2 buy-ins is lower than D for a 16-player tournament with an EV of 2 buy-ins. This illustrates an important point. As the field size increases, the risk you should be willing to take generally increases. Table 7.1 gives values of D for WTA tournaments as a function of the number of entrants, given that your mEV is always 2 buy-ins:

TABLE 7.1: D for WTA Tournaments When Your mEV Is 2 Buy-Ins

NUMBER OF ENTRANTS	D
8	.630
16	.595
32	.574
64	.561
128	.552
256	.545
512	.540
1,024	.536
2,048	.532

Most tournaments aren't WTA, so our next step is to make this model work for any tournaments of any payout structure. To do this, we simply need to come up with an expression for the probability of finishing in any place. Letting N denote the number of tournament entrants:

$$N = 2^n \tag{7.11}$$

$$n = \log_2 N \tag{7.12}$$

$$P(\text{1st}) = D^{\log_2 N} \tag{7.13}$$

(If logarithms aren't exactly your thing, just skim through the rest of this derivation. It's not that important that you understand the derivation exactly. You're okay as long as you understand the general idea of what I'm doing.)

P(2nd) equals the probability of doubling up to half the chips in the tournament minus the probability of winning the tournament. P(3rd) is the probability of doubling up to a third of the chips in the tournament minus the probabilities of finishing in second and first. In general, the probability of finishing in ith place is the probability of doubling up to a stack of $\frac{N}{i}$ minus the sums of the probabilities of finishing in a higher place.

$$\frac{N}{i} = 2^n \tag{7.14}$$

$$\log_2\left(\frac{N}{1}\right) = n \tag{7.15}$$

Therefore, the probability of doubling up to a stack of $\frac{N}{i}$ is $D^{\log_2\left(\frac{N}{i}\right)}$:

$$P(\text{1st}) = D^{\log_2\left(\frac{N}{i}\right)} \tag{7.15}$$

$$P(\text{2nd}) = D^{\log_2\left(\frac{N}{2}\right)} - D^{\log_2\left(\frac{N}{1}\right)} \tag{7.16}$$

$$P(\text{3rd}) = D^{\log_2\left(\frac{N}{3}\right)} - \left[D^{\log_2\left(\frac{N}{2}\right)} - D^{\log_2\left(\frac{N}{1}\right)}\right] - D^{\log_2\left(\frac{N}{1}\right)} =$$
$$D^{\log_2\left(\frac{N}{3}\right)} - D^{\log_2\left(\frac{N}{2}\right)} \tag{7.17}$$

$$P(\text{ith}) = D^{\log_2\left(\frac{N}{i}\right)} - D^{\log_2\left(\frac{N}{i-1}\right)} \tag{7.18}$$

Equation 7.18 is valid for all values of i greater than 1. To figure out your value of D for a tournament, you need to solve equation 7.19 for D:

$$\text{mEV(In Buy-Ins)} = \sum_i \left[\left(D^{\log_2(\frac{N}{i})} - D^{\log_2(\frac{N}{i-1})}\right)M(i)\right] \quad (7.19)$$

In equation 7.19, $M(i)$ represents the payout of ith place in terms of buy-ins. For example, if 1st place in a \$100 tournament is \$2,000, then $M(1) = 20$.

To this point, we've only been considering double ups. What about situations where you can triple up—or beyond? For the case of what I'll refer to as n ups, equation 7.19 can be generalized (p is the probability of winning an n up):

$$\text{mEV(In Buy-Ins)} = \sum_i \left[\left(p^{\log_n(\frac{N}{i})} - p^{\log_n(\frac{N}{i-1})}\right)M(i)\right] \quad (7.20)$$

Equation 7.20 represents the n up model of poker tournaments. Using it, you can do either one of two calculations:

1. Take a value of p and come up with the corresponding mEV.

2. Take an mEV and come up with the corresponding p for a particular kind of n up.

Working with equation 7.20 by hand is a huge pain—especially when dealing with a huge MTT. Therefore, I wrote a piece of software that does all the work. Using it, you can go from mEV to p and vice versa. Check out the free n up calculator at killerev.com.

Using Target ROI to Determine
Risk Threshold

If you go to a site like Official Poker Ranking (opranking .com), you can see the ROIs of every player who's ever played an MTT in the online poker rooms that OP Ranking tracks. Look at the results of players who've logged at least a few hundred tournaments, and you can see that an ROI above 100% puts you in a very elite class.

The typical chip preservation argument says that skilled players should preserve their chips in marginal situations so that they can outplay their opponents in later situations when they have a bigger edge. However, sitting and waiting for too long results in losing a chunk of your stack to the blinds; by the time you get your prime opportunity, you can't win as many chips.

Looking at the tables in appendix D, which were calculated using the payout structures found in many MTTs found on Poker Stars (pokerstars.com), you will see that 100% ROI players enjoy an edge in the 57%–60% range per double up for smaller tournaments (250 entrants or fewer). In larger tournaments (300–1,500 entrants), their edge per double up is 55%–56%. This isn't what most people think of when they say "big edge," but remember that since you're always playing against hand distributions, it's tough to be more than a 65% favorite against a single opponent.

All right, what about when some dead chips are in the pot? Or what about situations when 2 or maybe even 3 players are all-in. The basic guideline is that as the number of chips increases, the minimum winning percentage decreases. After all, you need fewer triple ups than double ups to win a tournament. The additional chips available in the pot make a big difference: the minimum winning percentage for a 100% ROI player begins to dip below 50% for 2.5 ups. And when it comes to triple ups, a 100% ROI player essentially progresses though a series of triple ups, where he wins each one about 40% of the time.

This is an extremely important point about tournament poker. Many players believe that they shouldn't even think about putting their tournament life on the line when they aren't at least at 50% to win. Those of you cash game players out there know that poker is really about pot odds. And although cEV and mEV aren't directly proportional in tournaments that pay multiple spots, additional chips in the pot reduce the minimum winning percentage required to call— even to below 50%.

And if you consider that this winning percentage is something of an average winning percentage (sometimes you'll have opportunities that are close to coin flips, and other times you'll be a much bigger favorite), you shouldn't really be shy about taking any sort of edge you can find. Avoid habitually engaging in just barely +cEV propositions for your stack. But if you're not taking any calculated risks to accumulate chips in MTTs with top-heavy payout structures, then your mEV will suffer considerably. From my experience, playing too conservatively in MTTs results in consistent top-third finishes where you either bubble or finish just barely in the money. And with the top-heavy payout structures of most MTTs, you won't be making much money; overly cautious tournament players are usually losing tournament players.

Chapter Summary

By performing some analysis on the results of top MTT players, we saw that the type of edge needed to contest a pot with a large fraction of your stack isn't nearly as high as some of the tournament literature hints at. As with the work we did with ICM, the n up model suggests only a slight buffer between the +cEV line and the +mEV line. Here's a good rule of thumb: when playing in an MTT with a top-heavy payout structure, be willing to risk large chunks of your stack—or your tournament life—whenever your winning percentage is at least 2 higher than the winning percentage corresponding to neutral cEV.

8

BLIND STRUCTURE

Introduction

Single-table tournaments, double *shootouts,* heads-up freeze-outs, speed tournaments, satellites, MTTs—and the list goes on! Many different types of tournaments exist, but all of them are the same on a fundamental level: they all feature blind structures and payout structures. We've done a lot of work up to now with tournament payout structures. It's now time to turn to blind structures.

Survival Time

Let's consider two different online NLHE tournaments. In Tournament A, everyone starts with 2,500 chips, and blinds start at 5–10. In Tournament B, everyone starts with 5,000 chips, and blinds start at 10–20. The starting number of chips is different in each tournament, but in both of these tournaments, players start with 250bb. These tournaments will play identically in the first round given the following:

1. The speed at which the blinds escalate doesn't affect how players play in a given round.

2. The absolute value of the chips involved has no psychological impact on how players will play. In other words, players view everything in terms of "number of big blinds" instead of "number of chips."

Let's now consider a third online NLHE tournament. In tournament C, each player begins with 1,000 chips, and the blinds start at 10–20; each player in this tournament starts with 50bb as opposed to 250bb. In tournaments A and B, players skilled at playing deeply stacked (DS) poker have a distinct advantage for a number of reasons including, but not limited to, the following:

1. Availability of lines of play that incorporate sophisticated bluffs on the turn and the river.

2. Sufficient implied odds from players who don't understand the unique dynamics of DSNLHE.

3. The ability to extract maximum value with made hands across all four rounds of betting.

4. A buffer to absorb a bad beat or two.

But it's really the combination of the starting stacks and the rate of blind escalation that determines how a tournament will play. One way of measuring the impact of blind structure is to calculate survival time—the number of hands a player will be dealt before he blinds out of the tournament given that he folds every single hand. Survival time can be interpreted as a measure of how tightly one can play. To calculate survival time, first find out the average number of chips lost per hand for each level. The number of chips you lose per hand for a given blind level is:

$$\text{Chips Lost Per Hand} = \frac{sb+bb}{N} + A \qquad (8.1)$$

In equation 8.1, sb is the amount of the small blind, bb is the amount of the big blind, N is the average number of players at the table (including you), and A is the ante. We can calculate how many chips are lost per level by multiplying equation 1.1 by H, the number of hands played per orbit:

$$\text{Chips Lost Per Level} = \left(\frac{sb+bb}{N} + A\right)H \qquad (8.2)$$

Some of you may object to equation 8.2 because the number of sbs and bbs paid is a function of your position at the start of a level. It's correct to identify that sbs and bbs paid in a particular tournament are a function of your starting position. But on average, across all starting positions, everything will even out, and you'll end up with equation 8.2.

Example 8.1: Calculate the survival time for tournament A given that it has the blind structure specified in table 8.1. Assume that tables are always 10-handed.

TABLE 8.1: Blind Structure for Tournament A

LEVEL	SB	BB	ANTE
1	5	10	0
2	10	20	0
3	15	30	0
4	20	40	0
5	25	50	0
6	30	60	0

(continued on p. 142)

LEVEL	SB	BB	ANTE
7	50	100	0
8	75	150	0
9	100	200	0
10	100	200	25
11	150	300	25
12	200	400	25
13	250	500	50
14	300	600	50
15	400	800	50
16	500	1,000	75
17	600	1,200	75
18	750	1,500	75
19	1,000	2,000	100
20	1,200	2,400	100

Each player begins with 2,500 chips, and blinds go up every 20 minutes.

Answer: Since this is an online tournament, assume that the average time per hand is one minute.[1] Use equation 8.2 to generate something along the lines of table 8.2, opposite. (I generated this table in a very short amount of time using Microsoft Excel, and by the time this book is in your hands, I probably will have ended up putting a survival time calculator up at killerev.com.):

1. I said this in *KPBTN,* and it's such an important idea that I'll say it again here: calculations are only as good as the assumptions that go into them. In that spirit, I try to make assumptions that accurately describe real playing conditions. But if the playing conditions you encounter differ from anything I describe, just take the thought processes I outline and apply them to the playing conditions that you encounter.

TABLE 8.2: Number of Chips You Lose Each Level in Tournament A

LEVEL	SB	BB	ANTE	CHIPS LOST PER HAND	HANDS PER LEVEL	CHIPS LOST	CUMULATIVE CHIPS LOST
1	5	10	0	1.5	20	30	30
2	10	20	0	3	20	60	90
3	15	30	0	4.5	20	90	180
4	20	40	0	6	20	120	300
5	25	50	0	7.5	20	150	450
6	30	60	0	9	20	180	630
7	50	100	0	15	20	300	930
8	75	150	0	22.5	20	450	1,380
9	100	200	0	30	20	600	1,980
10	100	200	25	55	20	1,100	3,080
11	150	300	25	70	20	1,400	4,480
12	200	400	25	85	20	1,700	6,180
13	250	500	50	125	20	2,500	8,680
14	300	600	50	140	20	2,800	11,480
15	400	800	50	170	20	3,400	14,880
16	500	1,000	75	225	20	4,500	19,380
17	600	1,200	75	255	20	5,100	24,480
18	750	1,500	75	300	20	6,000	30,480
19	1,000	2,000	100	400	20	8,000	38,480
20	1,200	2,400	100	460	20	9,200	47,680

The column labeled Cumulative Chips Lost was found by adding the number of chips lost in each level. Table 8.2 tells us that 1,980 chips are lost through level 9 and 3,080 chips are lost through level 10. Using x to denote the number of hands dealt in level 10, we can form equation 8.3 using the facts that 1,980 total chips are lost through level 9 and 55 chips are lost per hand in level 10. Solve for x:

$$1,980 + 55x = 2,500 \tag{8.3}$$

$$1,980 + 55x - 1,980 = 2,500 - 1,980 \tag{8.4}$$

$$55x = 520 \tag{8.5}$$

$$x = \tfrac{520}{55} \approx 9.4545 \tag{8.6}$$

TABLE 8.3: Blind Structure for Tournament B

LEVEL	SB	BB	ANTE
1	10	20	0
2	20	40	0
3	30	60	0
4	50	100	0
5	100	200	0
6	100	200	25
7	150	300	25
8	200	400	25
9	300	600	50
10	500	1,000	50
11	750	1,500	75
12	1,000	2,000	75
13	1,500	3,000	100
14	2,000	4,000	100
15	2,500	5,000	200
16	3,000	6,000	200
17	5,000	10,000	300
18	7,500	15,000	300
19	10,000	20,000	500
20	15,000	30,000	500

Since we're assuming that 20 hands per level are dealt before level 10, the survival time for tournament A is about $20(9) + 9.4545 = 189.4545$ hands.

Example 8.2: Calculate the survival time for tournament B given that it has the blind structure specified in table 8.3, opposite. Assume that tables are always 10-handed.

Answer: Since this is an online tournament, assume that the average time per hand is one minute.

Use equation 8.2 to generate something along the lines of table 8.4, below, which tells us that 4,956 chips are lost through level 9 and 7,356 chips are lost through level 10. Using x to denote the number of hands dealt in level 10, we can form equation 8.7 using the facts that 4,956 total chips

TABLE 8.4: Number of Chips You Lose Each Level in Tournament B

LEVEL	SB	BB	ANTE	CHIPS LOST PER HAND	HANDS PER LEVEL	CHIPS LOST	CUMULATIVE CHIPS LOST
1	10	20	0	3	12	36	36
2	20	40	0	6	12	72	108
3	30	60	0	9	12	108	216
4	50	100	0	15	12	180	396
5	100	200	0	30	12	360	756
6	100	200	25	55	12	660	1,416
7	150	300	25	70	12	840	2,256
8	200	400	25	85	12	1,020	3,276
9	300	600	50	140	12	1,680	4,956
10	500	1,000	50	200	12	2,400	7,356
11	750	1,500	75	300	12	3,600	10,956
12	1,000	2,000	75	375	12	4,500	15,456

LEVEL	SB	BB	ANTE	CHIPS LOST PER HAND	HANDS PER LEVEL	CHIPS LOST	CUMULATIVE CHIPS LOST
13	1,500	3,000	100	550	12	6,600	22,056
14	2,000	4,000	100	700	12	8,400	30,456
15	2,500	5,000	200	950	12	11,400	41,856
16	3,000	6,000	200	1,100	12	13,200	55,056
17	5,000	10,000	300	1,800	12	21,600	76,656
18	7,500	15,000	300	2,550	12	30,600	107,256
19	10,000	20,000	500	3,500	12	42,000	149,256
20	15,000	30,000	500	5,000	12	60,000	209,256

are lost through level 9 and 200 chips are lost per hand in level 10 and solve for x:

$$4,956 + 200x = 5,000 \qquad (8.7)$$

$$4,956 + 200x - 4,956 = 5,000 - 4,956 \qquad (8.8)$$

$$200x = 44 \qquad (8.9)$$

$$x = \tfrac{44}{200} \approx .22 \qquad (8.10)$$

Since we're assuming that 12 hands per level are dealt before level 10, the survival time for tournament B is about $12(9) + .22 = 108.22$ hands.

In tournament A, you get to see 81.2345 more hands before you get blinded off, implying that you can be much more patient in tournament A. However, the survival time in tournament B isn't short; the probability of seeing a few premium starting hands is quite high over the span of 108.22 hands.

Survival time indicates how patient you can be to some degree, but it unfortunately falls short of predicting the true dynamics of how you need to play. You aren't going to double up every time you get a premium hand. Sometimes, you'll just snag the blinds with your premium hands. And other times, you may even lose with your premium hands (and some of those losses will be big). In addition, your opponents will be accumulating chips while you sit back and wait for the nuts. Some of your other looser opponents will be eliminated in the process, and you'll move closer to the money; however, if you just sit back on your chips, it'll be very hard for you to reach a final table. And if you get blinded down too much before getting the superpremium hand you're waiting for, you won't be able to win as many chips since you'll have lost a substantial chunk of your stack to the blinds. Finally, on average, tournaments will feature the highest proportion of poor players in the early stages. If you're not in there mixing it up against players who you can easily exploit, then you're forcing yourself into a position in which you need to mix it up later on against players who, on average, are tougher to exploit.

If you play in MTTs with top-heavy payouts, you won't be profitable in the long run unless your game plan gets you to some final tables. And simply waiting around for superpremium hands won't do the trick—even in tournaments with somewhat slow structures. Imagine what the situation is when you're in tournaments featuring faster structures.

Example 8.3: Calculate the survival time of a $20+$2 tournament on Cake Poker (cakepoker.com). The first 20 levels of the blind structure are given in table 8.5 (p. 148). Assume that tables are always 10-handed.

Answer: Since this is an online tournament, assume that the average time per hand is one minute. Use equation 8.2 to generate something along the lines of table 8.6 (p. 149).

TABLE 8.5: Blind Structure for a Low Buy-In Tournament on Cake Poker

LEVEL	SB	BB	ANTE
1	10	20	0
2	15	30	0
3	25	50	0
4	50	100	0
5	75	150	0
6	100	200	0
7	100	200	25
8	200	400	25
9	300	600	50
10	400	800	50
11	600	1,200	75
12	800	1,600	75
13	1,000	2,000	100
14	1,250	2,500	125
15	1,500	3,000	150
16	2,000	4,000	200
17	2,500	5,000	250
18	3,000	6,000	300
19	4,000	8,000	400
20	5,000	10,000	500

Each player begins with 1,500 chips, and blinds go up every 12 minutes.

Table 8.6 tells us that at the end of level 6, after seeing about 72 hands, you'll have lost a total of 990 chips. Letting x denote how many hands you see in level 7, we can write equation 8.11 using the facts that 990 chips are lost through level 6 and 55 chips are lost per hand in level 7. Solve for x:

$$990 + 55x = 1,500 \qquad (8.11)$$

$$990 + 55x - 990 = 1,500 - 990 \qquad (8.12)$$

$$55x = 510 \tag{8.13}$$

$$x = \tfrac{510}{55} \approx 9.2727 \tag{8.14}$$

The survival time for this tournament is about 12(6) + 9.2727 = 81.2727 hands.

In the tournament from example 8.3, chances are still good that you'll see a couple of premium hands before being blinded off. However, a game plan involving more than sim-

TABLE 8.6: Number of Chips You Lose Each Level in a Low Buy-In Tournament on Cake Poker

LEVEL	SB	BB	ANTE	CHIPS LOST PER HAND	HANDS PER LEVEL	CHIPS LOST	CUMULATIVE CHIPS LOST
1	10	20	0	3	12	36	36
2	15	30	0	4.5	12	54	90
3	25	50	0	7.5	12	90	180
4	50	100	0	15	12	180	360
5	75	150	0	22.5	12	270	630
6	100	200	0	30	12	360	990
7	100	200	25	55	12	660	1,650
8	200	400	25	85	12	1,020	2,670
9	300	600	50	140	12	1,680	4,350
10	400	800	50	170	12	2,040	6,390
11	600	1,200	75	255	12	3,060	9,450
12	800	1,600	75	315	12	3,780	13,230
13	1,000	2,000	100	400	12	4,800	18,030
14	1,250	2,500	125	500	12	6,000	24,030
15	1,500	3,000	150	600	12	7,200	31,230
16	2,000	4,000	200	800	12	9,600	40,830
17	2,500	5,000	250	1,000	12	12,000	52,830
18	3,000	6,000	300	1,200	12	14,400	67,230
19	4,000	8,000	400	1,600	12	19,200	86,430
20	5,000	10,000	500	2,000	12	24,000	110,430

ple *hit-to-win* poker will be necessary to succeed—especially given that if you're blinded down through level 6 (72 hands), you'll only have 510 chips going into level 7, where the blinds will be 100–200 with an ante of 25. The only way you can get away with playing tight, straightforward poker is if your opponents yield huge implied odds, enabling you to get value consistently from your good hands.

Example 8.4: Calculate your survival time for event #1 at the 2006 Legends of Poker tournament hosted by the Bicycle Casino: $200+$30 NLHE. This blind structure is typical of many lower buy-in live tournaments in the Los Angeles area:

TABLE 8.7: Blind Structure for Event #1 at the 2006 Legends of Poker, for Example 8.4

LEVEL	SB	BB	ANTE
1	25	25	0
2	25	50	0
3	50	100	0
4	100	200	0
5	100	200	25
6	150	300	50
7	200	400	75
8	300	600	100
9	500	1,000	200
10	800	1,600	200
11	1,000	2,000	300
12	1,500	3,000	300

Each player begins with 1,500 chips, and blinds go up every 30 minutes.

Since this is a brick-and-mortar tournament featuring fullhanded tables, assume 10 players per table and that about 35 hands are dealt per hour.

Answer: Table 8.8 shows how many chips you lose in the first five levels:

TABLE 8.8: Chips Lost to the Blinds in the First Five Levels

LEVEL	SB	BB	ANTE	CHIPS LOST PER HAND	HANDS PER LEVEL	CHIPS LOST	CUMULATIVE CHIPS LOST
1	25	25	0	5	17.5	87.5	87.5
2	25	50	0	7.5	17.5	131.25	218.75
3	50	100	0	15	17.5	262.5	481.25
4	100	200	0	30	17.5	525	1,006.25
5	100	200	25	55	17.5	962.5	1,968.75

You lose 1,006.25 chips through the end of level 4 and 1,968.75 chips through the end of level 5. Since you lose 55 chips per hand in level 5, solving equation 8.15 for x will yield the number of hands played in level 5:

$$1{,}006.25 + 55x = 1{,}500 \tag{8.15}$$

$$1{,}006.25 + 55x - 1{,}006.25 = 1{,}500 - 1{,}006.25 \tag{8.16}$$

$$55x = 493.75 \tag{8.17}$$

$$x = \tfrac{493.75}{55} \approx 8.9773 \tag{8.18}$$

Your survival time is $(17.5)(4)+8.9773 = 78.9773$ hands.

TABLE 8.9: Blind Structure for Event #2 at the 2008 WSOP, for Example 8.5

LEVEL	SB	BB	ANTE
1	25	50	0
2	50	100	0
3	100	200	0
4	100	200	25
5	150	300	25
6	200	400	50
7	300	600	75
8	400	800	100
9	500	1,000	100
10	600	1,200	100
11	800	1,600	200
12	1,000	2,000	300
13	1,500	3,000	400
14	2,200	4,000	500

Each player begins with 3,000 chips, and blinds go up every 60 minutes.

Example 8.5: Calculate your survival time in event #2 at the 2008 World Series of Poker (WSOP): $1,500 buy-in NLHE.

Since this is a brick-and-mortar tournament featuring fullhanded tables, assume 10 players per table and that about 35 hands are dealt per hour.

Answer: Table 8.10, opposite, shows how many chips you lose in the first four levels.

TABLE 8.10: Chips Lost to the Blinds in the First Four Levels

LEVEL	SB	BB	ANTE	CHIPS LOST PER HAND	HANDS PER LEVEL	CHIPS LOST	CUMULATIVE CHIPS LOST
1	25	50	0	7.5	35	262.5	262.5
2	50	100	0	15	35	525	787.5
3	100	200	0	30	35	1,050	1,837.5
4	100	200	25	55	35	1,925	3,762.5

You lose 1,837.5 chips through the end of level 3 and 3,762.5 chips through the end of level 4. Since you lose 55 chips per hand in level 4, solving equation 8.19 for x will yield the number of hands played in level 4:

$$1,837.5 + 55x = 3,000 \qquad (8.19)$$

$$1,837.5 + 55x - 1,837.5 = 3,000 - 1,837.5 \qquad (8.20)$$

$$55x = 1,162.5 \qquad (8.21)$$

$$x = \tfrac{1,162.5}{55}; \; 21.1364 \qquad (8.22)$$

Your survival time is $35(3) + 21.1364 = 126.1364$ hands.

Example 8.6: Calculate your survival time in a Sunday Million at Poker Stars (pokerstars.com): $200+$15 NLHE:

TABLE 8.11: Blind Structure for Poker Stars' Sunday Million

LEVEL	SB	BB	ANTE
1	25	50	0
2	50	100	0
3	100	200	0
4	150	300	0

LEVEL	SB	BB	ANTE
5	200	400	0
6	300	600	0
7	400	800	0
8	400	800	50
9	500	1,000	75
10	600	1,200	100
11	750	1,500	150
12	1,000	2,000	200

Each player begins with 10,000 chips, and blinds go up every 15 minutes.

Since this is an online tournament featuring fullhanded tables, assume 10 players per table and figure about 60 hands are dealt per hour.

Answer: Table 8.12 shows how many chips you lose in the first nine levels:

TABLE 8.12: Chips Lost to the Blinds in the First Five Levels

LEVEL	SB	BB	ANTE	CHIPS LOST PER HAND	HANDS PER LEVEL	CHIPS LOST	CUMULATIVE CHIPS LOST
1	25	50	0	7.5	15	112.5	112.5
2	50	100	0	15	15	225	337.5
3	100	200	0	30	15	450	787.5
4	150	300	0	45	15	675	1,462.5
5	200	400	0	60	15	900	2,362.5
6	300	600	0	90	15	1,350	3,712.5
7	400	800	0	120	15	1,800	5,512.5
8	400	800	50	170	15	2,550	8,062.5
9	500	1,000	75	225	15	3,375	11,437.5

You lose 8,062.5 chips through the end of level 8 and 11,437.5 chips through the end of level 9. Since you lose 225 chips per hand in level 9, solving equation 8.23 for x will yield the number of hands played in level 9:

$$8,062.5 + 225x = 10,000 \tag{8.23}$$

$$8,062.5 + 225x - 8,062.5 = 10,000 - 8,062.5 \tag{8.24}$$

$$225x = 1,937.5 \tag{8.25}$$

$$x = \tfrac{1,937.5}{225} \approx 8.6111 \tag{8.26}$$

Your survival time is $15(8) + 8.6111 = 128.6111$ hands.

Double Ups Required

In conjunction with tournament survival time, the number of double ups required to reach a certain point in a tournament can be helpful—particularly when figuring out your approach to tournaments with flat payout structures.

Example 8.7: You enter a 20-player satellite with a $30+$3 buy-in. First through fifth, each wins an entry into a $110+$10 tournament. On average, how many chips do you need to win in order to win an entry given that everyone starts off with 1,000 chips?

Answer: Everyone starts with 1,000 chips, meaning that 20,000 chips in total are in play. The average stack of the top five players will be $\frac{20,000}{5} = 4,000$. Of course, it's possible to win your seat with much fewer chips, but basically, it just takes two double ups from your starting stack of 1,000 to win your seat.

Example 8.8: You enter a 100-player satellite with a $30+$3 buy-in. First through twenty-fifth, each player wins an entry into a $110+$10 tournament. On average, how many chips do you need to win in order to win an entry given that everyone starts off with 1,000 chips?

Answer: Everyone starts with 1,000 chips, meaning that 100,000 chips in total are in play. The average stack of the top 25 players will be $\frac{100,000}{25} = 4,000$. Just as in the tournament in question 4, you only need two double ups to put you in serious contention for the seat. Field size, the number of players who enter a tournament, has some affect on things, but a very important concept is that the average stack in a tournament is purely a function of the percentage of players left.

In a way, this tournament is effectively the same as the one described in example 8.7. However, for the short stacks, these tournaments will play somewhat differently close to and at the bubble.[2]

Chapter Summary

A good chunk of our exploration of NLHE tournaments has addressed the issue of chip preservation versus chip accumulation. Looking at tournament blind structures is just one other way of looking at the same question. And it also suggests an important point. Tournaments with ultrafast blind structures aren't necessarily the luck fests that players make them out to be. It's just that success in them sometimes requires lines of play that players aren't

---

2. The bubble is the time in a tournament at which the payouts are near. For example, the bubble in an STT where the top 3 players play is typically when the action is 4- or 5-handed. Meanwhile, the bubble in an MTT that pays the top 200 players might be when 210 or maybe even 220 players remain.

necessarily accustomed to. Without time to sit around and wait for superpremium hands, tournaments with fast blind structures require you to find ways of winning chips outside the realm of straightforward, hit-to-win poker.

9

THE ART OF THE DEAL

Introduction

Tournaments sometimes require more than just your poker playing skills. You might also need Donald Trumpish negotiating skills because it's possible to make deals in some tournaments. This chapter will discuss the dynamics of tournament dealmaking. It'll help you with the following:

- Identifying favorable deals.

- Identifying unfavorable deals.

- Forcing your opponents into taking deals that give you more than your fair share.

Chip Proportional Deals vs. ICM

The most popular way to calculate how to divide prize pools in a deal is the chip proportional method (CPM). CPM consists of the following steps:

1. Give last place money to everybody.

2. Divide the remaining money in the prize pool according to the fraction of tournament chips in each player's stack

Example 9.1: You're in a tournament that's down to four players. First pays $50,000, second pays $30,000, third pays $20,000, and fourth pays $15,000 (total prize pool of $115,000). You have T30,000, two of your opponents (to be creative, we'll call them Player A and Player B) have T20,000, and Player C has T10,000 (total of T80,000 in play). What's your share of the prize pool in a CPM deal?

Answer: Each player is guaranteed fourth-place money, (4)($15,000) = $60,000, leaving $55,000 to be divided up. You have T30,000 out of T80,000 in play, so your chip proportional share of the remaining prize pool is $\left(\frac{30,000}{80,000}\right)$ ($55,000) = $20,625. A CPM deal gives you $15,000 + $20,625 = $35,625.

CPM deals are common; after all, they're very easy to calculate. But to find the true mapping of chip counts to monetary equity, we need to turn to our good old friend from chapter 6: ICM. Table 9.1 (p. 160) takes example 9.1 and displays each player's monetary equity as calculated using both ICM and CPM:

Here, the ICM equities and the CPM equities are fairly close to each other, but notice how only the chip leader's CPM equity is higher than his ICM equity. CPM tends to overvalue chip leaders' equities.

Performing ICM on the fly in a live tournament is pretty much impossible, so just be aware of how CPM deviates from ICM. If you can, do some homework on your own using different payout schemes and stack distributions. Meanwhile,

TABLE 9.1: Comparison of ICM and CPM Equities from Example 9.1

PLAYER	STACK	ICM EQUITY	CPM EQUITY
You	T30,000	$33,767.86	$35,625
Player A	T20,000	$29,178.57	$28,750
Player B	T20,000	$29,178.57	$28,750
Player C	T10,000	$22,875.00	$21,875

Each player begins with 10,000 chips, and blinds go up every 15 minutes.

if you're playing in an online tournament, there's absolutely no excuse for not running a quick ICM calculation when a deal is being discussed.

Getting More Than Your Fair Share

Recall that ICM calculates players' monetary equities assuming all players play identically. This assumption rarely pans out in practice, but that's okay because ICM at least gives the benchmark for what the fair deal is. Now that we know how to establish that benchmark, we can move on to the fun part of deal making: getting more than your fair share. Here are some ideas that should control your exploitative deal making:

Estimate your skill relative to the rest of the field: If
you play better than your opponents, your actual
monetary equity is higher than that given by ICM.
And vice versa, if your opponents are better than
you (don't let pride get in the way of negotiating
a favorable deal), your actual monetary equity is

lower than that given by ICM. The true fair deal is obtained by applying a skill-based adjustment to the ICM equities. Just remember that big edges typically amount to differences on the order of only a few percent; if you overestimate the impact that skill has on monetary equities, then you may actually be costing yourself some very favorable deals.

Take advantage of risk aversion: Players are usually willing to take something that's guaranteed, even if it's less than their fair share. Most commonly, short stacks can use this to squeeze some equity from big stacks, but big stacks can sometimes squeeze some equity from short stacks facing elimination.

Take advantage of misconceptions regarding prize-pool equity: Many people take formulas on blind faith and don't understand how payout structures affect monetary equity. If you're the chip leader and everyone else is willing to take a CPM deal, don't say a word! In fact, go ahead and come out of the deal-making gates by proposing the CPM numbers! The great thing is that you don't even need to put forth the CPM numbers yourself. Poker Stars, for example, will suggest the CPM numbers as a default! And a deal suggested by hopefully impartial management will sound a lot better than a deal proposed by a greedy poker player.

Project how the next few hands might play out: Pay attention to the blinds and the depth of the stacks. For example, if you're solidly in second place with four players remaining and fourth place will have to make some desperation shoves to get into contention, consider holding off on a deal until after the fourth-place player *busts* or puts some bad beats on the chip leader who may, resultantly, become disheartened and highly risk averse.

Take advantage of players who might misplay a changed payout structure: Some deals chop up some part of the prize pool and leave the rest for the winner. Players can become a bit reckless when action is WTA—especially when they've already locked up a huge chunk of money from a deal. If you think that your opponents might play recklessly, consider proposing a deal that sets some money aside for the winner.

Don't play your hand faceup: If you say something like, "Well, I'm just happy to be here, so I'll be happy with whatever," you'll end up with whatever. Keep your proclivities concealed throughout the deal-making process.

Don't give in to peer pressure: If a deal isn't good, don't take it—no matter how much your opponents try to intimidate you into it. There's no rule in poker that says you have to do what your opponents tell you to. And honestly playing against angry opponents who take things personally can be good for your bottom line—as long as you're capable of maintaining your composure in the face of verbal tirades and whatever else.

Chapter Summary

This chapter covered some important considerations having to do with deal making in tournaments. When trying to make a deal, keep the following two-step process in mind:

1. Figure out the fair deal either by using ICM or by making an appropriate adjustment to CPM numbers.

2. Try to get more than your fair share.

And throughout the deal-making process, remember that you don't have to take a deal that you don't like. The poker table is no place to give in to peer pressure. If your opponents aren't willing to make a favorable deal, then simply play it out.

10

FINAL THOUGHTS

♧ ♤ ♢ ♡

Introduction

At this point, you have a very strong foundation in the theory behind tournament poker. We talked about how important the structure of a tournament is when it comes to influencing the decisions you make. Although we haven't covered a ton of unique situations, you now have the tools necessary to deduce the best line of play in any tournament situation you encounter. In this, the final chapter, we'll cover some random, but important topics, that didn't quite have a place in the development of the core theory.

Common Lines of Play

Poker is largely about betting patterns. Identify which betting patterns your opponents use in various circumstances, and you're in great shape to know when to avoid trouble and when to take advantage of your opposition. In addition, having a large set of predetermined scripts that you're used to running can make your decision-making process much easier. Here's a list of important lines of play:

Squeeze Play: Usually performed preflop, the *squeeze play* is when a player reraises after an opponent has raised and one or more opponents have called the raise. This play can be very powerful because of the strength that the squeezer conveys with his reraise. Theoretically, it's very tough for anyone to contest the squeezer. Look for your aggressive, highly successful foes to pull this play out of the tool belt when they need to make a move to accumulate some chips. Similarly, you should be looking to pull this play when you need chips. This is a great play to use when you have around 12bb, but it's also very effective when you have something like 25bb and you can reraise to just 12bb, leaving 13bb in your stack just in case the original raiser happens to have a monster. A word of caution: avoid going to this well too often. This play is very well known by now, and top players who know it and employ it won't be afraid of calling you somewhat light if they suspect that you're simply stealing. Don't necessarily pull this play with any two cards; look for a hand that will do somewhat well in an all-in confrontation in case you're called. And once you've pulled it once, don't pull it again against the same opponents as a pure steal; make sure you have the goods the second time.

Resteal: Usually performed preflop, a resteal is simply reraising a lone raiser preflop who's suspected of simply trying to steal the blinds. Like the squeeze play, this is a powerful play against weaker competition, but stronger foes will be willing to go to war with somewhat light holdings. This play is absolutely necessary if you're to be a top player—know it, and know when to employ it.

Limp-Reraise: Typically, this play is performed by someone with a very strong preflop hand in every EP when no other players have entered the pot. Simply put, the player with the monster preflop hand limps, and if there's a raise behind him, he'll reraise. If you're at a table where stacks are deep and there's likely to be only one raiser and no callers, this play isn't very strong when you have a huge hand: it immediately betrays the strength of your hand. When stacks are deep, this play is best used with a monster hand when there will most likely be a raiser and multiple callers. However, this play is more versatile than how most of your opponents will employ it—especially when your stack is around 10bb–15bb. With a 10bb–15bb stack, hands like TT and AJ can become a bit awkward to play. To maximize my value with these hands, I'll look to limp-reraise with them even from MP—when I open but also when other players have open limped and an aggressive foe has yet to act.

Continuation Bet (CB): A continuation bet is a bet made on the flop by a preflop raiser. The math of hold'em makes this play powerful—as long as you're playing an opponent who doesn't know what's up. These days, players are apt to play back against continuation bets, meaning that this play isn't as strong as it used to be. You still need to continuation bet, but don't commit tons of chips to your continuation bets. And don't continuation bet 100 percent of the time. Continuation bets that are too large, too frequent, and especially both are easily exploited.

Delayed Continuation Bet (DCB): A variation on the continuation bet where the preflop raiser checks the flop and bets the turn if his opponents still haven't shown any initiative. This line of play seems to be somewhat underrepresented; many players who check the flop and bet the turn tend to have hit the turn. You shouldn't really be in the business of defending against suspected DCBers unless you've seen them employ this line of play many times. Meanwhile, this line of play is highly effective—especially against straightforward, tight opponents. In fact, against such foes, the DCB should be your primary weapon of choice.

Stop-and-Go: Line of play where you call out of position and then lead on the next betting round. This line of play is often used as a bluffing line of play going from preflop to the flop, and it's sometimes superior to check-raise bluffing because it commits less chips. However, this line of play is also effective with good, but not great, hands. For example, you have top pair with a good kicker and you're heads-up out of position. You can check-call the turn and the lead out with a *blocking bet* on the river.

Check-Raise Bluff: This play can be employed on the flop occasionally to defend against habitual CBers. You can also consider employing this line of play on the turn—you can check-call the flop with air and then check-raise bluff the turn. The strength of this play is that the check-raise on the turn typically carries huge fold equity. The drawback is that it commits a lot of chips. You'll be seeing check-raise bluffs from your opponents more often on the flop than on the turn, and though you should have all check-raise bluffs in your arsenal, you usually shouldn't be in the business of putting in huge check-raise bluffs on the turn or the river.

Floating: Any line of play where a player calls a bet with the intention of bluffing on a future round of betting. A common float has to do with facing habitual CBers when you have position on them. You call the preflop raise, call the suspected CB on the flop no matter what you have, and then bet the turn if checked to you. The check-raise bluff on the turn is actually an example of a float that you can perform out of position, but in general, you shouldn't really be floating out of position. When you float, you should generally do so when you have position.

Checking It Down: When a player is all-in—particularly when payouts are increasing—players will often elect to check all the way to the river if an opponent is all-in. You should be aware of this line of play, because it'll sometimes be correct to check it out to maximize the chances that an all-in player is eliminated. However, checking it down isn't always the best line of play—no matter what the pundits say. It's best to perform ICM analysis on specific circumstances, but as a general rule, you shouldn't be shy about not checking it down when the pot is large and you're in a tournament with a top-heavy payout structure. For example, you're at the final table of a big MMT. Nine players remain, and you're in a hand with two players, one who is all-in. If you win the pot, you'll be chip leader. If you lose the pot, you'll be short stacked. Increasing your chance of eliminating the all-in player isn't nearly as important as putting yourself in a position to win the tournament. Don't isolate if there's a dry side pot and you have absolutely nothing, but definitely be willing to move your opponent off the pot if you have something like second board pair or better.

Exploitative Play vs. Equilibrium Play

Two types of poker analysis exist: exploitative and equilibrium. Exploitative analysis takes how your opponents play and seeks to find the best counter strategy. Reads are the key component to exploitative analysis; exploitative analysis involves putting opponents on hand distributions and action distributions. Most poker analysis is from the exploitative perspective. After all, you hope that your opponents can be exploited at least enough to overcome the rake (and hopefully more).

However, another approach to poker exists. Instead of being concerned with how your opponents play, consider how you can play so that no matter what, your opponents can't gain any mEV. By playing in this manner, you won't make as much as possible against any particular opponent (you'll be playing the same against someone shoving with any two cards as you will against someone who's only playing AA). But you guarantee that no opponent can exploit you. Such strategies are referred to as equilibrium strategies. Equilibrium play for deep-stacked NLHE isn't something that's been completely solved, but tons of work has been done on mini-games—such as the shove/fold endgame of STTs.

Solving for equilibrium strategies is a big aspect of the branch of mathematics known as game theory. For an excellent application of game theory to poker, I highly recommend Bill Chen and Jerrod Ankenman's *The Mathematics of Poker* (ConJelCo, 2006) with the following warning: it's a much tougher read than this book. But even if it makes your head spin, you should check out the table on p. 136, which gives the equilibrium strategy for the heads-up jam/fold game—it's a situation that I'm hoping you'll be in often.

Hourly Win Rate

Top online MTTers have ROIs around 100%. Top online STTers are lucky to have ROIs around 20%. If you're to make substantial money playing tournaments online, you need to multitable. Obviously, you shouldn't multitable when you're first starting out. But as you get competent, you need to begin working on your ability to multitask.

The other thing that's important when considering your hourly win rate is the rake. The ROIs I just cited are for tournaments that have a rake that's at most 10% of the entry. If a tournament has a buy-in of $X + .1X$ and a player's ROI is 20%, then he's getting an average prize of $1.32X$. If you bump up the rake from $.1X$ to $.2X$, that player's ROI will drop to 10%. When playing in tournaments, look for tournaments offering the best rake possible, and before playing in a tournament, figure out whether the rake can even be beaten by enough to make the tournament worth your time.

And if you're playing online, there's absolutely no excuse for playing without the best possible rakeback. Rakeback is when you get paid back a percentage of the rake that you pay. Offers vary from site to site—just make sure you're playing for the best rakeback available for the site you play at. If you already have an account with a site, but it's not a rakeback account, contact customer service for the site you play at. The current state of affairs is that some sites are very stubborn in converting nonrakeback players to rakeback players, but it's worth a shot.[1] Meanwhile, if you don't have an account for a site you'd like to play on, visit rakeback.killerev .com. There you'll find the best rakeback deals available for a wide range of online poker rooms.

Why Play Tournaments?

Although cash games are typically best when it comes to hourly win rate, exceptions exist and are a great reason to learn tournament poker. For example, there may be a tournament going on with a huge overlay. Or maybe a particular tournament is expected to draw an extremely weak field. In addition, changing things up is generally good for our mental well-being. Perhaps playing tournaments once in a while will keep your poker mind fresh and able to put in higher quality hours at the cash game tables.

---

1. If you're in such a position, one of my next poker goals has to do with getting all players on equal footing with respect to being eligible for the same benefits. I've no problem with sites like Poker Stars that have tiers of benefits based on a frequent player system. But I have a problem with sites that flat out refuse to convert players simply because they didn't know about rakeback when they first started playing (or even worse, players who tried to sign up for rakeback but, for some reason, weren't tracked properly).

Collusion

Collusion occurs when two or more players cooperate in an attempt to gain an unfair advantage. A few types of collusion exist. For example, players can share hole cards with one another and then use that information either to trap players into putting more chips in the pot or to narrow down the range of possible cards an opponent might have. This type of collusion is present in all forms of poker.

Chip dumping is a form of collusion unique to tournament poker (well, fine, players who purchase chips fraudulently online also engage in chip dumping, but that's the online poker room's problem instead of yours). It is widely accepted to be *the* way that a team of players can gain an unfair advantage in a tournament. Interestingly, chip dumping is about the worst thing that a team of players can do. If you perform ICM analysis on a tournament, you'll find that the chips carry higher mEV when kept in separate stacks than when the stacks are combined. I didn't think too deeply about this issue until Mike Caro spoke to me about an article I wrote for www.wizardofodds.com, and I thank him very much for bringing me back down to Earth.[2]

Love the Game, Play Hard, and Have Neither Fear Nor Regrets

Our treatment of NLHE has come to an end. Well, there's plenty of food for thought in the appendices, but at this

2. Having said that, I'm happy to engage in debates regarding anything I ever say. Either I'll get the satisfaction of winning a debate (always fun), or I'll get the satisfaction out of learning something new (always fun). It's a win-win situation, and unlike others, I'm not afraid to admit when I'm wrong (not that I make a habit out of being wrong—hehe).

point, you have the complete plot. After all the technical analyses we've undergone, now's a good time to take a step back.

Too many poker players are consumed by bad beats, should-haves, could-haves, and all that other unproductive negativity. In tournament NLHE, when one pot can literally mean the difference between nothing and a life-changing payday, turning to poker's dark side can be really easy. If you find yourself in a perpetual poker funk, like so many people I've encountered in cardrooms over the years, take a step back and try to see poker as you did when you first started playing: the fun, the excitement, the challenge. No matter how much playing you have under your belt, poker should always be about the fun, the excitement, and the challenge.

And while poker should be about those three things, there's one thing that poker shouldn't be about: fear. Well, let me rephrase that. Strike fear into your opponents, but never be scared. If you're eliminated from a tournament, there's always another one around the corner. If you make a mistake, you can learn from it and avoid making it in the future. The best tournament players in the world are fearless, and that's how you need to be if you're to be a top tournament player.

Love the game, play hard, and have neither fear nor regrets. Follow this creed, and your tournament poker will be both profitable and fun. May you always play to optimize your mEV!

Appendix A:
Preflop All-In Matchups

Introduction

A big part of NLHE tournaments is the endgame. In the endgame, blinds are typically high enough so that the only poker to be played is going all-in or folding preflop. There are 169 unique starting hands in hold'em, meaning that if you're playing against one opponent, there are (169)(169) = 28,561 possible starting hand arrangements. Eliminating the doubly counted matchups, there are 14,365 possible preflop matchups.[1] Obviously, knowing P(Win), P(Tie), and P(Lose) for all 14,365 matchups isn't feasible. However, the preflop all-in matchups can be classified in a way such that you can usually estimate P(Win) to within about .01 or .02.

---

1. To think about eliminating the double counts, imagine that you have all the preflop matchups in a giant table. The matchups on the diagonal of the table (like AA vs. AA, KK vs. KK, etc.) are only counted once. Since there are 169 matchups on the diagonal, subtract 169 from 28,561. The remaining 28,392 matchups are doubly counted; therefore, divide 28,392 by 2: $\frac{28,392}{2}$ = 14,196. Then, add back 169 to get 14,365.

And being able to estimate P(Win) to within about .01 or .02. will be more than sufficient.

This appendix will teach you how to estimate P(Win) quickly and accurately for all possible preflop all-in matchups:

- Specific hand versus specific hand.

- Specific hand versus a distribution.

The information in this appendix will allow you to look at your hole cards and accurately estimate your probability of winning against an opponent's pushing distribution, your probability of winning against an opponent's calling distribution, and your probability of picking up the pot uncontested if you shove.

Hand Simulators

A *hand simulator* is a program that takes a situation and evaluates the probability that each hand will win or tie. Basic hand simulators allow you to do calculations for matchups between specific hands. More advanced hand simulators—the type that you should be using—allow you to do calculations for matchups between hand distributions. My hand simulator of choice—the one I've used whenever a hand simulator was needed for something in this book—is Poker Stove. It's available at www.pokerstove.com. Surprisingly, it's free, so download it and use it.

Heads-Up Confrontations Involving Pocket Pairs

Six types of matchups involving pocket pairs exist:

1. Overpair versus underpair.

2. Pocket pair versus unpaired undercards.

3. Pocket pair versus a card of the same rank and an undercard.

4. Pocket pair versus an undercard and an overcard.

5. Pocket pair versus a card of the same rank and an *overcard*.

6. Pocket pair versus two overcards.

The rest of this section contains tables of results from representative matchups from each category along with steps to estimate the winning percentages associated with each category.

(Overpair vs. Underpair): Overpair wins about 80%.

Example A.1: Suppose you have KK and you know that your opponent has TT. What's your winning percentage?

Answer: You have an overpair versus an underpair; therefore, you'll win about 80% of the time. (Poker Stove says: winning percentage is about 80.93%; tying percentage is about .4%.)

Example A.2: Suppose you have 33, and you know that your opponent has 88. What's your winning percentage?

TABLE A.1: Overpair vs. Underpair (Sample Matchups)

HAND 1	HAND 2	P(1 WIN)	P(1 LOSE)	P(TIE)
AA	KK	0.8171	0.1782	0.0046
AA	QQ	0.8133	0.1824	0.0044
AA	77	0.8031	0.1935	0.0034
AA	22	0.8195	0.1751	0.0054
JJ	TT	0.8177	0.1780	0.0044
JJ	66	0.8077	0.1884	0.0038
TT	55	0.8070	0.1879	0.0050
TT	22	0.8156	0.1783	0.0060
33	22	0.7794	0.1708	0.0498

Answer: You have an underpair versus an overpair; therefore, you'll win about 20% of the time. (Poker Stove says: winning percentage is about 17.87%; tying percentage is about 1.02%.)

Step 1 (Pocket Pair vs. Two Undercards): Starting winning percentage for the pocket pair is 85%.

Step 2 (Pocket Pair vs. Two Undercards): Correction for connectivity: subtract up to 5% from the winning probability of the pocket pair (the more straights available to the unpaired hole cards, the more you subtract).

Step 3 (Pocket Pair vs. Two Undercards): Correction for suitedness: add 1% to the winning percentage of the pocket pair if the unpaired hole cards aren't suited, and subtract 3% from the winning percent-

TABLE A.2: Pocket Pair vs. Two Unpaired Undercards (Sample Matchups)

HAND 1	HAND 2	P(1 WIN)	P(1 LOSE)	P(TIE)
AA	KQo	0.8692	0.1268	0.0040
AA	KQs	0.8273	0.1686	0.0042
AA	KQ	0.8587	0.1372	0.0042
AA	76o	0.8116	0.1850	0.0034
AA	76s	0.7734	0.2229	0.0036
AA	76	0.8021	0.1945	0.0034
AA	86o	0.8248	0.1719	0.0034
AA	86s	0.7858	0.2106	0.0036
AA	86	0.8151	0.1815	0.0034
AA	K3o	0.8863	0.1092	0.0044
AA	K3s	0.8435	0.1521	0.0044
AA	K3	0.8756	0.1199	0.0044
AA	94o	0.8755	0.1205	0.0040
AA	94s	0.8334	0.1625	0.0040
AA	94	0.8650	0.1310	0.0040
TT	98o	0.8558	0.1397	0.0046
TT	98s	0.8146	0.1807	0.0046
TT	98	0.8455	0.1500	0.0046
TT	94o	0.8787	0.1165	0.0048
TT	94s	0.8363	0.1586	0.0050
TT	94	0.8681	0.1270	0.0050
TT	54o	0.8144	0.1804	0.0052
TT	54s	0.7759	0.2188	0.0054
TT	54	0.8048	0.1900	0.0052
TT	52o	0.8494	0.1451	0.0056
TT	52s	0.8087	0.1858	0.0054
TT	52	0.8392	0.1552	0.0056

age of the pocket pair if the unpaired hole cards are suited.[2]

Example A.3: Suppose you have QQ and your opponent has 64s. What's your winning percentage?

Answer: This is a pocket pair versus two undercards, so start with a winning percentage of 85%. Your opponent has a 1-gap that's far from your pair, so he has many ways to complete a straight. Bump your winning percentage down to 82%. Your opponent is suited, so subtract 3%. You'll win about 79% of the time (Poker Stove says: winning percentage is about 78.96%; tying percentage is about .4%.)

Example A.4: Suppose you have JTs and your opponent has AA. What's your winning percentage?

Answer: You have two undercards versus a pocket pair, so start with a winning percentage of 15%. JTs is maximally connected, meaning that you would normally bump your winning percentage up to 20%; however, AA consumes some of your straight outs, so estimate that you'll win about 19% of the time. Account for your suitedness by adding 3% to your winning percentage. We find 22% is a reasonable estimate. (Poker Stove says: winning percentage is about 20.97%; tying percentage is about .38%.)

---

2. The 4% swing between the suited and unsuited matchups corresponds to the percentage of the time that suited hole cards will make a flush with five board cards to come. The reason that the differences are asymmetric at +1% and −3% is that the ratio of unsuited hole card combinations to suited hole card combinations is 3:1.

Step 1 (Pocket Pair vs. One Matching Card and One Undercard): Starting winning percentage of the pocket pair is 90%.

Step 2 (Pocket Pair vs. One Matching Card and One Undercard): Correction for connectivity: subtract up to 5% from the winning probability of the pocket pair (the more straights available to the unpaired hole cards, the more you subtract).

Step 3 (Pocket Pair vs. Two Undercards): Correction for suitedness: add 1% to the winning percentage of the

TABLE A.3: Pocket Pair vs. a Card of the Same Rank and an Undercard (Sample Matchups)

HAND 1	HAND 2	P(1 WIN)	P(1 LOSE)	P(TIE)
AA	AK	0.9119	0.0751	0.0130
AA	AQ	0.9077	0.0794	0.0128
AA	AJ	0.9035	0.0837	0.0128
AA	AT	0.8993	0.0881	0.0126
AA	A9	0.9176	0.0687	0.0136
AA	A7	0.9134	0.0730	0.0136
QQ	QJ	0.8712	0.1126	0.0162
QQ	QT	0.8670	0.1169	0.0160
QQ	Q5	0.9074	0.0730	0.0196
JJ	JT	0.8477	0.1314	0.0210
JJ	J9	0.8657	0.1121	0.0222
JJ	J4	0.9055	0.0686	0.0258
88	87	0.8384	0.1265	0.0352
88	86	0.8516	0.1120	0.0364
88	82	0.8999	0.0599	0.0402
55	54	0.8195	0.1263	0.0542
55	52	0.8546	0.0887	0.0568
33	32	0.8472	0.0885	0.0642

pocket pair if the unpaired hole cards aren't suited, and subtract 3% from the winning percentage of the pocket pair if the unpaired hole cards are suited.

Example A.5: Suppose you have 99 and your opponent has 98o. What's your winning percentage?

Answer: You have a pocket pair against a matching card and an undercard, so begin with a winning percentage of 90%. Your opponent is maximally connected, so drop your winning percentage 5% to 85%. Since your opponent's hand is offsuit, add 1%; you'll win about 86% of the time. (Poker Stove says: winning percentage is about 85.46%; tying percentage is about 3.12%.)

Example A.6: Suppose you have KQs and your opponent has KK. What's your winning percentage?

Answer: You're facing a pocket pair with a matching card and an undercard. Start with a winning percentage of 10%. Your KQ is connected, but it can't make a lot of different straights. It's effectively a 2-gap, so bump your winning percentage up to 11%. Since you're suited, add 3% to get that your final winning percentage is about 14%. (Poker Stove says: winning percentage is about 13.27%; tying percentage is about 1.18%.)

> *Step 1 (Pocket Pair vs. One Undercard and One Overcard):* Starting winning percentage of the pocket pair is 70%.

> *Step 2 (Pocket Pair vs. One Undercard and One Overcard):* Correction for rank: subtract 2% from the winning percentage of the pocket pair if the pocket pair is among {44–22}.

TABLE A.4: Pocket Pair vs. an Undercard and an Overcard (Sample Matchups)

HAND 1	HAND 2	P(1 WIN)	P(1 LOSE)	P(TIE)
KK	AT	0.6991	0.2969	0.0040
KK	A6	0.7058	0.2904	0.0038
TT	A5	0.6940	0.3020	0.0040
TT	J9	0.6999	0.2960	0.0042
77	J3	0.6933	0.2995	0.0072
77	A6	0.6987	0.2976	0.0038
44	A3	0.6821	0.3120	0.0058
33	A2	0.6764	0.3170	0.0066

Step 3 (Pocket Pair vs. One Undercard and One Overcard): Correction for suitedness: add 1% to the winning percentage of the pocket pair if the unpaired hole cards aren't suited, and subtract 3% from the winning percentage of the pocket pair if the unpaired hole cards are suited.

Example A.7: Suppose you have 88 and your opponent has A7s. What's your winning percentage?

Answer: Your opponent has an undercard and an overcard, so start with a winning percentage of 70%. Since 88 isn't among {44–22}, there's no need to apply a correction for rank. Subtract 3% since your opponent's hand is suited. Your 88 will win about 67% of the time against your opponent's A7s. (Poker Stove says: winning percentage is about 67.17%; losing percentage is about .38%.)

Example A.8: Suppose you hold A3o and your opponent has 44. What's your winning percentage?

Answer: You have an undercard and an overcard against your opponent's pocket pair, so start with a winning percentage of 30%. 44 is a low pocket pair, so add 2% to get 32%. Since your hand isn't suited, subtract 1%. Your A3o will win against your opponent's 44 about 31% of the time. (Poker Stove says: winning percentage is about 30.32%; tying percentage is about .58%.)

> *Step 1 (Pocket Pair vs. One Matching Card and One Overcard):* Starting winning percentage of the pocket pair is 68%.

> *Step 2 (Pocket Pair vs. One Matching Card and One Overcard):* Correction for rank: subtract up to 4% from the winning percentage of the pocket pair

TABLE A.5: Pocket Pair vs. a Card of the Same Rank and an Overcard (Sample Matchups)

HAND 1	HAND 2	P(1 WIN)	P(1 LOSE)	P(TIE)
KK	AK	0.6846	0.3070	0.0084
JJ	QJ	0.6504	0.3343	0.0154
TT	AT	0.6706	0.3077	0.0216
TT	QT	0.6451	0.3351	0.0198
TT	JT	0.6304	0.3507	0.0188
77	J7	0.6578	0.3178	0.0244
77	A7	0.6722	0.3007	0.0272
33	A3	0.6446	0.3355	0.0198
33	43	0.6156	0.3333	0.0510
22	A2	0.6406	0.3431	0.0164

(the lower the pocket pair, the lower the winning percentage).

Step 3 (Pocket Pair vs. One Matching Card and One Overcard): Correction for connectivity: subtract up to 3% from the winning probability of the pocket pair (the more straights available to the unpaired hole cards, the more you subtract).

Step 4 (Pocket Pair vs. One Matching Card and One Overcard): Correction for suitedness: add 1% to the winning percentage of the pocket pair if the unpaired hole cards aren't suited, and subtract 3% from the winning percentage of the pocket pair if the unpaired hole cards are suited.

Example A.9: Suppose you have 66 and your opponent has A6o. What's your winning percentage?

Answer: You have a pocket pair against a matching card and an overcard, so start with a winning percentage of 68%. 66 is somewhat low, so bump your probability of winning down to about 66%. A6o isn't connected, so there's no need to adjust for connectivity of the unpaired hole cards. A6o is unsuited, so add 1% to your winning percentage. Your 66 will win about 67% of the time. (Poker Stove says: winning percentage is about 68.10%; tying percentage is about 2.80%.)

Example A.10: Suppose you have 98s and your opponent has 88. What's your winning percentage?

Answer: You're facing a pocket pair with a matching card and an overcard, so start with a winning percentage of 32%. Since 88 is a medium pocket pair, add 1% to get 33%. 98s is maximally connected, so add another 3% to get 36%. And finally, since your hand is suited, add another 3%. Your 98s will win about 39% of the time. (Poker Stove says: winning percentage is about 37.95%; tying percentage is about 2.10%.)

Step 1 (Pocket Pair. vs. Two Overcards): Starting winning percentage of the pocket pair is 56%.

Step 2 (Pocket Pair vs. Two Overcards): Correction for rank: subtract up to 4% from the winning percentage of the pocket pair (the lower the pocket pair, the lower the winning percentage).

Step 3 (Pocket Pair vs. Two Overcards): Correction for connectivity: subtract up to 3% from the winning probability of the pocket pair (the more straights available to the unpaired hole cards, the more you subtract).

Step 4: (Pocket Pair vs. Two Overcards): Correction for suitedness: add 1% to the winning percentage of the pocket pair if the unpaired hole cards aren't suited, and subtract 3% from the winning percent-

TABLE A.6: Pocket Pair vs. Two Overcards (Sample Matchups)

HAND 1	HAND 2	P(1 WIN)	P(1 LOSE)	P(TIE)
QQ	AK	0.5584	0.4373	0.0042
88	AK	0.543	0.4532	0.0038
55	AK	0.5372	0.4582	0.0046
55	A8	0.5436	0.4519	0.0044
55	JT	0.4901	0.5022	0.0072
55	T8	0.5024	0.4879	0.0096
22	AK	0.517	0.4767	0.0062
22	JT	0.471	0.5147	0.0144

age of the pocket pair if the unpaired hole cards are suited.

Example A.11: Suppose you hold 33 and your opponent has 98s. What's your winning percentage?

Answer: You have a pocket pair against two overcards, so start with a winning percentage of 56%. 33 is a really low pocket pair, so subtract 4% to get 52%. Since 98s is maximally connected, subtract 3% to get 49%. Finally, 98s is suited, so subtract another 3%. 33 will win about 46% of the time against 98s. (Poker Stove says: winning percentage is about 46.16%; tying percentage is about 1.68%.)

Example A.12: Suppose you hold KJs and your opponent has 99. What's your winning percentage?

Answer: You have two overcards against a pocket pair, so start with a winning percentage of 44%. Your opponent's 99 is a medium pocket pair, so add 1% to bring you to 45%. KJs is a high 1-gap, so it's effectively a 2-gap. Compound that with two dead 9s, and there's no need to apply a correction for connectivity. Since your hand is suited, add 3%. Your KJs will win about 48% of the time. (Poker Stove says: winning percentage is about 47.16%; tying percentage is about .40%.)

Table A.7 (p. 188) summarizes the steps to follow to estimate the winning probabilities associated with all preflop all-in matchups involving a pocket pair.

TABLE A.7: Summary of Pocket Pair Preflop Matchups

CASE	STARTING WINNING PERCENTAGE FOR POCKET PAIR	CORRECTION FOR RANK OF POCKET PAIR	CORRECTION FOR CONNECTIVITY OF UNPAIRED HOLE CARDS	CORRECTION FOR SUITEDNESS OF UNPAIRED HOLE CARDS
Overpair vs. Underpair	80%	None	None	None
Pocket Pair vs. Two Unpaired Undercards	85%	None	Subtract up to 5%	Add 1% if unsuited; Subtract 3% if suited
Pocket Pair vs. a Card of the Same Rank and an Undercard	90%	None	Subtract up to 5%	Add 1% if unsuited; Subtract 3% if suited
Pocket Pair vs. an Undercard and an Overcard	70%	Subtract 2% for {44-22}	None	Add 1% if unsuited; Subract 3% if suited
Pocket Pair vs. a Card of the Same Rank and an Overcard	68%	Subtract up to 4%	Subtract up to 3%	Add 1% if unsuited; Subtract 3% if suited
Pocket Pair vs. Two Unpaired Overcards	56%	Subtract up to 4%	Subtract up to 3%	Add 1% if unsuited; Subtract 3% if suited

Heads-Up Confrontations Not Involving Pocket Pairs

Four types of preflop all-in matchups don't involve pocket pairs:

1. Two higher cards versus two lower cards (AK vs. QJ, for example)

2. Alternating relative ranks (AJ vs. K9, for example)

3. Tweener matchups (A2 vs. 76, for example)

4. *Domination* matchups (AK vs. KQ and AQ vs. KQ, for example)

The rest of this section contains tables of results from representative matchups from each category along with steps to estimate the winning percentages associated with each category.

Step 1 (Two Higher Cards vs. Two Lower Cards): Start with a winning percentage of 67% for the two higher cards.

Step 2 (Two Higher Cards vs. Two Lower Cards): Correction for connectivity: subtract up to 5% from the winning percentage of the higher cards to account for the connectivity and available straights for the lower cards.

Step 3 (Two Higher Cards vs. Two Lower Cards): Correction for relative suitedness: if both sets of hole

TABLE A.8: Two Higher Cards vs. Two Lower Cards (Sample Matchups)

HAND 1	HAND 2	P(1 WIN)	P(1 LOSE)	P(TIE)
AK	QJ	0.6411	0.3541	0.0048
AK	76	0.6142	0.3817	0.0040
AK	75	0.6270	0.3685	0.0046
AK	74	0.6405	0.3549	0.0046
AK	72	0.6677	0.3273	0.0050
AT	98	0.6240	0.3719	0.0040
AT	76	0.6204	0.3755	0.0040
A9	54	0.6207	0.3743	0.0050
A9	72	0.6719	0.3233	0.0048
KT	54	0.6240	0.3689	0.0070
JT	54	0.6288	0.3593	0.0118
JT	82	0.6864	0.3017	0.0120

cards are unsuited or suited, then make no adjustment. If one set of hole cards is suited and the other set of hole cards is unsuited, then add 3% to the winning percentage of the suited cards. If the suitedness of only one set of hole cards is known, add 1% to the winning percentage if suited and subtract 1% from the winning percentage if unsuited.

Example A.13: Suppose you have QTo and your opponent has 98o. What's your winning percentage?

Answer: You have two higher cards against two lower cards, so start with a winning percentage of 67%. 98o is connected, but doesn't have all its straight combinations available, so subtract about 3%. Since both your hand and your opponent's hand are offsuit, there's no need to apply a correction for suitedness. Your approximate winning percent-age is 64%. (Poker Stove says: winning percentage is about 64.46%; tying percentage is about .88%.)

Example A.14: Suppose you have 76s and your opponent has AT. What's your winning percentage?

Answer: You have two lower cards against two higher cards, so start with a winning percentage of 33%. Since you have a connector and your opponent only has one of your possible straight cards in his hand (the ten), add 5% to your winning percentage. Because you're suited and don't know the suit-edness of your opponent's hand, add another 1% to your winning percentage. You'll win about 39% of the time. (Poker Stove says: winning percentage is about 40.10%; tying percentage is about .42%.)

> *Step 1 (Alternating Relative Ranks):* Start with a
> winning percentage of 63% for the set of hole cards
> containing the highest card.

TABLE A.9: Alternating Relative Ranks (Sample Matchups)

HAND 1	HAND 2	P(1 WIN)	P(1 LOSE)	P(TIE)
AQ	KJ	0.6222	0.3731	0.0048
AQ	K5	0.6375	0.3577	0.0048
A7	Q5	0.6282	0.3673	0.0046
A7	86	0.6000	0.3960	0.0040
A4	53	0.6135	0.3806	0.0058
KT	Q8	0.6446	0.3488	0.0066
J9	T4	0.6545	0.3319	0.0136
J9	T8	0.6255	0.3613	0.0132
64	53	0.5137	0.3562	0.1302

Step #2 (Alternating Relative Ranks): Correction for connectivity: if both sets of hole cards have the same type of connectivity, then apply no correction. Otherwise, add up to 2% to the winning percentage of the set of hole cards that can make more possible straights.

Step 3 (Alternating Relative Ranks): Correction for relative suitedness: if both sets of hole cards are unsuited or suited, then make no adjustment. If one set of hole cards is suited and the other set of hole cards is unsuited, then add 3% to the winning percentage of the suited cards. If the suitedness of only one set of hole cards is known, add 1% to the winning percentage if suited and subtract 1% from the winning percentage if unsuited.[3]

Example A.15: You have Q9s and your opponent has J8o. What's your winning percentage?

Answer: You're favored in this matchup between hole cards of alternating relative ranks, so start with a baseline percentage of 63%. You and your opponent have the same connectivity, so there's no need to apply a correction for connectivity. Since you're suited and your opponent is off-suit, add 3% to your winning percentage. You'll win about 66% of the time. (Poker Stove says: winning percentage is about 65.11%; tying percentage is about .9%.)

---

3. This 3-step approximation breaks down when both sets of hole cards are low because of the high probability of ties. When using this 3-step process with matchups between two sets of low hole cards (e.g., 64 vs. 53), you'll get estimates of the percentage of non-losses (i.e., percentage of wins and ties) instead of estimates of the percentage of wins. But most likely, you won't need to be concerned about this since decisions involving such matchups are rare.

Example A.16: You have 75s, and your opponent has A6o. What's your winning percentage?

Answer: You're the underdog in this matchup between hole cards of alternating relative ranks, so begin with a winning percentage of 37%. You have a 1-gap with no outs other than a 6 taken, so add 2% to bring you to 39%. Since you're suited and your opponent isn't suited, add another 3%. Your winning percentage is about 42%. (Poker Stove says: winning percentage is about 42.65%; tying percentage is about .46%.)

Step 1 (Tweener Matchups): Start with a winning percentage of 60% for the set of hole cards containing the highest card.

Step 2 (Tweener Matchups): Correction for connectivity: subtract up to 6% from the winning percentage of the hole cards with the highest card (the more straights that the tweener can make, the more you subtract).

Step 3 (Tweener Matchups): Correction for relative suitedness: If both sets of hole cards are unsuited or

TABLE A.10: Tweener Matchups (Sample Matchups)

HAND 1	HAND 2	P(1 WIN)	P(1 LOSE)	P(TIE)
AT	KQ	0.5931	0.4023	0.0046
A6	K7	0.5966	0.3993	0.0040
A5	JT	0.5434	0.4521	0.0046
A2	87	0.5419	0.4534	0.0048
T7	98	0.5640	0.4167	0.0192
A2	Q6	0.5835	0.4115	0.0050

suited, then make no adjustment. If one set of hole cards is suited and the other set of hole cards is unsuited, then add 3% to the winning percentage of the suited cards. If the suitedness of only one set of hole cards is known, add 1% to the winning percentage if suited and subtract 1% from the winning percentage if unsuited.

Example A.17: You have A2o, and your opponent has 76s. What's your winning percentage?

Answer: You're favored in this tweener matchup, so start with a baseline percentage of 60%. Your opponent's hand is connected and you don't have any of his straight outs, so subtract 6% from your winning percentage to get 54%. Then, since your hand is offsuit and your opponent's hand is suited, subtract another 3%. Your A2o will win about 51% of the time. (Poker Stove says: winning percentage is about 50.63%; tying percentage is about .52%.)

Example A.18: You have T8s, and your opponent has K5. What's your winning percentage?

Answer: You're the underdog in this tweener matchup, so start with a winning percentage of 40%. You have a 1-gap, and your opponent doesn't take any of your straight outs, so add about 4% to bring your winning percentage to 44%. Then, since your hand is suited and you don't know the suitedness of your opponent's K5, add an additional 1%. Your T8s will win about 45% of the time. (Poker Stove says: winning percentage is about 46.28%; tying percentage is about .70%.)

Step 1 (Domination Matchups): Start with a winning percentage of 73% for the dominating set of hole cards.

Step 2 (Domination Matchups): Correction for connectivity: subtract up to 5% from the winning percentage of the dominating hole cards (the more straights the dominated hole cards can make, the more you subtract).

Step 3 (Domination Matchups): Correction for relative suitedness: if both sets of hole cards are unsuited or suited, then make no adjustment. If one set of hole cards is suited and the other set of hole cards is unsuited, then add 3% to the winning percentage of the suited cards. If the suitedness of only one set of hole cards is known, add 1% to the winning percentage if suited and subtract 1% from the winning percentage if unsuited.

TABLE A.11: Domination Matchups (Sample Matchups)

HAND 1	HAND 2	P(1 WIN)	P(1 LOSE)	P(TIE)
AK	AT	0.707	0.2476	0.0454
AK	KT	0.7271	0.2616	0.0114
A7	A6	0.492	0.2354	0.2726
A7	76	0.6826	0.2919	0.0254
A7	97	0.6917	0.2863	0.022
A7	75	0.6984	0.2747	0.027
AQ	KQ	0.7319	0.2568	0.0114
A2	82	0.7321	0.2514	0.0164
JT	T9	0.6998	0.2496	0.0506
JT	T2	0.726	0.2192	0.0548

Example A.19: You have AQo, and your opponent has KQ. What's your winning percentage?

Answer: You dominate your opponent, so start with a winning percentage of 73%. Your opponent's hand, though connected, is effectively a 2-gap. In addition, you hold a card that your opponent can use to make a straight, so just subtract 1% from your winning percentage to account for your opponent's connectivity. Since your hand is offsuit and you don't know the suitedness of your opponent's hand, subtract 1% from your winning percentage. Your AQo will win about 71% of the time. (Poker Stove says: winning percentage is about 72.92%; tying percentage is about 1.14%.)

Example A.20: You have JTo, and your opponent has AJ. What's your winning percentage?

Answer: You're dominated, so start with a winning percentage of 27%. You have a connector, and your opponent takes away only one card from only one of the possible straights your JTo can make, so add 4% to your winning percentage to bring it up to 31%. Since your hand is offsuit and you don't know the suitedness of your opponent's AJ, subtract 1%. Your JTo will win about 30% of the time. (Poker Stove says: winning percentage is about 27.50%; tying percentage is about 1.78%.)

Table A.12, opposite, summarizes the results from our analysis of matchups not involving pocket pairs:

When dealing with heads-up matchups, we were able to organize the 14,365 possible matchups into 10 categories to which we could apply corrections to come up with very reasonable estimates regarding the winning percentages of most matchups. At most, the estimates derived using the material in the previous two sections will be off by about

TABLE A.12: Summary of Preflop All-In Matchups Not Involving Pocket Pairs

CASE	STARTING WINNING PERCENTAGE FOR HAND WITH HIGHEST CARD	CORRECTION FOR CONNECTIVITY	CORRECTION FOR RELATIVE SUITEDNESS
Two Higher Cards vs. Two Lower Cards	67%	Subtract up to 5% depending on connectivity of two lower cards	Suited vs. Offsuit: +3% Offsuit vs. Suited: −3% Suited vs. ?: +1% Offsuit vs. ?: −1%
Alternating Relative Ranks	63%	Same connectivity: None otherwise: Add or subtract up to 2%	Suited vs. Offsuit: +3% Offsuit vs. Suited: −3% Suited vs. ?: +1% Offsuit vs. ?: −1%
Tweener Matchups	60%	Subtract up to 6% depending on connectivity of tweener	Suited vs. Offsuit: +3% Offsuit vs. Suited: −3% Suited vs. ?: +1% Offsuit vs. ?: −1%
Domination Matchups	73%	Subtract up to 5% depending on connectivity of dominated hand	Suited vs. Offsuit: +3% Offsuit vs. Suited: −3% Suited vs. ?: +1% Offsuit vs. −1%

2%. The cases in which those estimates are further off are typically those in which there are a large percentage of ties:

1. Situations like A3 versus A2, where there's a good chance that the kicker won't play.

2. Situations like 54 versus 32, where there's a non-negligible chance that the board will play.

In those cases, the estimates will usually give you the sum of the winning and tying percentage. And although it's nice to know these percentages separately, if nothing else, you'll get your survival percentage.

Probabilities of Being Dealt Certain Hands Preflop

Many categories of hole cards exist. People talk about suited connectors, pocket pairs, unsuited 1-gaps, ace-rag, and all sorts of other things. Such classifications are necessary for talking about hold'em; however, to do calculations involving the probability of being dealt a certain class of hole cards, we can use a more streamlined classification scheme.

Hole cards fall into one of two categories:

1. Paired

2. Unpaired

If your hole cards are unpaired, they can be suited or unsuited. The final classification scheme we'll use is the following:

1. Paired

2. Unpaired and Unsuited

3. Unpaired and Suited

With that in mind, let's calculate the number of combinations that exist for a specific pocket pair. Since all pairs are equivalent for this type of calculation, let's go with AA. As long as you're playing in a game in which there are four cards of each rank in the deck, there are 4 aces in the deck. To have AA, you're getting 2 aces out of a pool of 4 aces, meaning that there are $\frac{4\cdot3}{2!}$ = 6 combinations of AA. In general, there are 6 combinations for a specific pocket pair.

Let's now consider the number of combinations existing for a specific set of hole cards that are unpaired and unsuited. We'll use AKo as our representative hand here. For the first card, there are 8 possibilities (4 aces and 4 kings). After you're dealt the first card, there are only 3 possibilities left. For example, if you're dealt A♣, the only cards that you can have for your second hole card are K♦, K♥, and K♠. This means that there are 24 permutations of AKo. Taking away the double counts to convert to number of combinations, we get that there are $\frac{24}{2}$ = 12 combinations of AKo. In general, there are 12 combinations for a specific set of unpaired, unsuited hole cards.

Finally, let's consider the number of combinations existing for a specific set of unpaired, suited hole cards. Using AKs as our example, we know without doing any calculations that there are 4 combinations of AKs: A♣K♣, A♦K♦, A♥K♥, and A♠K♠. There's no other combination of AKs. In general, there are 4 combinations for a specific set of unpaired, unsuited hole cards. (Note that if suitedness doesn't matter, there are 12 + 4 = 16 combinations for a specific set of unpaired hole cards.)

To determine the probability of being dealt hole cards from some set, the only other number we need is the total number of combinations of hole cards, which as you should recall is 1,326. Table 5.13 (p. 200) summarizes our discussion thus far.

TABLE A.13: Numbers You Should Know Involving Combinations of Hole Cards

TYPE OF HOLE CARDS	REPRESENTATIVE HAND	COMBINATIONS
Specific Pocket Pair	AA	6
Specific Unpaired, Unsuited Hole Cards	AKo	12
Specific Unpaired, Suited Hole Cards	AKs	4
Specific Unpaired Hole Cards	AK	16
Total Number of Combinations of Hole Cards	N/A	1,326

You can calculate many probabilities having to do with being dealt specific sets of hole cards using the numbers in table A.13. All you do is take the total number of combinations of hole cards in the distribution and then divide by 1,326, the total number of combinations of hole cards.

Example A.21: What's the probability of being dealt AA?

Answer: Take the number of AA combinations (6) and divide by the number of hole card combinations (1,326): $\frac{6}{1,326} \approx$ .0045.

Example A.22: What's the probability of being dealt AKo?

Answer: Take the number of AKo combinations (12) and divide by the number of hole card combinations (1,326): $\frac{12}{1,326} \approx$ .0090.

Example A.23: What's the probability of being dealt AKs?

Answer: Take the number of AKs combinations (4) and divide by the number of hole card combinations (1,326): $\frac{4}{1,326}$ .0030.

Example A.24: What's the probability of being dealt AK?

Answer: 12 AKo combinations plus 4 AKs combinations makes 16 AK combinations in total. Since 1,326 hole card combinations are possible: $\frac{16}{1,326} \approx$ .0121.

Now, let's talk about the probability of being dealt hole cards from a distribution. What's the probability of being dealt {AA–22, AK–AT, A9s–A8s}? We know that AA–22 accounts for (13)(6) = 78 combinations, AK–AT accounts for (4)(16) = 64 combinations, and that A9s–A8s accounts for (4)(2) = 8 combinations. Adding these numbers up, we get 78 + 64 + 8 = 150 combinations. The probability of being dealt a hand in the {AA–22, AK–AT, A9s–A8s} distribution is $\frac{150}{1,326} \approx$ .113.

This type of calculation can be useful in determining what distribution you should be pushing all-in with as you're becoming short stacked because it gives you how many hands you'll have to wait for before being dealt a hand from a distribution. For example, if the probability of being dealt {AA–22, AK–AT, A9s–A8s} is .113, then the probability of not being dealt {AA–22, AK–AT, A9s–A8s} is 1 − .113 = .887. The odds against your being dealt {AA–22, AK–AT, A9s–A8s} are .887:.113 ≈ 7.85:1, which means that you'll be dealt {AA–22, AK–AT, A9s–A8s} 1 out of every 8.85 hands.

Can you do this type of analysis in your head while you're at the table? Sure you can! You just need to make some estimates. If I'm at the poker table, the following is my thought process:

13 pocket pairs means (13)(6) = 78 combinations. {AK–AT} means (4)(16) = 64 combinations. 78 + 64 = 142.

{A9s–A8s} means (2)(4) = 8 combinations. 142 + 8 = 150. $\frac{150}{1,326} \approx \frac{150}{1,300} = \frac{15}{130} \approx$ .11 or .12. I should therefore expect to see a hand in this distribution about every 9 hands.

You should learn two things from this internal dialogue. First, notice how I don't keep lots of pieces of information in my head. When doing mental math, I never keep more than two or three pieces of information in my head at one time. I get two numbers, and I immediately combine them into one; I keep things simple! Second, notice how I did some quick estimating in the end. Sure, it would be awesome if I could instantly do $\frac{150}{1,326}$ in my head. But, there's no need to because dividing by 1,326 and dividing by 1,300 are almost the same thing, and being off by .01 or .02 in the heat of battle won't kill me, especially when I'm battling with so much other uncertainty at the table. Since it won't kill me, it won't kill you either!

Estimating Winning Percentages Against Distributions

With all this information, you now know everything you need to know to estimate winning percentages against distributions on the fly. It'll take a lot of practice, but the more you stick to it, the easier it'll become when you're faced with tough decisions. Here are some examples:

Example A.25: Suppose you have A7s and your opponent has {AA–22, AK–A2, KQ–KT}. Estimate your winning percentage.

Answer: Deal with the pocket pairs first. You're about 13% against AA, but only 3 possible combinations make it a very small part of the range. You're about 33% against KK–77 and 47% against 66–22. 66–22 is five pocket pairs and KK–77 is seven pocket pairs. Your winning percentage against the pocket pairs will be the average of 47% and 33%—which is 40%; plus a small shift toward 47% since those hands are more prevalent—and a small shift down to account for AA. A good estimate is 40% against these 72 combinations (which is about 70 combinations). Against the unpaired aces, you're about 30% against AK–A8 and 76% against A6–A2 (though a large chunk of this 76% is actually ties). Estimate that P(win) against AK–A2 is a little more than halfway between 30% and 76%—55% isn't a bad estimate, acknowledging that a chunk of that will come from ties. AK–A2 represents close to 140 combinations, so against {AA–22, AK–A2}, you're about two thirds of the way between 40% and 55%, which is about 50%. Against the approximately 60 {KQ–KT} combinations, you're about 63%. Your winning percentage will be much closer to 50% than 63%, so something like 52%–53% is a reasonable estimate, acknowledging that something like 5%–10% will be ties. (Poker Stove says: winning percentage is about 41.32% and tying percentage is about 11.68%.)

Example A.26: Suppose you have 55, and your opponent has {AA–22, AK–A2, KQ–KT, QJ}. Estimate your winning percentage.

Answer: For the pocket pair matchups, 44–22 cancels out 66–88, leaving AA–99, against which you're 20%. You're effectively 50% against 6 pairs and 20% against another 6 pairs, meaning that you're about 35% against about 75 combinations. Against pretty much all the unpaired hole cards, you're about 55%, and the unpaired hole cards comprise (16)(16) combinations (about 250). Halfway between 35% and 55% is 45%, but the high proportion of unpaired hole cards means that you'll win about 50% of the time. (Poker Stove says: winning percentage is about 51.35%; tying percentage is about 1.04%.)

Example A.27: Suppose you have KQs and your opponent has {AA–22, AK–A2}. Estimate your winning percentage.

Answer: You're about 15% against AA–KK and about 30% against QQ, meaning that you're about 20% against AA–QQ. You're about 48% against all the underpairs. Since there are many more underpairs, your winning percentage will be skewed closer to 48% than to 20%. The midway point is 34%, so 40% is a reasonable assumption against the pocket pairs. Against the unpaired aces, your winning percentage will be in the 40%–45% range except against AK and AQ, against which you'll be about 30%. Against the unpaired aces, it's fair to estimate that you'll be about 40% to win. Since you're about 40% against the pocket pairs and the unpaired aces, then 40% is a good estimate of your winning percentage. (Poker Stove says: winning percentage is about 42.68%; tying percentage is about .58%.)

Appendix A Summary

We covered pretty much everything there is to know regarding the winning percentages for preflop all-in matchups. Being able to play quality deep-stacked poker is important, but a lot of equity changes hands in the fast and furious shove/fold game that happens late in tournaments—particularly in STTs. To do well in this dynamic, you need to perform quick estimates of your winning probability against your opponents' hand distributions. Besides the drills in this book, a great way to work on your estimates is to fire up Poker Stove and to come up with estimates that you can then verify.

Knowing your probability of winning a showdown is important, but you also need to perform quick estimates of how often your opponents will fold to your all-ins, given that you can reasonably approximate their calling distributions. Fold equity is a huge weapon in tournament poker. As seen in this appendix, once you assess an opponent's calling distribution, determining your fold equity at the table is just about hand combinations and being comfortable with estimating.

Problems

1. Suppose you have A6s in the big blind. Action folds to a player who shoves all-in to 7BB, and then action folds to you. You put your opponent on {AA–22, AK–A2}. What's your winning percentage?

2. Suppose you're in the small blind with 76s and your opponent will call an all-in with {AA–22, AK–A2}. Estimate how often your opponent will fold and how often you'll win if called.

3. An aggressive player with 15bb raises to 3bb from MP. You're on the button with 10bb, and you have 86s. You put MP on {AA–22, AK–A2, KQ–K7, QJ–Q7, JT–76, 65s–54s, J9s–53s}, and if you go all-in, you think that MP will call with {AA–22, AK–A9}. You put the blinds on somewhat tighter distributions—something along the lines of {AA–77, AK–AJ}. If you go all-in, estimate the probability that everybody will fold, and estimate the probability that you'll win when called (since this is an estimate, assume you'll only get one caller).

Answers

1. You're about 13% against AA, 33% against KK–66, and 47% against 55–22. There are more 55–22 combinations, but 13% is further from 33% than 47%, so estimate about 33% against the pocket pairs. Against AK–A7, you're about 33%, and against A5–A2 you're about 73% except that a bulk of the A5–A2 hands will actually be ties. Therefore, estimate your winning percentage against A5–A2 to be somewhere around 50%. The average of 33% and 50% is 40.5%, but since there are more AK–A7 combinations, shift down to about 37%. You're 33% against the pocket pairs and 37% against AL–A2. The average of 33% and 37% is 35%, but since there are more AK–A2 combinations shift up a little to 36%. Around 36% is a reasonable estimate of your winning percentage. (Poker Stove says: winning percentage is about 33.06%; tying percentage is about 16.32%.)

2. AA–22 is 11 hands of 6 combinations each and 2 hands of 3 combinations each, making 72 combinations.

Round down to 70 combinations. AK–A2 is 10 hands of 16 combinations each and 2 hands of 12 combinations each, making 184 combinations total. Round this down to 180 combinations. In total, {AA–22, AK–A2} is about 250 combinations. The probability that your opponent will call is approximately $\frac{250}{1,225} \approx$ $\frac{250}{1,200} = \frac{25}{120} = \frac{5}{24} \approx .2$ (since you know your 2 hole cards, your opponent's hand distribution consists of $_{50}C_2 = 1,225 \approx 1,200$ combinations). Your opponent will fold about 80% of the time. (The exact number of combinations in your opponent's calling distribution is $11(6) + 2(3) + 10(16) + 2(12) = 256$, and the exact probability that he'll fold is therefore $\frac{1,225-256}{1,225} = \frac{969}{1,225} \approx .7910$.)

The next part of this problem is figuring out the probability that you'll win the 20% of the time that you're called. Against AA–88, you're about 22% since TT–88 kills some of your straight outs. You're about $\frac{13\% + 33\%}{2} = 23\%$ against 77–66, meaning that you're about 22% against AA–66. You're about 50% against 55–22. Your winning percentage will be skewed closer to 22% than 50%, and since 36% is halfway between, something around 30% is a reasonable estimate against the pocket pairs. Against the unpaired hole cards, you're about 40% against AK–A8, 35% against A7–A6, and 50% against A5–A2. The larger number of AK–A8 combinations along with the A7–A6 combinations puts your winning percentage somewhere just about 40%. (Poker Stove says: winning percentage is about 38.65%; tying percentage is about .86%.)

This is a very important hand to keep in mind. You have high fold equity, and even when you're called, you're still 40% to win. You can't let opportunities like these pass you by.

3. This is the type of question that takes pages of work to get the precise answer and just a few estimates and approximations to get an answer close enough for government work.[4] The raiser's hand distribution is quite wide. AA–22 is about 70 combinations; plus about 180 AK–A2 combinations is about 250; plus about 90 KQ–K7 combinations is about 340; plus about 70 QJ–Q7 combinations is about 410; plus about 70 JT–76 combinations is about 480; plus about 5 65s–54s combinations is about 485; plus about 25 J9s–53s combinations is about 510 combinations. In total, the raiser's hand distribution is about 500 combinations.

Meanwhile, his calling distribution is about 70 AA–22 combinations plus about 80 AK–A9 combinations. The approximate probability that the raiser will call is $\frac{150}{500} = \frac{15}{50} = .3$; therefore, the approximate probability that the raiser will fold is .7.

Next, we need to tend to the blinds. Although the hands that the blinds hold aren't independent and we should technically account for the raiser's range, we're just approximating here, and as I showed in *KPBTN,* assuming independence in situations with hand ranges that aren't restrictively narrow will get you answers that are sufficiently accurate. So with that being said, AA–77 is about 45 combinations plus about 50 AK–AJ combinations makes 95 combinations. This estimate $\frac{95}{1,225}$ is close enough to $\frac{100}{1,200} \approx \frac{1}{12} \approx \frac{1}{10} = .1$. The probability that a particular blind will fold is .9. The probability that all three of your opponents will fold is about $(.7)(.9)(.9) = (.7)(.81) \approx .57$.

---

4. Okay—considering that DMV is a U.S. government agency, we're looking for something a bit better than government work. The bottom line: a few estimates and approximations will get us something close enough to be useful at the table.

The 43% of the time you're called, you'll be against {AA–22, AK–A9} one third of the time and {AA–77, AK–AJ} two thirds of the time. Let's first consider the {AA–22, AK–A9} distribution. Against AA–99, you're a little bit less than 20% to win; against 88 you're about 15% to win; against 77–66, you're about 35% to win; and against 55–22, you're about 48% (close to 50%) to win. AA–99 and 77–22 are about the same number of combinations, and 77–22 average out to a little over 40%, so 30% is a good ballpark estimate of your winning probability against AA–22. Meanwhile, against AK–A9, you're about 40%. AA–22 and AK–A9 have about the same number of combinations, so when you're called, you'll win about 35% of the time. (Poker Stove says: winning percentage is about 35.63%; tying percentage is about .78%.)

Now, let's consider the {AA–77, AK–AJ} distribution. You're a little bit less than 20% to win against AA–99, about 15% against 88, and about 35% against 77. 20% is a good estimate of your winning percentage against AA–77. Meanwhile, you're about 40% against AK–AJ. AK–AJ and AA–77 have about the same number of combinations; therefore, you're about 30% the two thirds of the time you're against {AA–77, AK–AJ}. (Poker Stove says: winning percentage is about 30.69%; tying percentage is about .56%.)

You're about 35% one third of the time and about 30% two thirds of the time, so you'll win about 32% of the time you're called. Note how different this situation is from the one in problem 2.

Appendix B:
The Math of Postflop Play

Introduction

Knowledge of preflop all-in matchups is essential. But even though many think of the high profile all-in confrontations often seen on TV, tournament poker is about more than pre-flop play. To excel at poker tournaments, you need to know how to play across all betting rounds. This chapter is a crash course on the math having to do with postflop play. For a much more thorough treatment, pick up *Killer Poker by the Numbers*.

Drawing with One Card to Come

When drawing with one card to come, your probability of winning the hand is simply the number of outs you have divided by the total number of cards left in the deck. The odds against you wining the hand are the ratio of non-outs to outs. Evaluating the probability of hitting a hand with one card to come is nothing more than an exercise in honestly and accurately assessing where you are in the hand.

Situations in which you'll be drawing with one card to come are the following:

- It's the turn.

- It's the flop, and you think your opponent(s) will bet in a way that shuts you out of the pot on the turn.

Example B.1: It's the turn, the board is A♦9♦2♥6♠, and you have 7♦6♦. Your opponent makes a small bet, and you think he has a pair of aces with a hand like AJ or AT. What's the probability that you'll win the hand?

Answer: {AJ–AT} represents 24 combinations. The probability that your opponent has a diamond is $\frac{6}{24}$, and the probability that your opponent doesn't have a diamond is $\frac{18}{24}$. When your opponent has a diamond, you have 8 outs out of 44 cards; when your opponent doesn't have a diamond, you have 9 outs out of 44 cards. The probability that you hit your flush is:

$$\left(\tfrac{6}{24}\right)\left(\tfrac{8}{44}\right) + \left(\tfrac{18}{24}\right)\left(\tfrac{9}{44}\right) \approx .1989 \qquad (B.1)$$

In addition, 5 cards give you two pair or trips. The probability of hitting two pair or trips is therefore $\frac{5}{44} \approx .1136$. In total, the probability that you'll win is about .1989 + .1136 = .3125.

Most players in the situation described in example B.1 would simply say that they have 14 outs in a deck of 46 cards. These players would assess their winning probability to be $\frac{14}{46} \approx .3043$. Notice that this isn't too far off from the answer found by accounting for the opponent's precise distribution. Generally, as long as your opponents' distributions aren't heavy in cards that you're drawing to, there won't be a significant difference between the exact distribution-dependent answers and the distribution-independent answers. This is good news since the distribution-independent answers are much easier to calculate mentally. And although we want to be as accurate as possible away from the table, it's also important to have analytic tools to take with you to the tables.

Drawing with Two Cards to Come

If you have a draw on the flop, then sometimes you'll be drawing with two cards to come:

1. You or your opponent(s) will be all-in on the flop, meaning that you get to the river without any more betting action.

2. You know your opponents' action distributions so you know you'll get the proper price when considering the hands across both betting rounds.

3. Your opponent calls a semibluff on the flop and checks to you when you have position, giving you the opportunity to check behind to see the river without putting any chips in on the turn.

To find the probability of drawing with two cards to come, first count your outs and then use table B.1 (p. 214).

A common trick that people use is to take the number of outs they have and then to multiply by 4 to get the approximate percentage of hitting with two cards to come. This approximation is good when you don't have many outs, but it breaks down as the number of outs you have increases.

TABLE B.1: Probability of Hitting a Draw with Two Cards to Come

NUMBER OF OUTS ON THE FLOP	P(COMPLETE DRAW WITH TWO CARDS TO COME)	ODDS AGAINST HITTING DRAW WITH TWO CARDS TO COME
1	.04	22.50:1
2	.08	10.88:1
3	.12	7.00:1
4	.16	5.07:1
5	.20	3.91:1
6	.24	3.14:1
7	.28	2.59:1
8	.31	2.18:1
9	.35	1.86:1
10	.38	1.60:1
11	.42	1.40:1
12	.45	1.22:1
13	.48	1.08:1
14	.51	.95:1
15	.54	.85:1
16	.57	.75:1
17	.60	.67:1
18	.62	.60:1
19	.65	.54:1
20	.68	.48:1
21	.70	.43:1

Notice, for example, how a 13-outer will hit 48% of the time instead of 52% of the time; a 14-outer is the first draw that hits more than 50% of the time with two cards to come. But you can use this rule when you have up to 10 outs, and from there, you just need to know that 14+ outs will hit more than 50% of the time.

When counting your outs, make sure that you honestly assess your outs. For example, if you have A♦Q♦ and the board is J♦9♦6♥, aces and queens are probably not outs against a tight opponent willing to put a lot of chips in the pot when stacks are deep. Your flush draw with two over-cards, sometimes thought of as a 15-outer, is most likely a 9-outer. And it's most likely a 9-outer that will win less than 35% of the time because your opponent will have redraws to a boat.[1] In *KPBTN,* I showed that redraws aren't typically a big concern unless your opponent has a set—in which case your probability of winning drops about 10%.

Example B.2: Early in an MTT, action happens as described in table B.2 (p. 216).

What's your probability of winning the hand?

Answer: To figure this out, we need the following two pieces of information:

1. How many outs you have.

2. Whether you'll see the flop or both the flop and the turn.

The obvious-looking answer to #1 is that you have 9 outs. However, the betting in this hand strongly suggests that at least one of your other opponents is drawing. While it *could* be possible that someone is drawing purely to a *gutshot straight draw,* the more likely scenario is that someone is

---

1. Generally speaking, sets are the only hands where redraws substantially devalue your draw. Check out *KPBTN* for a more thorough treatment of redraws.

TABLE B.2: Action for Example B.2

	STACKS	PREFLOP	STACKS	FLOP K♠T♦9♥	STACKS
SB xx	1,600	sb15 / 30	1,570	250	
BB xx	1,800	bb30 / 30	1,770	–	
UTG xx	3,000	30	2,970	100 / 250	
UTG+1 xx	500	–			
UTG+2 xx	860	30	830	100 / 250	
UTG+3 xx	1,140	30	1,110	100 / 250	
CO−2 xx	2,000	–			
CO−1 (6♣4♣)	1,700	30	1,670	100 / ?	
CO xx	1,300	30	1,270	–	
B xx	2,350	–			
POT		210			

drawing to a flush draw. And someone else with a flush draw is very likely drawing to a higher flush than you are. There's a good chance that you have 0 outs here, and therefore, it doesn't even matter how many cards you'd get to see—you should simply fold and not see any more cards.

Example B.3: You have 44. If you don't flop a 4, what's the probability that you'll hit a 4 with two cards to come?

Answer: Two 4's are left in the deck, (2)(4) = 8; therefore, the probability of hitting a 4 with two cards to come is about .08. This low probability makes unimproved small pocket pairs a dangerous proposition postflop—if your opponent has an overpair, chances are very slim that you'll catch up.

Drawing in NLHE involves knowing the percentages and honestly assessing your true outs. The easiest mistake to make is to be too optimistic when counting your outs. If you habitually overestimate how many outs you have, you'll be taking risks that you shouldn't be taking. However, being overly pessimistic is also bad when assessing your outs. If you're trying to come up with *runner-runner* chop situations to justify a call, you're probably overdoing it. But if you're always counting hands like 7♥6♠ on a 5♥4♥T♦ board as 6 outers, you're probably folding in some situations where you should be calling.

Pocket Pairs

For an extremely thorough treatment behind the math of pocket pairs (in particular, playing them under the hit-to-win paradigm), check out chapter 4 in *KPBTN*. The brief summary of playing pocket pairs is as follows:

1. The odds against flopping a set or better are about 7.5:1.

2. The probability of flopping an overpair to an unpaired board is given in table B.3 (p. 218).

TABLE B.3: Probability of Flopping an Overpair to an Unpaired Board

POCKET PAIR	P(UNPAIRED BOARD AND OVERPAIR)
AA	0.72
KK	0.54
QQ	0.39
JJ	0.27
TT	0.18
99	0.11
88	0.07
77	0.03
66	0.01
55	0.003
44	0
33	0
22	0

Unpaired Hole Cards

With unpaired hole cards, the probability of missing the flop entirely is:

$$\left(\tfrac{44}{50}\right)\left(\tfrac{43}{49}\right)\left(\tfrac{42}{48}\right) \approx .68 \tag{B.2}$$

The probability of flopping one of your cards (for one pair on an unpaired board and two is:

$$3\left(\tfrac{6}{50}\right)\left(\tfrac{44}{49}\right)\left(\tfrac{43}{48}\right) \approx .29 \tag{B.3}$$

The probability of flopping two of your cards is:

$$3\left(\tfrac{6}{50}\right)\left(\tfrac{5}{49}\right)\left(\tfrac{44}{48}\right) \approx .03 \tag{B.4}$$

Finally, the probability of flopping three of your cards is:

$$\left(\tfrac{6}{50}\right)\left(\tfrac{5}{49}\right)\left(\tfrac{4}{48}\right) \approx .001 \qquad\qquad (B.5)$$

Equations B.3 and B.4 show that the odds against flopping two pair or better are 27.82:1. When are you going to have proper odds, accounting for implied odds and *reverse implied odds,* to play a hand like 83o? You'll virtually never have odds to call with junk—even from the small blind. If your only line of play is to play hit-to-win poker, then you simply can't afford to play junk hands. Junk hands are only playable if you have lines of play that can make your opponents fold.

When it comes to hitting straights and flushes with five cards to come, check out table B.4:

TABLE B.4: Odds Involving Getting Straights and Flushes with Five Cards to Come

TYPE OF HAND HELD	APPROXIMATE ODDS AGAINST HITTING DRAW WITH FIVE CARDS TO COME
Unsuited, Connected	6.66:1
Suited, Not Connected	14.63:1
Suited, Connected	4.44:1

From this table, we see that under most playing conditions, you need bets to go into the pot postflop to get proper odds to draw (the exception is suited connectors in pots with 3 or more limpers). Because of the odds involved, we want to play these hands in situations similar to those in which we played pocket pairs. The big difference with pocket pairs, though, is that with pocket pairs, hit-to-win play is largely based on whether we hit the flop. When we hit the flop with a pocket pair, we have a huge hand. When we hit the flop with a connector or a suited hand, most of the time, we will end up flopping a *draw* as opposed to a made hand—we'll need to hit a card on the turn or river to complete our draw and win the hand. This means that we'd like to be involved in pots with a low potential for huge action on the flop. From that perspective, we don't really want to be playing these hands in raised pots. We want to see the flop cheaply and make a good chunk of profit from implied odds.

Your Opponents' Hands

NLHE isn't just a game of your own cards. It's also a game of your opponents' cards. And when it comes to your opponents' cards, equation B.2 tells a good chunk of the story. When you have unpaired hole cards, you'll miss the flop about two thirds of the time. When your opponents have unpaired hole cards, they'll miss the flop about two thirds of the time. In other words, *shorthanded* pots in NLHE are contested over little or nothing. Put constant pressure on your opponents in shorthanded pots. Although the chips from any individual pot may not seem like much, all the extra chips you win through aggressive shorthanded play will quickly add up. Of course, don't be mindlessly aggressive—you can't push the gas pedal all the way to the floor. But look to be active in shorthanded pots so that you can win more hands than your opponents can in the situations where neither you nor they have a good hand.

Appendix B Summary

This appendix was a crash course on some of the math having to do with the numbers of postflop play. All the material in this appendix is fundamental to the play of NLHE tournaments. From drawing postflop to making judgments about what hands to enter pots with in the first place, the numbers in this appendix will factor heavily into your NLHE tournament decisions.

Appendix C:
Tournament Simulation
Results

Tables C.1 and C.2 are simulations of heads-up tournament situations in which P1 and P2 begin with varying numbers of big blinds each and play the same strategy versus each other. For the simulation in table C.1, both players go all-in preflop every hand. For the simulation in table C.2, the small blind limps, the big blind checks, and both players check all the way down. In both simulations, the percentage of times that P1 finishes in first very closely matches the percentage of tournament chips in P1's stack. Meanwhile, table C.3 is from a three-handed simulation, where all three players go all-in preflop. Again, the percentage of times that P1 finishes in first very closely matches the percentage of tournament chips in P1's stack.

Although these simulations are only for tournaments down to two or three players, they at least provide some empirical verification of the notion that a player's P(1st) equals the proportion of total tournament chips in his stack (given that everyone is playing identically). And although I prove this idea in chapter 6, it's nice to have empirical evidence that corresponds with the theory. Much thanks to my friend, Ryan Patterson, for these!

TABLE C.1: Heads-Up; Both Players All-In Every Hand

TOTAL BIG BLINDS IN TOURNAMENT	BIG BLINDS IN P1'S STACK	SIMULATED P(P1 WINS)	EXPECTED P(P1 WINS)	DIFFERENCE BETWEEN THEORY AND SIMULATION
4	3	0.74995 ± 0.00004	0.75000	0.00005
6	4	0.66666 ± 0.00005	0.66667	0.00001
6	5	0.83333 ± 0.00004	0.83333	0.00000
10	6	0.60007 ± 0.00005	0.60000	−0.00007
10	7	0.69996 ± 0.00005	0.70000	0.00004
10	8	0.79999 ± 0.00004	0.80000	0.00001
10	9	0.90000 ± 0.00003	0.90000	0.00000
14	8	0.57147 ± 0.00005	0.57143	−0.00004
14	9	0.64287 ± 0.00005	0.64286	−0.00001
14	10	0.71431 ± 0.00005	0.71429	−0.00002
14	11	0.78576 ± 0.00004	0.78571	−0.00005
14	12	0.85714 ± 0.00003	0.85714	0.00000
14	13	0.92855 ± 0.00003	0.92857	0.00002
20	11	0.55006 ± 0.00005	0.55000	−0.00006
20	12	0.60004 ± 0.00005	0.60000	−0.00004
20	13	0.64997 ± 0.00005	0.65000	0.00003
20	14	0.69995 ± 0.00005	0.70000	0.00005
20	15	0.75000 ± 0.00004	0.75000	0.00000
20	16	0.79996 ± 0.00004	0.80000	0.00004
20	17	0.84996 ± 0.00004	0.85000	0.00004
20	18	0.90001 ± 0.00003	0.90000	−0.00001
20	19	0.95001 ± 0.00002	0.95000	−0.00001
30	16	0.53332 ± 0.00005	0.53333	0.00001
30	17	0.56667 ± 0.00005	0.56667	0.00000
30	18	0.59999 ± 0.00005	0.60000	0.00001
30	19	0.63328 ± 0.00005	0.63333	0.00005
30	20	0.66666 ± 0.00005	0.66667	0.00001
30	21	0.70010 ± 0.00005	0.70000	−0.00010
30	22	0.73332 ± 0.00004	0.73333	0.00001
30	23	0.76664 ± 0.00004	0.76667	0.00003
30	24	0.80002 ± 0.00004	0.80000	−0.00002

TOTAL BIG BLINDS IN TOURNAMENT	BIG BLINDS IN P1'S STACK	SIMULATED P(P1 WINS)	EXPECTED P(P1 WINS)	DIFFERENCE BETWEEN THEORY AND SIMULATION
30	25	0.83335 ± 0.00004	0.83333	−0.00002
30	26	0.86669 ± 0.00003	0.86667	−0.00002
30	27	0.90002 ± 0.00003	0.90000	−0.00002
30	28	0.93329 ± 0.00002	0.93333	0.00004
30	29	0.96667 ± 0.00002	0.96667	0.00000
50	26	0.51996 ± 0.00005	0.52000	0.00004
50	27	0.54007 ± 0.00005	0.54000	−0.00007
50	28	0.56004 ± 0.00005	0.56000	−0.00004
50	29	0.58012 ± 0.00005	0.58000	−0.00012
50	30	0.59998 ± 0.00005	0.60000	0.00002
50	31	0.61997 ± 0.00005	0.62000	0.00003
50	32	0.63992 ± 0.00005	0.64000	0.00008
50	33	0.66003 ± 0.00005	0.66000	−0.00003
50	34	0.68001 ± 0.00005	0.68000	−0.00001
50	35	0.69997 ± 0.00005	0.70000	0.00003
50	36	0.71993 ± 0.00004	0.72000	0.00007
50	37	0.73989 ± 0.00004	0.74000	0.00011
50	38	0.75999 ± 0.00004	0.76000	0.00001
50	39	0.77997 ± 0.00004	0.78000	0.00003
50	40	0.79993 ± 0.00004	0.80000	0.00007
50	41	0.81999 ± 0.00004	0.82000	0.00001
50	42	0.84001 ± 0.00004	0.84000	−0.00001
50	43	0.85999 ± 0.00003	0.86000	0.00001
50	44	0.87997 ± 0.00003	0.88000	0.00003
50	45	0.89998 ± 0.00003	0.90000	0.00002
50	46	0.91998 ± 0.00003	0.92000	0.00002
50	47	0.94002 ± 0.00002	0.94000	−0.00002
50	48	0.96000 ± 0.00002	0.96000	0.00000
50	49	0.98000 ± 0.00001	0.98000	0.00000

TABLE C.2: Heads-Up; Limp Every Hand

TOTAL BIG BLINDS IN TOURNAMENT	BIG BLINDS IN P1'S STACK	SIMULATED P(P1 WINS)	EXPECTED P(P1 WINS)	DIFFERENCE BETWEEN THEORY AND SIMULATION
4	3	0.75017 ± 0.00014	0.75000	−0.00017
6	4	0.66679 ± 0.00015	0.66667	−0.00012
6	5	0.83329 ± 0.00012	0.83333	0.00004
10	6	0.60062 ± 0.00049	0.60000	−0.00062
10	7	0.70046 ± 0.00046	0.70000	−0.00046
10	8	0.80098 ± 0.00040	0.80000	−0.00098
10	9	0.89988 ± 0.00030	0.90000	0.00012
14	8	0.57106 ± 0.00049	0.57143	0.00037
14	9	0.64319 ± 0.00048	0.64286	−0.00033
14	10	0.71493 ± 0.00045	0.71429	−0.00064
14	11	0.78608 ± 0.00041	0.78571	−0.00037
14	12	0.85766 ± 0.00035	0.85714	−0.00052
14	13	0.92861 ± 0.00026	0.92857	−0.00004
20	11	0.54988 ± 0.00050	0.55000	0.00012
20	12	0.60052 ± 0.00049	0.60000	−0.00052
20	13	0.65116 ± 0.00048	0.65000	−0.00116
20	14	0.69946 ± 0.00046	0.70000	0.00054
20	15	0.74982 ± 0.00043	0.75000	0.00018
20	16	0.79968 ± 0.00040	0.80000	0.00032
20	17	0.85009 ± 0.00036	0.85000	−0.00009
20	18	0.89991 ± 0.00030	0.90000	0.00009
20	19	0.94999 ± 0.00022	0.95000	0.00001
30	16	0.53224 ± 0.00050	0.53333	0.00109
30	17	0.56682 ± 0.00050	0.56667	−0.00015
30	18	0.60033 ± 0.00049	0.60000	−0.00033
30	19	0.63238 ± 0.00048	0.63333	0.00095
30	20	0.66746 ± 0.00047	0.66667	−0.00079
30	21	0.70017 ± 0.00046	0.70000	−0.00017
30	22	0.73319 ± 0.00044	0.73333	0.00014
30	23	0.76690 ± 0.00042	0.76667	−0.00023
30	24	0.79987 ± 0.00040	0.80000	0.00013

TOTAL BIG BLINDS IN TOURNAMENT	BIG BLINDS IN P1'S STACK	SIMULATED P(P1 WINS)	EXPECTED P(P1 WINS)	DIFFERENCE BETWEEN THEORY AND SIMULATION
30	25	0.83359 ± 0.00037	0.83333	−0.00026
30	26	0.86698 ± 0.00034	0.86667	−0.00031
30	27	0.90036 ± 0.00030	0.90000	−0.00036
30	28	0.93325 ± 0.00025	0.93333	0.00008
30	29	0.96692 ± 0.00018	0.96667	−0.00025
50	26	0.52033 ± 0.00050	0.52000	−0.00033
50	27	0.54070 ± 0.00050	0.54000	−0.00070
50	28	0.55947 ± 0.00050	0.56000	0.00053
50	29	0.57859 ± 0.00049	0.58000	0.00141
50	30	0.59966 ± 0.00049	0.60000	0.00034
50	31	0.61948 ± 0.00049	0.62000	0.00052
50	32	0.63954 ± 0.00048	0.64000	0.00046
50	33	0.66012 ± 0.00047	0.66000	−0.00012
50	34	0.68000 ± 0.00047	0.68000	0.00000
50	35	0.69988 ± 0.00046	0.70000	0.00012
50	36	0.72033 ± 0.00045	0.72000	−0.00033
50	37	0.73888 ± 0.00044	0.74000	0.00112
50	38	0.75970 ± 0.00043	0.76000	0.00030
50	39	0.78075 ± 0.00041	0.78000	−0.00075
50	40	0.79972 ± 0.00040	0.80000	0.00028
50	41	0.82003 ± 0.00038	0.82000	−0.00003
50	42	0.84022 ± 0.00037	0.84000	−0.00022
50	43	0.85984 ± 0.00035	0.86000	0.00016
50	44	0.88017 ± 0.00032	0.88000	−0.00017
50	45	0.90029 ± 0.00030	0.90000	−0.00029
50	46	0.91971 ± 0.00027	0.92000	0.00029
50	47	0.94015 ± 0.00024	0.94000	−0.00015
50	48	0.96006 ± 0.00020	0.96000	−0.00006
50	49	0.98020 ± 0.00014	0.98000	−0.00020

TABLE C.3: Three-Way All-In Every Hand

TOTAL BIG BLINDS IN TOURNAMENT	BIG BLINDS IN P1'S STACK	BIG BLINDS IN P2'S STACK	SIMULATED P(P1 WINS)	EXPECTED P(P1 WINS)	DIFFERENCE BETWEEN THEORY AND SIMULATION
4	2	1	0.49991 ± 0.00016	0.50000	0.00009
6	2	2	0.33350 ± 0.00015	0.33333	−0.00017
6	3	2	0.49992 ± 0.00016	0.50000	0.00008
6	4	1	0.66656 ± 0.00015	0.66667	0.00011
10	4	3	0.39994 ± 0.00015	0.40000	0.00006
10	4	4	0.40007 ± 0.00015	0.40000	−0.00007
10	5	3	0.50003 ± 0.00016	0.50000	−0.00003
10	5	4	0.49995 ± 0.00016	0.50000	0.00005
10	6	2	0.60010 ± 0.00015	0.60000	−0.00010
10	6	3	0.59998 ± 0.00015	0.60000	0.00002
10	7	2	0.70002 ± 0.00014	0.70000	−0.00002
10	8	1	0.79978 ± 0.00013	0.80000	0.00022
14	5	5	0.35719 ± 0.00015	0.35714	−0.00005
14	6	4	0.42863 ± 0.00016	0.42857	−0.00006
14	6	5	0.42847 ± 0.00016	0.42857	0.00010
14	6	6	0.42881 ± 0.00016	0.42857	−0.00024
14	7	4	0.49995 ± 0.00016	0.50000	0.00005
14	7	5	0.49999 ± 0.00016	0.50000	0.00001
14	7	6	0.49977 ± 0.00016	0.50000	0.00023
14	8	3	0.57132 ± 0.00016	0.57143	0.00011
14	8	4	0.57153 ± 0.00016	0.57143	−0.00010
14	8	5	0.57164 ± 0.00016	0.57143	−0.00021
14	9	3	0.64276 ± 0.00015	0.64286	0.00010
14	9	4	0.64322 ± 0.00015	0.64286	−0.00036
14	10	2	0.71415 ± 0.00014	0.71429	0.00014
14	10	3	0.71436 ± 0.00014	0.71429	−0.00007
14	11	2	0.78566 ± 0.00013	0.78571	0.00005
14	12	1	0.85701 ± 0.00011	0.85714	0.00013
20	7	7	0.35020 ± 0.00015	0.35000	−0.00020
20	8	6	0.40011 ± 0.00015	0.40000	−0.00011

TOTAL BIG BLINDS IN TOUR-NAMENT	BIG BLINDS IN P1'S STACK	BIG BLINDS IN P2'S STACK	SIMULATED P(P1 WINS)	EXPECTED P(P1 WINS)	DIFFERENCE BETWEEN THEORY AND SIMULATION
20	8	7	0.39986 ± 0.00015	0.40000	0.00014
20	8	8	0.39992 ± 0.00015	0.40000	0.00008
20	9	6	0.45005 ± 0.00016	0.45000	−0.00005
20	9	7	0.45011 ± 0.00016	0.45000	−0.00011
20	9	8	0.44982 ± 0.00016	0.45000	0.00018
20	9	9	0.44991 ± 0.00016	0.45000	0.00009
20	10	5	0.50012 ± 0.00016	0.50000	−0.00012
20	10	6	0.49983 ± 0.00016	0.50000	0.00017
20	10	7	0.49990 ± 0.00016	0.50000	0.00010
20	10	8	0.49987 ± 0.00016	0.50000	0.00013
20	10	9	0.50019 ± 0.00016	0.50000	−0.00019
20	11	5	0.54999 ± 0.00016	0.55000	0.00001
20	11	6	0.55003 ± 0.00016	0.55000	−0.00003
20	11	7	0.55006 ± 0.00016	0.55000	−0.00006
20	11	8	0.55019 ± 0.00016	0.55000	−0.00019
20	12	4	0.60004 ± 0.00015	0.60000	−0.00004
20	12	5	0.59995 ± 0.00015	0.60000	0.00005
20	12	6	0.60006 ± 0.00015	0.60000	−0.00006
20	12	7	0.59974 ± 0.00015	0.60000	0.00026
20	13	4	0.65003 ± 0.00015	0.65000	−0.00003
20	13	5	0.64987 ± 0.00015	0.65000	0.00013
20	13	6	0.65005 ± 0.00015	0.65000	−0.00005
20	14	3	0.70008 ± 0.00014	0.70000	−0.00008
20	14	4	0.70011 ± 0.00014	0.70000	−0.00011
20	14	5	0.69971 ± 0.00014	0.70000	0.00029
20	15	3	0.75035 ± 0.00014	0.75000	−0.00035
20	15	4	0.74989 ± 0.00014	0.75000	0.00011
20	16	2	0.80003 ± 0.00013	0.80000	−0.00003
20	16	3	0.79983 ± 0.00013	0.80000	0.00017
20	17	2	0.85017 ± 0.00011	0.85000	−0.00017
20	18	1	0.90008 ± 0.00009	0.90000	−0.00008
30	10	10	0.33305 ± 0.00015	0.33333	0.00028
30	11	10	0.36661 ± 0.00015	0.36667	0.00006

Table C.3 *(cont.)*

TOTAL BIG BLINDS IN TOUR- NAMENT	BIG BLINDS IN P1'S STACK	BIG BLINDS IN P2'S STACK	SIMULATED P(P1 WINS)	EXPECTED P(P1 WINS)	DIFFERENCE BETWEEN THEORY AND SIMULATION
30	11	11	0.36645 ± 0.00015	0.36667	0.00022
30	12	9	0.39994 ± 0.00015	0.40000	0.00006
30	12	10	0.40013 ± 0.00015	0.40000	− 0.00013
30	12	11	0.40001 ± 0.00015	0.40000	− 0.00001
30	12	12	0.39997 ± 0.00015	0.40000	0.00003
30	13	9	0.43322 ± 0.00016	0.43333	0.00011
30	13	10	0.43340 ± 0.00016	0.43333	− 0.00007
30	13	11	0.43321 ± 0.00016	0.43333	0.00012
30	13	12	0.43325 ± 0.00016	0.43333	0.00008
30	13	13	0.43311 ± 0.00016	0.43333	0.00022
30	14	8	0.46664 ± 0.00016	0.46667	0.00003
30	14	9	0.46659 ± 0.00016	0.46667	0.00008
30	14	10	0.46654 ± 0.00016	0.46667	0.00013
30	14	11	0.46673 ± 0.00016	0.46667	− 0.00006
30	14	12	0.46660 ± 0.00016	0.46667	0.00007
30	14	13	0.46655 ± 0.00016	0.46667	0.00012
30	14	14	0.46655 ± 0.00016	0.46667	0.00012
30	15	8	0.50012 ± 0.00016	0.50000	− 0.00012
30	15	9	0.49995 ± 0.00016	0.50000	0.00005
30	15	10	0.50010 ± 0.00016	0.50000	− 0.00010
30	15	11	0.49993 ± 0.00016	0.50000	0.00007
30	15	12	0.50038 ± 0.00016	0.50000	− 0.00038
30	15	13	0.49980 ± 0.00016	0.50000	0.00020
30	15	14	0.50030 ± 0.00016	0.50000	− 0.00030
30	16	7	0.53323 ± 0.00016	0.53333	0.00010
30	16	8	0.53343 ± 0.00016	0.53333	− 0.00010
30	16	9	0.53340 ± 0.00016	0.53333	− 0.00007
30	16	10	0.53305 ± 0.00016	0.53333	0.00028
30	16	11	0.53323 ± 0.00016	0.53333	0.00010
30	16	12	0.53353 ± 0.00016	0.53333	− 0.00020
30	16	13	0.53350 ± 0.00016	0.53333	− 0.00017
30	17	7	0.56668 ± 0.00016	0.56667	− 0.00001
30	17	8	0.56676 ± 0.00016	0.56667	− 0.00009

TOTAL BIG BLINDS IN TOUR- NAMENT	BIG BLINDS IN P1'S STACK	BIG BLINDS IN P2'S STACK	SIMULATED P(P1 WINS)	EXPECTED P(P1 WINS)	DIFFERENCE BETWEEN THEORY AND SIMULATION
30	17	9	0.56644 ± 0.00016	0.56667	0.00023
30	17	10	0.56707 ± 0.00016	0.56667	−0.00040
30	17	11	0.56671 ± 0.00016	0.56667	−0.00004
30	17	12	0.56647 ± 0.00016	0.56667	0.00020
30	18	6	0.59968 ± 0.00015	0.60000	0.00032
30	18	7	0.59963 ± 0.00015	0.60000	0.00037
30	18	8	0.59998 ± 0.00015	0.60000	0.00002
30	18	9	0.60029 ± 0.00015	0.60000	−0.00029
30	18	10	0.59979 ± 0.00015	0.60000	0.00021
30	18	11	0.60018 ± 0.00015	0.60000	−0.00018
30	19	6	0.63331 ± 0.00015	0.63333	0.00002
30	19	7	0.63345 ± 0.00015	0.63333	−0.00012
30	19	8	0.63362 ± 0.00015	0.63333	−0.00029
30	19	9	0.63363 ± 0.00015	0.63333	−0.00030
30	19	10	0.63343 ± 0.00015	0.63333	−0.00010
30	20	5	0.66650 ± 0.00015	0.66667	0.00017
30	20	6	0.66683 ± 0.00015	0.66667	−0.00016
30	20	7	0.66684 ± 0.00015	0.66667	−0.00017
30	20	8	0.66651 ± 0.00015	0.66667	0.00016
30	20	9	0.66686 ± 0.00015	0.66667	−0.00019
30	21	5	0.70003 ± 0.00014	0.70000	−0.00003
30	21	6	0.69993 ± 0.00014	0.70000	0.00007
30	21	7	0.69986 ± 0.00014	0.70000	0.00014
30	21	8	0.70012 ± 0.00014	0.70000	−0.00012
30	22	4	0.73356 ± 0.00014	0.73333	−0.00023
30	22	5	0.73333 ± 0.00014	0.73333	0.00000
30	22	6	0.73338 ± 0.00014	0.73333	−0.00005
30	22	7	0.73362 ± 0.00014	0.73333	−0.00029
30	23	4	0.76649 ± 0.00013	0.76667	0.00018
30	23	5	0.76660 ± 0.00013	0.76667	0.00007
30	23	6	0.76638 ± 0.00013	0.76667	0.00029
30	24	3	0.79994 ± 0.00013	0.80000	0.00006
30	24	4	0.79996 ± 0.00013	0.80000	0.00004

Table C.3 *(cont.)*

TOTAL BIG BLINDS IN TOUR-NAMENT	BIG BLINDS IN P1'S STACK	BIG BLINDS IN P2'S STACK	SIMULATED P(P1 WINS)	EXPECTED P(P1 WINS)	DIFFERENCE BETWEEN THEORY AND SIMULATION
30	24	5	0.79997 ± 0.00013	0.80000	0.00003
30	25	3	0.83336 ± 0.00012	0.83333	−0.00003
30	25	4	0.83312 ± 0.00012	0.83333	0.00021
30	26	2	0.86662 ± 0.00011	0.86667	0.00005
30	26	3	0.86664 ± 0.00011	0.86667	0.00003
30	27	2	0.90003 ± 0.00009	0.90000	−0.00003
30	28	1	0.93343 ± 0.00008	0.93333	−0.00010
50	17	17	0.33993 ± 0.00015	0.34000	0.00007
50	18	16	0.36012 ± 0.00015	0.36000	−0.00012
50	18	17	0.35994 ± 0.00015	0.36000	0.00006
50	18	18	0.35991 ± 0.00015	0.36000	0.00009
50	19	16	0.38003 ± 0.00015	0.38000	−0.00003
50	19	17	0.37990 ± 0.00015	0.38000	0.00010
50	19	18	0.37990 ± 0.00015	0.38000	0.00010
50	19	19	0.37988 ± 0.00015	0.38000	0.00012
50	20	15	0.40018 ± 0.00015	0.40000	−0.00018
50	20	16	0.40012 ± 0.00015	0.40000	−0.00012
50	20	17	0.40012 ± 0.00015	0.40000	−0.00012
50	20	18	0.40008 ± 0.00015	0.40000	−0.00008
50	20	19	0.39984 ± 0.00015	0.40000	0.00016
50	20	20	0.40023 ± 0.00015	0.40000	−0.00023
50	21	15	0.41997 ± 0.00016	0.42000	0.00003
50	21	16	0.42004 ± 0.00016	0.42000	−0.00004
50	21	17	0.41986 ± 0.00016	0.42000	0.00014
50	21	18	0.41982 ± 0.00016	0.42000	0.00018
50	21	19	0.41993 ± 0.00016	0.42000	0.00007
50	21	20	0.41996 ± 0.00016	0.42000	0.00004
50	21	21	0.41999 ± 0.00016	0.42000	0.00001
50	22	14	0.44008 ± 0.00016	0.44000	−0.00008
50	22	15	0.43990 ± 0.00016	0.44000	0.00010
50	22	16	0.43991 ± 0.00016	0.44000	0.00009
50	22	17	0.44032 ± 0.00016	0.44000	−0.00032
50	22	18	0.44011 ± 0.00016	0.44000	−0.00011

TOTAL BIG BLINDS IN TOURNAMENT	BIG BLINDS IN P1'S STACK	BIG BLINDS IN P2'S STACK	SIMULATED P(P1 WINS)	EXPECTED P(P1 WINS)	DIFFERENCE BETWEEN THEORY AND SIMULATION
50	22	19	0.44001 ± 0.00016	0.44000	−0.00001
50	22	20	0.44007 ± 0.00016	0.44000	−0.00007
50	22	21	0.43981 ± 0.00016	0.44000	0.00019
50	22	22	0.44013 ± 0.00016	0.44000	−0.00013
50	23	14	0.46008 ± 0.00016	0.46000	−0.00008
50	23	15	0.46011 ± 0.00016	0.46000	−0.00011
50	23	16	0.45983 ± 0.00016	0.46000	0.00017
50	23	17	0.46016 ± 0.00016	0.46000	−0.00016
50	23	18	0.45995 ± 0.00016	0.46000	0.00005
50	23	19	0.46007 ± 0.00016	0.46000	−0.00007
50	23	20	0.46012 ± 0.00016	0.46000	−0.00012
50	23	21	0.46002 ± 0.00016	0.46000	−0.00002
50	23	22	0.45992 ± 0.00016	0.46000	0.00008
50	23	23	0.46022 ± 0.00016	0.46000	−0.00022
50	24	13	0.48006 ± 0.00016	0.48000	−0.00006
50	24	14	0.47997 ± 0.00016	0.48000	0.00003
50	24	15	0.47980 ± 0.00016	0.48000	0.00020
50	24	16	0.47975 ± 0.00016	0.48000	0.00025
50	24	17	0.48019 ± 0.00016	0.48000	−0.00019
50	24	18	0.47997 ± 0.00016	0.48000	0.00003
50	24	19	0.48009 ± 0.00016	0.48000	−0.00009
50	24	20	0.48003 ± 0.00016	0.48000	−0.00003
50	24	21	0.47968 ± 0.00016	0.48000	0.00032
50	24	22	0.48003 ± 0.00016	0.48000	−0.00003
50	24	23	0.47992 ± 0.00016	0.48000	0.00008
50	24	24	0.48003 ± 0.00016	0.48000	−0.00003
50	25	13	0.50006 ± 0.00016	0.50000	−0.00006
50	25	14	0.50019 ± 0.00016	0.50000	−0.00019
50	25	15	0.49994 ± 0.00016	0.50000	0.00006
50	25	16	0.49986 ± 0.00016	0.50000	0.00014
50	25	17	0.50021 ± 0.00016	0.50000	−0.00021
50	25	18	0.50009 ± 0.00016	0.50000	−0.00009
50	25	19	0.49990 ± 0.00016	0.50000	0.00010

Table C.3 *(cont.)*

TOTAL BIG BLINDS IN TOURNAMENT	BIG BLINDS IN P1'S STACK	BIG BLINDS IN P2'S STACK	SIMULATED P(P1 WINS)	EXPECTED P(P1 WINS)	DIFFERENCE BETWEEN THEORY AND SIMULATION
50	25	20	0.50011 ± 0.00016	0.50000	−0.00011
50	25	21	0.49999 ± 0.00016	0.50000	0.00001
50	25	22	0.50020 ± 0.00016	0.50000	−0.00020
50	25	23	0.49970 ± 0.00016	0.50000	0.00030
50	25	24	0.50006 ± 0.00016	0.50000	−0.00006
50	26	12	0.51973 ± 0.00016	0.52000	0.00027
50	26	13	0.52002 ± 0.00016	0.52000	−0.00002
50	26	14	0.51994 ± 0.00016	0.52000	0.00006
50	26	15	0.51986 ± 0.00016	0.52000	0.00014
50	26	16	0.51994 ± 0.00016	0.52000	0.00006
50	26	17	0.52007 ± 0.00016	0.52000	−0.00007
50	26	18	0.52017 ± 0.00016	0.52000	−0.00017
50	26	19	0.51999 ± 0.00016	0.52000	0.00001
50	26	20	0.52017 ± 0.00016	0.52000	−0.00017
50	26	21	0.51997 ± 0.00016	0.52000	0.00003
50	26	22	0.52002 ± 0.00016	0.52000	−0.00002
50	26	23	0.52017 ± 0.00016	0.52000	−0.00017
50	27	12	0.53978 ± 0.00016	0.54000	0.00022
50	27	13	0.54016 ± 0.00016	0.54000	−0.00016
50	27	14	0.54014 ± 0.00016	0.54000	−0.00014
50	27	15	0.54013 ± 0.00016	0.54000	−0.00013
50	27	16	0.53986 ± 0.00016	0.54000	0.00014
50	27	17	0.53995 ± 0.00016	0.54000	0.00005
50	27	18	0.54014 ± 0.00016	0.54000	−0.00014
50	27	19	0.53993 ± 0.00016	0.54000	0.00007
50	27	20	0.53989 ± 0.00016	0.54000	0.00011
50	27	21	0.54008 ± 0.00016	0.54000	−0.00008
50	27	22	0.54004 ± 0.00016	0.54000	−0.00004
50	28	11	0.56011 ± 0.00016	0.56000	−0.00011
50	28	12	0.55976 ± 0.00016	0.56000	0.00024
50	28	13	0.56003 ± 0.00016	0.56000	−0.00003
50	28	14	0.56005 ± 0.00016	0.56000	−0.00005
50	28	15	0.56001 ± 0.00016	0.56000	−0.00001

TOTAL BIG BLINDS IN TOUR- NAMENT	BIG BLINDS IN P1'S STACK	BIG BLINDS IN P2'S STACK	SIMULATED P(P1 WINS)	EXPECTED P(P1 WINS)	DIFFERENCE BETWEEN THEORY AND SIMULATION
50	28	16	0.56016 ± 0.00016	0.56000	− 0.00016
50	28	17	0.56019 ± 0.00016	0.56000	− 0.00019
50	28	18	0.56025 ± 0.00016	0.56000	− 0.00025
50	28	19	0.56005 ± 0.00016	0.56000	− 0.00005
50	28	20	0.56021 ± 0.00016	0.56000	− 0.00021
50	28	21	0.56027 ± 0.00016	0.56000	− 0.00027
50	29	11	0.58016 ± 0.00016	0.58000	− 0.00016
50	29	12	0.58035 ± 0.00016	0.58000	− 0.00035
50	29	13	0.58018 ± 0.00016	0.58000	− 0.00018
50	29	14	0.58009 ± 0.00016	0.58000	− 0.00009
50	29	15	0.58013 ± 0.00016	0.58000	− 0.00013
50	29	16	0.58012 ± 0.00016	0.58000	− 0.00012
50	29	17	0.58001 ± 0.00016	0.58000	− 0.00001
50	29	18	0.58018 ± 0.00016	0.58000	− 0.00018
50	29	19	0.58002 ± 0.00016	0.58000	− 0.00002
50	29	20	0.58009 ± 0.00016	0.58000	− 0.00009
50	30	10	0.60012 ± 0.00015	0.60000	− 0.00012
50	30	11	0.59993 ± 0.00015	0.60000	0.00007
50	30	12	0.60019 ± 0.00015	0.60000	− 0.00019
50	30	13	0.59996 ± 0.00015	0.60000	0.00004
50	30	14	0.59999 ± 0.00015	0.60000	0.00001
50	30	15	0.59997 ± 0.00015	0.60000	0.00003
50	30	16	0.60015 ± 0.00015	0.60000	− 0.00015
50	30	17	0.60008 ± 0.00015	0.60000	− 0.00008
50	30	18	0.60001 ± 0.00015	0.60000	− 0.00001
50	30	19	0.60001 ± 0.00015	0.60000	− 0.00001
50	31	10	0.61995 ± 0.00015	0.62000	0.00005
50	31	11	0.61987 ± 0.00015	0.62000	0.00013
50	31	12	0.61966 ± 0.00015	0.62000	0.00034
50	31	13	0.61997 ± 0.00015	0.62000	0.00003
50	31	14	0.62012 ± 0.00015	0.62000	− 0.00012
50	31	15	0.61990 ± 0.00015	0.62000	0.00010
50	31	16	0.61980 ± 0.00015	0.62000	0.00020

Table C.3 *(cont.)*

TOTAL BIG BLINDS IN TOUR- NAMENT	BIG BLINDS IN P1'S STACK	BIG BLINDS IN P2'S STACK	SIMULATED P(P1 WINS)	EXPECTED P(P1 WINS)	DIFFERENCE BETWEEN THEORY AND SIMULATION
50	31	17	0.62011 ± 0.00015	0.62000	− 0.00011
50	31	18	0.62000 ± 0.00015	0.62000	0.00000
50	32	9	0.63980 ± 0.00015	0.64000	0.00020
50	32	10	0.64008 ± 0.00015	0.64000	− 0.00008
50	32	11	0.63987 ± 0.00015	0.64000	0.00013
50	32	12	0.64008 ± 0.00015	0.64000	− 0.00008
50	32	13	0.64000 ± 0.00015	0.64000	0.00000
50	32	14	0.64001 ± 0.00015	0.64000	− 0.00001
50	32	15	0.64010 ± 0.00015	0.64000	− 0.00010
50	32	16	0.63996 ± 0.00015	0.64000	0.00004
50	32	17	0.63997 ± 0.00015	0.64000	0.00003
50	33	9	0.65970 ± 0.00015	0.66000	0.00030
50	33	10	0.65993 ± 0.00015	0.66000	0.00007
50	33	11	0.65989 ± 0.00015	0.66000	0.00011
50	33	12	0.66002 ± 0.00015	0.66000	− 0.00002
50	33	13	0.65984 ± 0.00015	0.66000	0.00016
50	33	14	0.66018 ± 0.00015	0.66000	− 0.00018
50	33	15	0.65975 ± 0.00015	0.66000	0.00025
50	33	16	0.65974 ± 0.00015	0.66000	0.00026
50	34	8	0.67992 ± 0.00015	0.68000	0.00008
50	34	9	0.68020 ± 0.00015	0.68000	− 0.00020
50	34	10	0.67996 ± 0.00015	0.68000	0.00004
50	34	11	0.67991 ± 0.00015	0.68000	0.00009
50	34	12	0.67990 ± 0.00015	0.68000	0.00010
50	34	13	0.67992 ± 0.00015	0.68000	0.00008
50	34	14	0.68017 ± 0.00015	0.68000	− 0.00017
50	34	15	0.68016 ± 0.00015	0.68000	− 0.00016
50	35	8	0.69981 ± 0.00014	0.70000	0.00019
50	35	9	0.70000 ± 0.00014	0.70000	0.00000
50	35	10	0.70005 ± 0.00014	0.70000	− 0.00005
50	35	11	0.69963 ± 0.00014	0.70000	0.00037
50	35	12	0.70003 ± 0.00014	0.70000	− 0.00003
50	35	13	0.69998 ± 0.000014	0.70000	0.00002

TOTAL BIG BLINDS IN TOUR-NAMENT	BIG BLINDS IN P1'S STACK	BIG BLINDS IN P2'S STACK	SIMULATED P(P1 WINS)	EXPECTED P(P1 WINS)	DIFFERENCE BETWEEN THEORY AND SIMULATION
50	35	14	0.70005 ± 0.00014	0.70000	−0.00005
50	36	7	0.72004 ± 0.00014	0.72000	−0.00004
50	36	8	0.72009 ± 0.00014	0.72000	−0.00009
50	36	9	0.72010 ± 0.00014	0.72000	−0.00010
50	36	10	0.71993 ± 0.00014	0.72000	0.00007
50	36	11	0.71994 ± 0.00014	0.72000	0.00006
50	36	12	0.72011 ± 0.00014	0.72000	−0.00011
50	36	13	0.72007 ± 0.00014	0.72000	−0.00007
50	37	7	0.74011 ± 0.00014	0.74000	−0.00011
50	37	8	0.73980 ± 0.00014	0.74000	0.00020
50	37	9	0.74008 ± 0.00014	0.74000	−0.00008
50	37	10	0.74003 ± 0.00014	0.74000	−0.00003
50	37	11	0.74003 ± 0.00014	0.74000	−0.00003
50	37	12	0.73997 ± 0.00014	0.74000	0.00003
50	38	6	0.76010 ± 0.00014	0.76000	−0.00010
50	38	7	0.76016 ± 0.00014	0.76000	−0.00016
50	38	8	0.76015 ± 0.00014	0.76000	−0.00015
50	38	9	0.75986 ± 0.00014	0.76000	0.00014
50	38	10	0.76016 ± 0.00014	0.76000	−0.00016
50	38	11	0.75994 ± 0.00014	0.76000	0.00006
50	39	6	0.78035 ± 0.00013	0.78000	−0.00035
50	39	7	0.78012 ± 0.00013	0.78000	−0.00012
50	39	8	0.78003 ± 0.00013	0.78000	−0.00003
50	39	9	0.78013 ± 0.00013	0.78000	−0.00013
50	39	10	0.77998 ± 0.00013	0.78000	0.00002
50	40	5	0.79993 ± 0.00013	0.80000	0.00007
50	40	6	0.80007 ± 0.00013	0.80000	−0.00007
50	40	7	0.80013 ± 0.00013	0.80000	−0.00013
50	40	8	0.79998 ± 0.00013	0.80000	0.00002
50	40	9	0.79986 ± 0.00013	0.80000	0.00014
50	41	5	0.82011 ± 0.00012	0.82000	−0.00011
50	41	6	0.82000 ± 0.00012	0.82000	0.00000
50	41	7	0.82004 ± 0.00012	0.82000	−0.00004

Table C.3 *(cont.)*

TOTAL BIG BLINDS IN TOUR- NAMENT	BIG BLINDS IN P1'S STACK	BIG BLINDS IN P2'S STACK	SIMULATED P(P1 WINS)	EXPECTED P(P1 WINS)	DIFFERENCE BETWEEN THEORY AND SIMULATION
50	41	8	0.82011 ± 0.00012	0.82000	−0.00011
50	42	4	0.83999 ± 0.00012	0.84000	0.00001
50	42	5	0.83989 ± 0.00012	0.84000	0.00011
50	42	6	0.84010 ± 0.00012	0.84000	−P0.00010
50	42	7	0.83992 ± 0.00012	0.84000	0.00008
50	43	4	0.85986 ± 0.00011	0.86000	0.00014
50	43	5	0.86009 ± 0.00011	0.86000	−0.00009
50	43	6	0.85981 ± 0.00011	0.86000	0.00019
50	44	3	0.88010 ± 0.00010	0.88000	−0.00010
50	44	4	0.88003 ± 0.00010	0.88000	−0.00003
50	44	5	0.88006 ± 0.00010	0.88000	−0.00006
50	45	3	0.90002 ± 0.00009	0.90000	−0.00002
50	45	4	0.89990 ± 0.00009	0.90000	0.00010
50	46	2	0.91990 ± 0.00009	0.92000	0.00010
50	46	3	0.91984 ± 0.00009	0.92000	0.00016
50	47	2	0.94000 ± 0.00008	0.94000	0.00000
50	48	1	0.95998 ± 0.00006	0.96000	0.00002

Appendix D:
N-Up Tables for Poker Stars MTTs

For MTTs that take place as a series of n ups, these tables provide the minimum edge required to achieve various target ROIs (for an explanation of the n up model of tournaments, refer to chapter 7). The payout structure used to come up with these tables is that found in many tournaments at Poker Stars—a fairly typical top-heavy payout structure. The MTTs you're playing in might not have the same exact payout structure, but since many top-heavy payout structures are somewhat similar, these tables should at least give you a rough idea of how much risk you should be willing to accept for large chunks of your stack. If you want more than just a rough idea for a particular MTT, just go to my website, www.killerev.com, and check out the free n up calculator I have there.

TABLE D.1: Target ROI = 20%

TYPE OF N UP	ENTRANTS	MINIMUM WINNING PERCENTAGE	TYPE OF N UP	ENTRANTS
2	50	52.3979%	3	50
2	500	51.5479%	3	500
2	1500	51.4175%	3	1500
2.25	50	46.9482%	3.25	50
2.25	500	46.0583%	3.25	500
2.25	1500	45.9221%	3.25	1500
2.5	50	42.5552%	3.5	50
2.5	500	41.6450%	3.5	500
2.5	1500	41.5059%	3.5	1500
2.75	50	38.9365%	3.75	50
2.75	500	38.0181%	3.75	500
2.75	1500	37.8780%	3.75	1500

TABLE D.2: Target ROI = 40%

TYPE OF N UP	ENTRANTS	MINIMUM WINNING PERCENTAGE	TYPE OF N UP	ENTRANTS
2	50	54.4938%	3	50
2	500	52.8717%	3	500
2	1500	52.6130%	3	1500
2.25	50	49.1525%	3.25	50
2.25	500	47.4452%	3.25	500
2.25	1500	47.1737%	3.25	1500
2.5	50	44.8198%	3.5	50
2.5	500	43.0647%	3.5	500
2.5	1500	42.7864%	3.5	1500
2.75	50	41.2303%	3.75	50
2.75	500	39.4515%	3.75	500
2.75	1500	39.1701%	3.75	1500

MINIMUM WINNING PERCENTAGE	TYPE OF N UP	ENTRANTS	MINIMUM WINNING PERCENTAGE
35.9023%	4	50	27.4554%
34.9836%	4	500	26.5719%
34.8435%	4	1500	26.4376%
33.3204%	4.25	50	25.9464%
32.4064%	4.25	500	25.0755%
32.2672%	4.25	1500	24.9434%
31.0957%	4.5	50	24.5998%
30.1899%	4.5	500	23.7420%
30.0521%	4.5	1500	23.6120%
29.1583%	4.75	50	23.3904%
28.2629%	4.75	500	22.5460%
28.1268%	4.75	1500	22.4181%

MINIMUM WINNING PERCENTAGE	TYPE OF N UP	ENTRANTS	MINIMUM WINNING PERCENTAGE
38.2049%	4	50	29.6957%
36.4183%	4	500	27.9542%
36.1363%	4	1500	27.6813%
35.6183%	4.25	50	28.1601%
33.8344%	4.25	500	26.4387%
33.5533%	4.25	1500	26.1693%
33.3799%	4.5	50	26.7850%
31.6058%	4.5	500	25.0852%
31.3268%	4.5	1500	24.8195%
31.4226%	4.75	50	25.5462%
29.6632%	4.75	500	23.8686%
29.3870%	4.75	1500	23.6068%

TABLE D.3: Target ROI = 60%

TYPE OF N UP	ENTRANTS	MINIMUM WINNING PERCENTAGE	TYPE OF N UP	ENTRANTS
2	50	56.3610%	3	50
2	500	54.0303%	3	500
2	1500	53.6473%	3	1500
2.25	50	51.1285%	3.25	50
2.25	500	48.6638%	3.25	500
2.25	1500	48.2605%	3.25	1500
2.5	50	46.8610%	3.5	50
2.5	500	44.3166%	3.5	500
2.5	1500	43.9018%	3.5	1500
2.75	50	43.3081%	3.75	50
2.75	500	40.7195%	3.75	500
2.75	1500	40.2990%	3.75	1500

TABLE D.4: Target ROI = 80%

TYPE OF N UP	ENTRANTS	MINIMUM WINNING PERCENTAGE	TYPE OF N UP	ENTRANTS
2	50	58.0482%	3	50
2	500	55.0616%	3	500
2	1500	54.5593%	3	1500
2.25	50	52.9237%	3.25	50
2.25	500	49.7522%	3.25	500
2.25	1500	49.2216%	3.25	1500
2.5	50	48.7243%	3.5	50
2.5	500	45.4381%	3.5	500
2.5	1500	44.8910%	3.5	1500
2.75	50	45.2133%	3.75	50
2.75	500	41.8588%	3.75	500
2.75	1500	41.3026%	3.75	1500

MINIMUM WINNING PERCENTAGE	TYPE OF N UP	ENTRANTS	MINIMUM WINNING PERCENTAGE
40.3004%	4	50	31.7655%
37.6912%	4	500	29.1927%
37.2687%	4	1500	28.7803%
37.7184%	4.25	50	30.2118%
35.1048%	4.25	500	27.6625%
34.6827%	4.25	1500	27.2547%
35.4755%	4.5	50	28.8165%
32.8686%	4.5	500	26.2932%
32.4487%	4.5	1500	25.8904%
33.5075%	4.75	50	27.5560%
30.9150%	4.75	500	25.0604%
30.4984%	4.75	1500	24.6629%

MINIMUM WINNING PERCENTAGE	TYPE OF N UP	ENTRANTS	MINIMUM WINNING PERCENTAGE
42.2293%	4	50	33.6959%
38.8378%	4	500	30.3178%
38.2777%	4	1500	29.7671%
39.6585%	4.25	50	32.1305%
36.2517%	4.25	500	28.7761%
35.6912%	4.25	1500	28.2308%
37.4181%	4.5	50	30.7213%
34.0112%	4.5	500	27.3944%
33.4525%	4.5	1500	26.8549%
35.4463%	4.75	50	29.4452%
32.0499%	4.75	500	26.1485%
31.4947%	4.75	1500	25.6153%

TABLE D.5: Target ROI = 100%

TYPE OF N UP	ENTRANTS	MINIMUM WINNING PERCENTAGE	TYPE OF N UP	ENTRANTS
2	50	59.5899%	3	50
2	500	55.9917%	3	500
2	1500	55.3752%	3	1500
2.25	50	54.5719%	3.25	50
2.25	500	50.7369%	3.25	500
2.25	1500	50.0838%	3.25	1500
2.5	50	50.4422%	3.5	50
2.5	500	46.4556%	3.5	500
2.5	1500	45.7805%	3.5	1500
2.75	50	46.9764%	3.75	50
2.75	500	42.8948%	3.75	500
2.75	1500	42.2071%	3.75	1500

TABLE D.6: Target ROI = 120%

TYPE OF N UP	ENTRANTS	MINIMUM WINNING PERCENTAGE	TYPE OF N UP	ENTRANTS
2	50	61.0112%	3	50
2	500	56.8395%	3	500
2	1500	56.1136%	3	1500
2.25	50	56.0978%	3.25	50
2.25	500	51.6368%	3.25	500
2.25	1500	50.8661%	3.25	1500
2.5	50	52.0388%	3.5	50
2.5	500	47.3877%	3.5	500
2.5	1500	46.5893%	3.5	1500
2.75	50	48.6206%	3.75	50
2.75	500	43.8459%	3.75	500
2.75	1500	43.0311%	3.75	1500

MINIMUM WINNING PERCENTAGE	TYPE OF N UP	ENTRANTS	MINIMUM WINNING PERCENTAGE
44.0208%	4	50	35.5096%
39.8828%	4	500	31.3507%
39.1890%	4	1500	30.6641%
41.4662%	4.25	50	33.9376%
37.2992%	4.25	500	29.8001%
36.6035%	4.25	1500	29.1192%
39.2335%	4.5	50	32.5193%
35.0567%	4.5	500	28.4085%
34.3621%	4.5	1500	27.7340%
37.2631%	4.75	50	31.2323%
33.0902%	4.75	500	27.1519%
32.3988%	4.75	1500	26.4844%

MINIMUM WINNING PERCENTAGE	TYPE OF N UP	ENTRANTS	MINIMUM WINNING PERCENTAGE
45.6965%	4	50	37.2237%
40.8442%	4	500	32.3073%
40.0205%	4	1500	31.4874%
43.1621%	4.25	50	35.6493%
38.2647%	4.25	500	30.7498%
37.4374%	4.25	1500	29.9357%
40.9411%	4.5	50	34.2259%
36.0219%	4.5	500	29.3501%
35.1947%	4.5	1500	28.5428%
38.9762%	4.75	50	32.9319%
34.0522%	4.75	500	28.0849%
33.2277%	4.75	1500	27.2850%

TABLE D.7: Target ROI = 140%

TYPE OF N UP	ENTRANTS	MINIMUM WINNING PERCENTAGE	TYPE OF N UP	ENTRANTS
2	50	62.3311%	3	50
2	500	57.6189%	3	500
2	1500	56.7884%	3	1500
2.25	50	57.5202%	3.25	50
2.25	500	52.4662%	3.25	500
2.25	1500	51.5824%	3.25	1500
2.5	50	53.5322%	3.5	50
2.5	500	48.2486%	3.5	500
2.5	1500	47.3313%	3.5	1500
2.75	50	50.1633%	3.75	50
2.75	500	44.7261%	3.75	500
2.75	1500	43.7883%	3.75	1500

TABLE D.8: Target ROI = 160%

TYPE OF N UP	ENTRANTS	MINIMUM WINNING PERCENTAGE	TYPE OF N UP	ENTRANTS
2	50	63.5643%	3	50
2	500	58.3406%	3	500
2	1500	57.4097%	3	1500
2.25	50	58.8538%	3.25	50
2.25	500	53.2357%	3.25	500
2.25	1500	52.2433%	3.25	1500
2.5	50	54.9367%	3.5	50
2.5	500	49.0490%	3.5	500
2.5	1500	48.0171%	3.5	1500
2.75	50	51.6183%	3.75	50
2.75	500	45.5460%	3.75	500
2.75	1500	44.4893%	3.75	1500

MINIMUM WINNING PERCENTAGE	TYPE OF N UP	ENTRANTS	MINIMUM WINNING PERCENTAGE
47.2732%	4	50	38.8517%
41.7355%	4	500	33.1994%
40.7859%	4	1500	32.2492%
44.7619%	4.25	50	37.2781%
39.1612%	4.25	500	31.6365%
38.2061%	4.25	1500	30.6920%
42.5559%	4.5	50	35.8530%
36.9196%	4.5	500	30.2305%
35.9633%	4.5	1500	29.2928%
40.5999%	4.75	50	34.5551%
34.9481%	4.75	500	28.9580%
33.9938%	4.75	1500	28.0280%

MINIMUM WINNING PERCENTAGE	TYPE OF N UP	ENTRANTS	MINIMUM WINNING PERCENTAGE
48.7642%	4	50	40.4042%
42.5669%	4	500	34.0362%
41.4955%	4	1500	32.9587%
46.2782%	4.25	50	38.8343%
39.9988%	4.25	500	32.4693%
38.9196%	4.25	1500	31.3972%
44.0897%	4.5	50	37.4100%
37.7595%	4.5	500	31.0580%
36.6776%	4.5	1500	29.9927%
42.1454%	4.75	50	36.1109%
35.7875%	4.75	500	29.7796%
34.7065%	4.75	1500	28.7221%

TABLE D.9: Target ROI = 180%

TYPE OF N UP	ENTRANTS	MINIMUM WINNING PERCENTAGE	TYPE OF N UP	ENTRANTS
2	50	64.7225%	3	50
2	500	59.0128%	3	500
2	1500	57.9856%	3	1500
2.25	50	60.1103%	3.25	50
2.25	500	53.9540%	3.25	500
2.25	1500	52.8570%	3.25	1500
2.5	50	56.2638%	3.5	50
2.5	500	49.7974%	3.5	500
2.5	1500	48.6549%	3.5	1500
2.75	50	52.9966%	3.75	50
2.75	500	46.3139%	3.75	500
2.75	1500	45.1422%	3.75	1500

TABLE D.10: Target ROI = 200%

TYPE OF N UP	ENTRANTS	MINIMUM WINNING PERCENTAGE	TYPE OF N UP	ENTRANTS
2	50	65.8150%	3	50
2	500	59.6421%	3	500
2	1500	58.5225%	3	1500
2.25	50	61.2990%	3.25	50
2.25	500	54.6278%	3.25	500
2.25	1500	53.4300%	3.25	1500
2.5	50	57.5226%	3.5	50
2.5	500	50.5007%	3.5	500
2.5	1500	49.2513%	3.5	1500
2.75	50	54.3072%	3.75	50
2.75	500	47.0365%	3.75	500
2.75	1500	45.7535%	3.75	1500

MINIMUM WINNING PERCENTAGE	TYPE OF *N* UP	ENTRANTS	MINIMUM WINNING PERCENTAGE
50.1799%	4	50	41.8900%
43.3469%	4	500	34.8251%
42.1572%	4	1500	33.6234%
47.7211%	4.25	50	40.3260%
40.7857%	4.25	500	33.2551%
39.5859%	4.25	1500	32.0583%
45.5522%	4.5	50	38.9049%
38.5494%	4.5	500	31.8398%
37.3453%	4.5	1500	30.6495%
43.6218%	4.75	50	37.6067%
36.5779%	4.75	500	30.5565%
35.3735%	4.75	1500	29.3739%

MINIMUM WINNING PERCENTAGE	TYPE OF *N* UP	ENTRANTS	MINIMUM WINNING PERCENTAGE
51.5290%	4	50	43.3161%
44.0819%	4	500	35.5718%
42.7776%	4	1500	34.2489%
49.0989%	4.25	50	41.7599%
41.5281%	4.25	500	33.9997%
40.2112%	4.25	1500	32.6810%
46.9514%	4.5	50	40.3440%
39.2957%	4.5	500	32.5812%
37.9726%	4.5	1500	31.2686%
45.0366%	4.75	50	39.0488%
37.3254%	4.75	500	31.2939%
36.0007%	4.75	1500	29.9888%

Glossary

Most of these are words and acronyms used in the text. I've included a few items here not used in the text that are, nonetheless, commonly used in talking about poker.

3-Bet: Same as reraise.

6-max: Tournament where full tables have at most six players.

AF: *See* Aggression Factor.

Aggression Factor (AF): An attempted measure of aggression. The expression used to generate a player's aggression factor is $\frac{\text{Bets + Raises}}{\text{Calls}}$. Note that checks and folds aren't included in the denominator of this expression.

Aggression Frequency: A measure of aggression obtained by the expression $\frac{\text{Bets + Raises}}{\text{Checks + Folds + Calls}}$. Aggression frequency is the percentage of times a player is aggressive when given the chance.

Aggressive: A player who bets and raises more often than he checks and calls. This term is the opposite of passive (note that aggressive players can be either loose or tight).

ASB: Percentage of the time a player Attempts to Steal Blinds when the opportunity arises.

Autopilot: Mental mode in which your decisions are automatic and not completely thought out. You think that you've been in a situation so many times that you simply act before thoroughly thinking. For me, I have to fight autopilot because I'm used to playing many online games simultaneously with the aid of Poker Tracker and Poker Ace HUD. Autopilot for you may have other causes. The bottom line is that autopilot is to be avoided at all costs.

B: *See* Button.

Backdoor: A draw that needs two cards to complete: one on the turn, and the other on the river.

BB: Big Bet. An amount of chips equal to twice the big blind.

BB: *See* Big Blind.

Big Blind (BB): The big blind is a forced bet made before a hand is dealt. It's usually placed by the player two positions to the left of the button, and it's typically twice the small blind. If no one raises, the player who posts the big blind has an option of raising. BB is also used to designate the player who posts the BB in a hand.

Big Slickina: AQ. *See* also *Slickerella*.

Blinds: Forced bets that are made before the hand starts. In a Texas hold'em hand, there are usually two blinds: a small blind and a big blind. The player immediately to the left of the button posts the small blind, and the player immediately to the left of the small blind posts the big blind. The word "blinds" can be used to refer to both the bets and the players who post them.

Blocking Bet: An undersized lead bet made out of position designed to discourage a larger one from someone in position.

Broadway: The ace-high straight, TJQKA.

Broadway Cards: Cards that are ten or higher.

Bubble: The last few spots in a tournament before the money. In a multitable tournament, the bubble is usually when there's one table of players to eliminate before payouts begin. In single-table tournaments where the top 3 get paid; bubble time is when the tournament is down to 4 players. If you finish on the bubble, you're said to have "bubbled out."

Bust: Usually refers to when you are eliminated from a tournament. However, this can also refer to when you lose money in a cash game and have no more money with which to buy in.

Button (B): The player who acts last on all betting rounds except the first round. The button is denoted by a white disc that usually has the word "dealer" written on it. Online, dealer is replaced by D since the disc on-screen is too small.

CB: *See* Continuation Bet.

cEV: *See* Chip EV.

Check-Raise: Play where you initially check only to raise later in the same round of betting. For example, you have 4 opponents. You flopped a set and are first to act. You check. The person to your left bets, everyone folds, and you raise when the action gets back to you.

Clean Outs: Outs where you improve your hand and aren't beaten by another hand. Say the board is J52, and you have AQ. If your opponent has JT, aces and queens are clean outs. However, if your opponent has AJ, aces are no longer clean outs since your top pair will be beaten by your opponent's two pair.

Chip EV (cEV): Expectation value in terms of the number of chips you have in front of you. In cash games, your decisions are usually based on optimizing your chip EV. In tournaments, there's chip EV associated with each hand, but your goal isn't necessarily to optimize chipEV.

Clumping: Effect in which players in late position are more likely to have good cards given that all the early-position players fold.

CO: *See* Cutoff.

Combination: A particular set of objects for which ordering does not matter.

Complete Information: A game is said to be a game of "complete information" when all players have the same state of knowledge. The board game Monopoly, for example, is a game of complete information since there's no hidden information—everyone has their property, money, and "Get Out of Jail Free" cards laid out for everyone to see.

Conditional Probability: The chance of an outcome that's dependent on previous outcomes.

Connectors: Hole cards containing cards of consecutive ranks (JT and 54, for example).

Continuation Bet (CB): A bet made by a preflop raiser on the flop when he misses the flop.

CPM: Chip Proportional Method. Way of determining the monetary equity of stacks in a tournament by assuming that all chips have an equal value.

Crippled Deck: Situation that occurs when you have a monster hand and hold most of the cards that could make good hands for your opponents. For example, if the flop is AAK and you hold AK, there aren't many cards left that your opponents could have so that they could justify staying in the hand with you.

Cutoff (CO): The player to the right of the button. Aggressive players in the CO will often open for a raise, cutting the button off from entering the hand.

DCB: *See* Delayed Continuation Bet.

Delayed Continuation Bet (DCB): A bet made on the turn by the preflop raiser after all parties have checked the flop.

Domination: Situation when players have hole cards with one card in common. The set of hole cards with the higher kicker is said to dominate. For example, preflop, AQ dominates AJ.

Donk Bet: Pejorative term for a stop-and-go.

Double Gutshot Straight Draw: A straight draw where you simultaneously have two inside straight draws. If you hold 75, and the flop is 369, you have such a draw. Notice that you have eight outs with a double gutshot, which is the same number of outs you have with an outside straight draw.

Double-Paired Board: Board with two pair on it. An example of a double-paired board is KK552.

Drag: To slow play.

Early Position (EP): At a fullhanded table, this term usually applies to UTG, UTG + 1, and UTG + 2. More generally, it refers to approximately the first third of players to act in a hand, so at a 6-handed table, UTG and UTG + 1 can be considered to be EP.

EP: *See* Early Position.

EV: *See* Expectation Value.

Event Odds: The odds corresponding to an event happening. These are usually simply referred to as "odds," but sometimes a distinction needs to be made between event odds and pot odds. As an example, the event odds against drawing an ace from a full deck of cards are 12:1.

Expectation (or Expected) Value (EV): The amount of money you expect to win or lose in the long run per random event. If I flip a coin and I make a bet where I profit $5 for a head and lose $10 for a tail, my EV would be − $2.50. Negative EV events like this one are to be avoided.

Exposed Card: A card that shouldn't be known but is somehow shown to one or more players at the table. Cards are usually shown via dealer mistakes or by players who expose their cards either willingly or unwillingly.

Fixed Strategy: Game plan in which a player always performs the same action in a specific situation. An example of a fixed preflop strategy is always raising with [AA,JJ]||[AK,AQ], limping with [AJ,A9]||[KQ,K9]||[QJ,Q9]||[JT,J9]||[TT,55], and folding all other hands.

Fold Equity: The part of EV that arises from considering the probability that an opponent will fold and multiplying it by the amount of money to be won when he folds.

Fullhanded: A table with seven or more players.

Ghost: To "inhabit" your opponent's point of view and see the hand or hands through his eyes.

Grandstand Overbet: An all-in bet well out of proportion to the size of the pot, either for show or for ego or for both.

Gutshot Straight Draw: A straight draw where only one rank can complete the straight, meaning that there are only 4 outs to complete the straight. An example is if you hold AK and the board is QJ5.

Hack: A strategy or counterstrategy derived and developed from observing your opponents' betting patterns.

Hand Distribution: The group of hands that you assign to your opponent.

Hand Simulator: Software that takes as its input hole cards and a board and outputs the winning, losing, and tying probabilities associated with each hand.

Hand Tracker: Software that keeps track of hands played online and sorts the data according to many statistics. These statistics include such things as the percentage of pots a player enters voluntarily, or VPIP, the percentage with which a player attempts to steal blinds, or ASB, and the percentage of times an opponent will fold to a bet on the flop.

Heads-Up Display (HUD): Software that takes the data stored in a hand tracker's database and that displays your opponents' statistics in real time while playing online.

Hit-To-Win: Paradigm for playing poker in which the primary plan is to sit and wait to hit a hand.

HUD: *See* Heads-Up Display.

ICM: *See* Independent Chip Modeling.

Idiot End of Straight: Straight made with a board of 4 connected cards that can be beaten by a higher straight. Suppose the board is 4567. If you make a 7-high straight with a 3 in your hand, you have the idiot end of the straight. This is sometimes also referred to as the "ass end" of the straight.

Implied Odds: Payout odds gained because of money that opponents will put in the pot on future betting rounds.

Incomplete Information: State in a game where not all players have the same state of knowledge. Poker isn't a game of complete information since players' cards are unknown to other players.

Independence: Term from probability referring to events whose outcomes don't influence each other. Independent events are convenient to work with because the probability of both events happening is equal to the product of their individual probabilities. An example of independent probabilities is the outcome of consecutive coin flips (the coin doesn't remember what the result of the previous flip was).

Independent Chip Modeling (ICM): Mathematical model that calculates a player's finishing distribution as a pure function of players' stacks. ICM assumes that all players play identically.

In the Dark: Phrase referring to an action (betting, checking, raising) done to begin the next betting round before the board card(s) for the next betting round is/are exposed.

In the Money (ITM): The point in a tournament where payouts begin.

Iso Play: Reraising the initial raiser to isolate against him and induce heads-up play (used more in limit hold'em than in no-limit hold'em).

ITM: *See* In the Money.

JV: Nickname (and probably not coincidentally the initials) for the founder of *Killer Poker,* John Vorhaus.

Ka-chingaling: Word synonymous with "major payday." Here's an example. In the last hour of cash game play on the PPMIV cruise, I was playing $2–$5 blind no-limit hold'em with a $200–$500 buy-in. UTG raised to $25, UTG + 1 called, and UTG + 2 raised to $50. UTG + 3 folded, and I looked down and saw AA. I reraised to $150. I got 5 cold callers. The blinds folded, along with UTG and UTG + 1. UTG + 2 reraised all-in to $1,250, I called my remaining $750 or so, and everyone else folds except for the button who called off his remaining $500. UTG + 2 had KK and the button, believe it or not, called his remaining $500 with 22! I took down a $3,000 pot—ka-chingaling!

Ka-chingo: Term my friends and I sometimes use when referring to the casino. "Our pockets go ka-chingo after visiting the casino."

LAG: *See* Loose-Aggressive.

LAP: *See* Loose-Aggressive-Passive

LHE: Limit hold'em.

Limpede: A preflop phenomenon where an early position limp encourages everyone else at the table to limp along as well. Also known as a *limpfest*.

Limp-Reraise: Play where you limp only to raise later within the same round of betting.

Loose: A player who plays a lot of hands. Loose is the opposite of tight (loose players can be either passive or aggressive).

Loose-Aggressive (LAG): General categorization applied to someone who plays many pots and plays them by doing lots of betting and raising.

Loose-Aggressive-Passive (LAP): Acronym referring to a loose player who's aggressive preflop and passive postflop.

Loose-Passive-Aggressive (LPA): Acronym referring to a loose player who's passive preflop and aggressive postflop.

LPA: *See* Loose-Passive-Aggressive.

MCU Poker Chart: Chart used to relay the play of poker hands. These are the charts Mike Caro first introduced in *Mike Caro's Book of Poker Tells.*

Mixed Strategy: Game plan in which someone executes different actions given the same situation. In the most ideal sense, the action chosen for a specific instance is determined by a random event having the same probability distribution as the mixed strategy to be employed. An example of a mixed strategy is calling with KK 10% of the time and raising with KK 90% of the time. To accomplish this, you can use the second hand of a watch. If the hand is from 0–53, you raise, and if the hand is from 54–59, you call. A second hand is appropriate because with respect to the play of hands, the location of a second hand is a random event.

Monetary EV: Your expected payday. In cash games, chip EV and monetary EV are synonymous. In tournaments, chip EV and monetary EV are different. In tournaments, your goal is ultimately to optimize your monetary EV.

MP: Middle Position.

MTT: *See* Multitable Tournament.

Multitable Tournament (MTT): Tournament that starts with more than one table. A majority of no-limit hold'em MTTs features fullhanded tables, but once in a while, one will feature 6-max tables.

NLHE: No-Limit Hold'em.

N-Up Modeling: Mathematical model that treats poker tournaments as a series of double ups, triple ups, and so on. It can be used to approximate the average winning percentage a player with a given ROI has per hand.

Nuts: The absolute best hand that someone can have given the board cards. If the board is T♠J♠Q♠, you have the nuts if you have A♠K♠ for the royal flush.

Odds: Term referring to the ratio of (Outcomes of Interest): (Outcomes Not of Interest).

One-Gap or **1-Gap:** Hole cards such as 8T, where there's a single rank in between the two cards.

OOP: *See* Out of Position.

Open: The first person to put money in a pot voluntarily in a particular betting round is said to open.

Outcomes of Interest: Outcomes for which a probability, the odds in favor of, or the odds against are calculated.

Outcome Space: Set of all possible outcomes for a random event. If I'm flipping a coin, the outcome space is (heads, tails).

Out of Position (OOP): You're out of position when you have to act before your opponent(s).

Outs: Cards available in the deck that can improve your hand. If you've two hearts in your hand and there are two hearts on the board, you have 9 outs with which you can complete your flush.

Outside Straight Draw: Straight draw where you have 4 consecutive cards and you have 8 outs. For example, if the board is 674 and you hold 89, you have an outside straight draw. Note that even though you have 4 consecutive cards with JQKA, this isn't considered an outside straight draw because you only have 4 outs.

Overcaller: If there's a raise and a call, any additional players who call the raise are referred to as overcallers.

Overcard: This term has multiple applications, but it has the same fundamental meaning. First, an overcard is a hole card that's bigger than any of the cards on the board. Reciprocally, an overcard is also a board card greater than a pair you have (either a pocket pair or a pair made using a board card).

Paired Board: A board with a pair on it (TTJ2, for example).

P&P: *See* Push and Pray.

Partial Outs: After considering your opponents' hand distribution, partial outs are cards that win the hand for you against some, but not all, hands in your opponents' distributions. For example, suppose your opponent is on [AA,KK], you have AK, and the board is 4567. Aces are partial outs, because they only win the hand for you when your opponent has KK.

Passive: Term referring to a player who checks and calls more often than he bets and raises. This term is the opposite of aggressive (passive players can be either loose or tight).

Payout Odds: For a wager, this ratio is defined as (money available to win):(money you wager).

Permutations: Number of arrangements that exist for a set of objects.

PFR: Preflop Raising percentage. The percentage of times that a player raises preflop.

Physical Deck: The deck that the dealer actually holds. The physical deck doesn't include the burn cards or the muck. It's not used in probability calculations unless for some strange reason all the burn cards and mucked cards are known.

Pot Odds: The payout odds when only factoring the money currently in the pot.

Probability: The relative frequency with which an outcome occurs. If you take a probability and multiply it by 100%, you get the percentage with which an outcome occurs.

Probe Bet: A type of bet, particularly on the flop, where a player who wasn't the last aggressor in the previous round's betting makes a bet into the previous round's final aggressor.

Push: To bet all your chips. Sometimes, you'll hear this as "I pushed all-in." Other times, it'll be abbreviated as "I pushed."

Push and Pray (P&P): Move done with a short stack late in a tournament where you shove all-in hoping that you steal the blinds or get lucky and win when called (since you'll probably be called by a better hand).

Put (on a Hand or **Hand Distribution):** The act of assigning possible holdings to your opponents.

Rake: The amount of money that the cardroom takes from a pot. Casinos usually take a rake in low- and medium-stakes games (a timed collection is usually employed at high-stakes games). As poker players, it's desirable to play in games with the lowest possible rake; however, we should also acknowledge that cardrooms couldn't possibly exist without the rake. Every business needs to make money, and quite frankly, I wouldn't be able to make my money if the cardrooms couldn't make theirs. Remember to account for the rake when calculating your pot odds.

Random Event: An occurrence where the precise outcome is unknown, and each possible outcome has a known or unknown probability associated with it.

Resteal: Play in which you raise a player with a marginal hand when you suspect that he's being aggressive with a very wide hand distribution.

Reverse Domination: Situation in which a hand that is originally dominant falls behind because the other player hits his kicker. For example, before the flop, AQ dominates over AJ. However, when the flop comes J52, the AQ becomes dominated because an ace gives AJ two pair.

Reverse Implied Odds: Payout odds lost because of money that you may lose on future betting rounds.

ROI: Return of Investment. ROI is used as a measure of tournament success. To find your ROI, take your net profit or loss, divide it by the total amount of entries and fees, and then multiply by 100%. Usually, players calculate ROIs for different stakes separately. As an example of an ROI calculation, assume that I play 10 $20+$2 single-table tournies, and I've won $240. I've paid $220 in entries and fees, so my net profit is therefore $20. My ROI would be $\left(\frac{\$20}{\$220}\right)(100\%) \approx +9.09\%$.

Runner-Runner: Refers to a draw made by hitting both the turn and river cards. For example, if you hold two hearts and there's one heart on the flop, you need to "hit runner-runner" to complete your flush.

Satellite: Tournament whose prize is an entry into a higher stakes tournament.

SB: *See* Small Blind.

Semibluff: Play where you bet or raise with a hand that is currently behind but has the potential to improve to the best hand on a later round. An example of a semibluff is raising with a four-flush.

Shootout: Multitable tournament format played in rounds, where the top player or top few players from each table advance to the next round.

Shorthanded: Table with six or fewer players.

Single-Table Tournament (STT): Tournament starting with one table. STTs typically start ten-, nine-, six-, or two-handed.

Sit-n-Go (SNG): Originally, SNGs were synonymous with single-table tournaments; however, today's SNGs can start with anywhere from 2 to 20 tables! Today, an SNG is simply a tournament with no scheduled start time: it starts whenever enough people sign up.

Slickerella: AQ, aka *Big Slickina*.

Small Blind (SB): Forced bet made by the player to the left of the button. It's usually equal to half the big blind, but it can range from one third of the big blind to two thirds of the big blind.

SNG: *See* Sit-n-Go.

Sniffer: Term referring to software that tracks the play of your online opponents.

Squeeze Play: Sophisticated play, usually preflop, where after a raise and one or more callers, you reraise representing a monster hand. Against most opponents, you usually end up squeezing the original raiser and all the subsequent callers out of the hand unless they have monster hands.

Stop-and-Go: Line of play from early position where you check/call the flop or turn and then bet out immediately on the next round. Aka Donk Bet.

Straddle: A voluntarily posted blind equal to double the big blind. Since it's a blind, the person posting the straddle has an option to raise if no one else raises. There are different types of straddles. The usual straddle bet is made by the player immediately to the big blind's left. Another type of straddle, referred to as a "Mississippi Straddle," is a straddle where the option to straddle works from the button to UTG. If a person posts a Mississippi straddle, he acts last preflop—preflop action skips him and returns to him after the big blind acts.

STT: *See* Single-Table Tournament.

TAG: *See* Tight Aggressive.

TAP: *See* Tight-Aggressive-Passive.

Theoretical Deck: The pool of all the unknown cards (includes burn cards and the muck). Because of burn cards and mucked cards, the theoretical deck and the physical deck are different things. The theoretical deck is the deck that must be used in probability calculations.

Tight: Term referring to a player who doesn't play a lot of hands. This term is the opposite of loose (tight players can be either aggressive or passive).

Tight-Aggressive (TAG): Playing style defined by not playing many hands (tight) and by betting and raising a lot in hands played (aggressive).

Tight-Aggressive-Passive (TAP): Playing style defined by not playing many hands and by playing them in a way that's generally aggressive preflop and passive postflop.

Tight-Passive-Aggressive (TPA): Playing style defined by not playing many hands and by playing them in a way that's generally passive preflop and aggressive postflop.

TPA: *See* Tight-Passive-Aggressive.

TPTK: Top-pair-top-kicker.

Tree Diagram: Visual aid in which different outcomes and actions are represented by branches.

Tripped Board: Board with three of a kind (KKK54, for example).

Under the Gun (UTG): Player immediately to the left of the big blind. He's the first one to act preflop.

UTG: *See* Under the Gun.

Variance: Numerical measure of the spread of payouts pertaining to a random event. Take the following two sets of outcomes: A = {$5, $0, −$5} B = {$500, $0, −$500} (assume that each outcome has an equal probability). Set B has a much higher variance associated with it even though both A and B have the same EV.

Voluntarily Puts Chips in Pot (VPIP): The percentage of hands that a player puts money in the pot preflop when given the opportunity. You'll sometimes see VP$IP used instead of VPIP.

VPIP: *See* Voluntarily Puts Chips in Pot.

Wheelhouse Card: A card that completes a huge hand. For example, if you hold A♠K♠ and the board is Q♠J♠5♣, T♠ would be considered a "wheelhouse card."

WTA: Winner take all.

Index